150 LEADING CASES

English Legal System

150 Leading Cases

English Legal System

Consultant Editor: Lord Templeman
Editor: Charles P Reed
LLB, Barrister

Old Bailey Press

OLD BAILEY PRESS
200 Greyhound Road, London W14 9RY

ISBN 1 85836 279 2

British Library Cataloguing-in-Publication Data

A catalogue record for this book is available from the British Library.

5 4 3 2 1

Printed and bound in Great Britain

Contents

Acknowledgements

The publishers and author would like to thank the Incorporated Council of Law Reporting for England and Wales for kind permission to reproduce extracts from the Weekly Law Reports, and Butterworths for their kind permission to reproduce extracts from the All England Law Reports.

Preface

Old Bailey Press Casebooks are intended as companion volumes to the Textbooks but they are also invaluable reference tools in themselves. Their aim is to supplement and enhance a student's understanding and interpretation of a particular area of law and provide essential background reading. Companion Revision WorkBooks and Statutes are also published.

The emphasis of the '150 Leading Cases' series is on recent developments, which for the *English Legal System* include: *Westdeutsche Landesbank Girozentrale* v *Islington London Borough Council* (1996) (judicial law reform and doctrine of precedent in the House of Lords); *O'Hara* v *Chief Constable of the Royal Ulster Constabulary* (1997) (definition of 'reasonable suspicion' for making an arrest); *R* v *Khan (Sultan)* (1996) (scope of common law and statutory discretions to exclude illegally obtained evidence); *Williams* v *Bedwellty Justices* (1996) (reviewability of committal proceedings); *John* v *MGN Ltd* (1996) (guidance to civil juries in defamation cases); *Thompson* v *Commissioner of Police of the Metropolis* (1997) (guidance to civil juries in assault and false imprisonment cases); *Shtun* v *Zalejska* (1996) (dismissal for want of prosecution); *R* v *Graham (HK) and Others* (1997) ('unsafe' convictions under the Criminal Appeal Act 1995); and *R* v *Jones (Steven Martin)* (1996) (receiving fresh evidence under the Criminal Appeal Act 1995).

Developments up to 1 January 1998 have been taken into account.

Table of Cases

Cases in bold type are the leading cases. Page numbers in bold indicate the main references to them.

1 Sources of Law

Costa v *ENEL Case 6/64* [1964] CMLR 425 Court of Justice of the European Communities

- *European Community legislation*

Facts

A lawyer in Milan refused to pay an electricity bill, arguing that the recent nationalisation of the Italian electricity industry was contrary to several articles in the EEC Treaty. The Milanese judge referred the case to the ECJ for interpretation under art 177.

Held

The court had jurisdiction under art 177 to hear the case. It considered art 37(2) which creates individual rights to protect Community nationals and prohibits any new rule which discriminates between nationals of Member States in regard to monopolies. Since the nationalisation constituted subsequent domestic legislation which conflicted with the Treaty, it was not enforceable.

Maurice Lagrange M:

> 'The common market system is based on the creation of a legal order separate from that of the Member States, and if we reached the stage where a constitutional judge of one of the Member States feels that ordinary national laws which are contrary to the Treaty could prevail over the Treaty without any judge having the power to nullify their application so that they could only be repealed or modified by parliament, such a decision would create an insoluble conflict between the two orders and would undermine the very foundations of the Treaty.'

Comment

One of the leading cases in European Community law which established the primacy of EC law over national legal systems.

Furniss v *Dawson* [1984] 2 WLR 226 House of Lords (Lords Fraser, Scarman, Roskill, Bridge and Brightman)

- *Social legislation: development of law by judicial reasoning*

Facts

In 1971 the taxpayers, a father and his two sons, wished to sell their shareholdings in two small family companies. In order to reduce their capital gains tax liability they entered into a scheme which consisted of a series of artificial share transactions. The Inland Revenue assessed them for capital gains but this was quashed by the special commissioners. An appeal by the Crown was dismissed by Vinelott J and his decision was affirmed by the Court of Appeal. The Crown appealed.

Held

The appeal would be upheld. The series of transactions was planned as a single scheme and therefore should be treated as a whole rather than as individual transactions.

Lord Scarman:

> 'My Lords, I would allow the appeals for the reasons given by my noble and learned friend, Lord Brightman. I add a few observations only because I am aware, and the legal profession (and others) must understand, that the law in this area is in an early stage of development. Speeches in your Lordships' House and judgments in the appellate courts of the United Kingdom are

concerned more to chart a way forward between principles accepted and not to be rejected than to attempt anything so ambitious as to determine finally the limit beyond which the safe channel of acceptable tax avoidance shelves into the dangerous shallows of unacceptable tax evasion. The law will develop from case to case. … the determination of what does, and what does not, constitute an unacceptable tax evasion is a subject suited to development by judicial process. The best chart that we have for the way forward appears to me, with great respect to all engaged on the map-making process, to be the words of Lord Diplock in *IRC* v *Burmah Oil Co Ltd* [1982] STC 30 at 32 … These words leave space in the law for the principle enunciated by Lord Tomlin in *IRC* v *Duke of Westminster* [1936] AC 1 that every man is entitled if he can to order his affairs so as to diminish the burden of tax. The limits within which this principle is to operate remain to be probed and determined judicially. Difficult though the task may be for judges, it is one which is beyond the power of the blunt instrument of legislation. Whatever a statute may provide, it has to be interpreted and applied by the courts; and ultimately it will prove to be in this area of judge-made law that our elusive journey's end will be found.'

Comment

A major judicial revision of the law concerning tax planning. The comments of Lord Scarman are particularly useful as a guide to the potential scope of judicial law reform as a source of law.

Lim Poh Choo* v *Camden & Islington Area Health Authority [1980] AC 174 House of Lords (Viscount Dilhorne, Lords Diplock, Simon of Glaisdale and Scarman)

- *Damages – judicial law reform*

Facts

Having been admitted to hospital for a minor operation, the plaintiff suffered irreparable brain damage, due to the defendants' negligence. Damages were awarded for pain, suffering and loss of amenities, loss of earnings, cost of future care and future inflation. Both parties appealed.

Held

Both appeals would be dismissed.

Lord Scarman:

> 'It cannot be said that any of the time judicially spent on these protracted proceedings has been unnecessary. The question, therefore, arises whether the state of the law which gives rise to such complexities is sound. Lord Denning MR in the Court of Appeal declared that a radical reappraisal of the law is needed. I agree. But I part company with him on ways and means. Lord Denning MR believes it can be done by the judges, whereas I would suggest to your Lordships that such a reappraisal calls for social, financial, economic and administrative decisions which only the legislature can take. The perplexities of the present case, following on the publication of the report of the Royal Commission on Civil Liability and Compensation for Personal Injury ("the Pearson report"), emphasise the need for reform of the law.
>
> The course of the litigation illustrates, with devastating clarity, the insuperable problems implicit in a system of compensation for personal injuries which (unless the parties agree otherwise) can yield only a lump sum assessed by the court at the time of judgment. Sooner or later, and too often later rather than sooner, if the parties do not settle, a court (once liability is admitted or proved) has to make an award of damages. The award, which covers past, present and future injury and loss, must, under our law, be of a lump sum assessed at the conclusion of the legal process. The award is final; it is not susceptible to review as the future unfolds, substituting fact for estimate.

Knowledge of the future being denied to mankind, so much of the award as is to be attributed to future loss and suffering (in many cases the major part of the award) will almost surely be wrong. There is really only one certainty: the future will prove the award to be either too high or too low.

Lord Denning MR appeared, however, to think, or at least to hope, that there exists machinery in the rules of the Supreme Court which may be adapted to enable an award of damages in a case such as this to be "regarded as an interim award". It is an attractive, ingenious suggestion, but, in my judgment, unsound. For so radical a reform can be made neither by judges nor by modification of rules of court. It raises issues of social, economic and financial policy nor amenable to judicial reform, which will almost certainly prove to be controversial and can be resolved by the legislature only after full consideration of factors which cannot be brought into clear focus, or be weighed and assessed, in the course of the forensic process. The judge, however wise, creative, and imaginative he may be, is "cabin'd, cribb'd, confin'd, bound in" not, as was Macbeth, to his "saucy doubts and fears" but by the evidence and arguments of the litigants. It is this limitation, inherent in the forensic process, which sets bounds to the scope of judicial law reform.'

Comment

An important case illustrating the limits to judicial law reform. The contrasting attitudes of Lord Denning MR and Lord Scarman should be noted – they are typical of the clashes of opinion between Lord Denning and senior Law Lords on the role of the judge.

R* v *Fisher [1969] 1 All ER 100 Court of Appeal Criminal Division (Widgery and Fenton Atkinson LJJ and O'Connor J)

- *Operation of statute*

Facts

On 28 October 1967 the appellant was arrested and on 2 January 1968 he was charged with being an accessory after the fact. On 5 March 1968 he was arraigned. The Criminal Law Act 1967 came into force on 1 January 1968 abolishing the offence. Counsel for the defence moved to quash the appropriate count on the indictment claiming that it disclosed no offence known to law. The chairman ruled against the appellant and he was tried and convicted. He appealed against the ruling.

Held

The appeal would be dismissed. The offence existed at the time the act was committed and therefore the statutory provisions for its indictment punishment remained in force.

O'Connor J:

> 'We can find nothing in the Criminal Law Act 1967 that requires us to hold that the change in the law as from 1st January 1968 means that the offence of accessory after the fact has never existed. We are satisfied that the offence did exist at the time the appellant committed it, and that the statutory provisions providing for its indictment and punishment remained in force. We conclude by saying that without the clearest words we cannot think that Parliament intended that accessories after the fact to serious crime, say murder or armed robbery, in the latter part of 1967 should not be guilty of any offence.'

Comment

The case is a simple one, showing the general presumption against retrospective operation of statutes.

Wilson* v *Dagnall [1972] 1 QB 509 Court of Appeal (Lord Denning MR, Megaw and Stephenson LJJ)

- *Statute – effective date*

Facts

The plaintiff's husband was killed in a motor accident in 1969. On 19 March 1970 she commenced proceedings claiming, inter alia, damages under the Fatal Accident Acts. The hearing was on 27 July 1971: the defendant admitted liability and formal judgment was entered on 30 July. On 1 July 1971 the Law Reform (Miscellaneous Provisions) Act 1971 received the Royal Assent and the Act stipulated that it was to come into force on 1 August 1971. The Act provided (in s4) that, in assessing damages under the Fatal Accidents Acts, no longer was account to be taken of a widow's prospects of remarriage. As the 21 year old plaintiff enjoyed such prospects, the judge assessed her damages as though the 1971 Act were already in force. The defendant's appeal was heard in December 1971.

Held (Lord Denning MR dissenting)

The judge had been wrong to apply the 1971 Act and the plaintiff's damages would therefore be reduced to take account of her prospects of remarriage.

Megaw LJ:

> 'It is natural to feel sympathy for this young widow, as against an anonymous insurance company. But it cannot be proper for a court of law to decide a case in favour of a plaintiff on the basis of sympathy, if the law of the land, as laid down in an Act of Parliament, provides otherwise. Whenever the law is changed by an Act of Parliament, there are likely to be cases which can be regarded as hard cases. That would not have been avoided if, for example, Parliament had provided – as it deliberately did not provide – that the change in the law was to take effect on the date when the Act was passed, 1st July 1971. For in that event the cases decided by the courts in the days or weeks preceding 1st July (instead of, as now, 1st August) could equally have been regarded as hard cases: hard, because they fell so close to the dividing line but on the wrong side of it for the plaintiff concerned. yet a dividing line there must be. The only question is: what is the dividing line which Parliament has chosen to lay down?
>
> Parliament has unambiguously said that the Act is to come into operation on 1st August 1971. To my mind there is no ambiguity about that nor any doubt as to its effect. It means that Parliament has ordained that up to that date, 1st August 1971, the law is to remain as before. I do not know why Parliament so provided. But that it did so provide is beyond dispute. I should have thought it was also beyond dispute, as an essential part of the unwritten constitutional law of England, by which courts of law are ineluctably bound, that those courts must loyally give effect to what Parliament has provided, and not seek to give effect to what they may think that Parliament ought to have provided. If Parliament has made a mistake, it has full sovereign power to correct the mistake. It follows that in my judgment the learned judge could not lawfully treat s4 of the Act as though it was already in force on 27th July. The judge's decision was wrong and contrary to law. It ordered the defendant to pay money which, in law, the defendant could not lawfully be ordered to pay to the plaintiff.'

Comment

The case is a simple one, showing that judges will give literal effect to any date stipulated by Parliament for the coming into force of an Act.

Wolstanton Ltd and Duchy of Lancaster v ***Newcastle-under-Lyme Borough Council*** [1940] 3 All ER 101 House of Lords (Viscount Maugham, Lords Atkin, Wright, Romer and Porter)

- *Custom*

Facts

The appellant owned some houses near the respondents' coal and ironstone mine. The houses were damaged by subsidence due to

the mine workings, but the respondents denied being liable to pay compensation, claiming, inter alia, that they had a customary right to work the mine without being liable to pay compensation for damage caused by subsidence. The appellant sought an injunction to prevent the respondents from working the mine.

Held

The custom was unreasonable and oppressive and therefore void.

Viscount Maugham:

> 'My Lords, it has long been beyond dispute that to give validity to a custom it must possess three characteristics. It must be certain, reasonable in itself, and of immemorial origin. As regards the last, it means that the custom must have been in existence from a time preceding the memory of man, which has been fixed as meaning 1189, the first year of the reign of Richard I: see, for the explanation of this date, the opinion of Lord Blackburn in *Dalton* v *Angus* (1881) 6 App Cas 740. The courts, however, have decided that, in the case of an alleged custom, it is sufficient to prove facts from which it may be presumed that the custom existed at that remote date, and that this presumption should in general be raised by evidence showing continuous user as of right going as far back as living testimony can go. The presumption is rebuttable, and, for instance, can be rebutted by proof that the custom alleged could not have existed in the time of Richard I. The presumption itself in most cases is little more than a fiction. It was applicable in the case of common law prescriptions ... and in most cases no one supposed that the enjoyment really went back to 1189. In the present case, however, I think that we are called upon to assume, in determining the point of law, that the custom is being attacked only on the point that it is unreasonable, and we must, therefore, assume that in other respects it either has been, or can be, proved to be valid.'

Comment

One of the rare cases to reach the House of Lords on the validity of a custom. The case shows how a custom will not be recognised if it conflicts with common law principles, in this case by being oppressive. The comments of Viscount Maugham are a useful summary of the basic elements that need to be proved to establish a lawful custom.

Woolwich Building Society v *Inland Revenue Commissioners* [1992] 3 WLR 366 House of Lords (Lords Keith of Kinkel, Goff of Chieveley, Jauncey of Tullichettle, Browne-Wilkinson and Slynn of Hadley)

- *Tax paid pursuant to unlawful demand – taxpayer's right to interest – judicial law reform*

Facts

The plaintiffs paid tax in accordance with a demand made under statutory regulations which, in subsequent proceedings by way of judicial review, were held to be ultra vires and void. The defendants repaid the capital but refused to pay interest on the money for the period between the date of payment and the judgment at judicial review.

Held (Lords Keith of Kinkel and Jauncey of Tullichettle dissenting)

By virtue of their rights at common law, the plaintiffs' claim to the interest would be successful.

Lord Goff of Chieveley:

> 'I ... turn to the submission of Woolwich that your Lordships' House should, despite the authorities to which I have referred, reformulate the law so as to establish that the subject who makes a payment in response to an unlawful demand of tax acquires forthwith a prima facie right in restitution to the repayment of the money.

This is the real point which lies at the heart of the present appeal …

In all the circumstances, I do not consider that [counsel for the Revenue's] argument, powerful though it is, is persuasive enough to deter me from recognising, in law, the force of the justice underlying Woolwich's case. Furthermore, there are particular reasons which impel me to that conclusion. The first is that this opportunity will never come again. If we do not take it now, it will be gone forever. The second is that I fear that, however compelling the principle of justice may be, it would never be sufficient to persuade a government to propose its legislative recognition by Parliament; caution, otherwise known as the Treasury, would never allow this to happen. The third is that, turning [counsel's] argument against him, the immediate practical impact of the recognition of the principle will be limited, for (unlike the present case) most cases will continue for the time being to be regulated by the various statutory regimes now in force. The fourth is that, if the principle is to be recognised, this is an almost ideal moment for that recognition to take place. This is because the Law Commission's consultation paper is now under active consideration, calling for a fundamental review of the law on this subject, including a fresh look at the various, often inconsistent, statutory regimes under which overpaid taxes and duties either may or must be repaid. The consultation may acquire a greater urgency and sense of purpose if set against the background of a recognised right of recovery at common law… In this way, legislative bounds can be set to the common law principle … Fifth, it is well established that, if the Crown pays money out of the consolidated fund without authority, such money is ipso facto recoverable if it can be traced (see *Auckland Harbour Board* v *R* [1924] AC 318). It is true that the claim in such a case can be distinguished as being proprietary in nature. But the comparison with the position of the citizen, on the law as it stands at present, is most unattractive.

There is a sixth reason which favours this conclusion. I refer to the decision of the Court of Justice of the European Communities in *Amministrazione delle Finanze dello Stato* v *San Giorgio SpA* Case 199/82 [1983] ECR 3595, which establishes that a person who pays charges levied by a member state contrary to the rules of Community law is entitled to repayment of the charge, such right being regarded as a consequence of, and an adjunct to, the rights conferred on individuals by the Community provisions prohibiting the relevant charges … The *San Giorgio* case is also of interest for present purposes in that it accepts that Community law does not prevent a national legal system from disallowing repayment of charges where to do so would entail unjust enrichment of the recipient, in particular where the charges have been incorporated into the price of goods and so passed on to the purchaser. I only comment that, at a time when Community law is becoming increasingly important, it would be strange if the right of the citizen to recover overpaid charges were to be more restricted under domestic law than it is under Community law.

I would therefore hold that money paid by a citizen to a public authority in the form of taxes or other levies paid pursuant to an ultra vires demand by the authority is prima facie recoverable by the citizen as of right …'

Comment

An important case illustrating the potential growth of equitable principles so as to keep pace with modern developments, including the implications of membership of the European Union. The fact that the Law Lords were divided 3 to 2 on the issue of whether to reformulate the principles of restitution shows the sensitivity of the subject of judicial law reform. Lord Goff's judgment gives six cogent reasons for such reform.

2 The Judiciary and Magistrates

R* v *Human Fertilisation and Embryology Authority, ex parte Blood [1997] 2 All ER 687 Court of Appeal (Lord Woolf MR, Waite and Henry LJJ)

- *Statutory regulation of fertilisation procedures – effect of breach of statutory rules – flexible nature of judicial review to grant appropriate remedy in exceptional circumstances – discretion of judges to make law in novel situations*

Facts

The applicant and her husband had wanted to start a family but before the applicant could conceive the husband contracted meningitis and lapsed into a coma. The applicant asked for samples of his sperm to be collected for future use in artificial insemination. The samples were entrusted to a research trust for storage. The husband died. Subsequently the Human Fertilisation and Embryology Authority prevented the research trust from releasing the samples from storage on the ground that the written consent of the donor to the taking of his sperm had not been obtained as required by the relevant statute. The applicant sought judicial review of the Authority's decision.

Held

Judicial review would be granted so as to enable the applicant to obtain the sperm samples and undergo treatment for an artificially assisted pregnancy. The Authority's decision had been lawful under the terms of the statute but the circumstances were exceptional and had not been foreseen by Parliament when passing the regulatory legislation. Judicial discretion was sufficiently flexible to grant the remedy which the compassionate circumstances demanded, particularly as the legal situation had never before been explored. (Subsequently the Authority gave permission for Mrs Blood to export her husband's sperm provided she attended a fertility clinic in Belgium for treatment.)

Lord Woolf MR:

> '... it is reasonably clear that it was a concern of the authority that if they gave Mrs Blood consent to export, this would create an undesirable precedent which could result in the flouting of the 1990 Act. While as already indicated this can, in the appropriate case, be a legitimate reason for impeding the provision of services in another Member Sstate it is a consideration which cannot have any application here. The fact that storage cannot lawfully take place without written consent, from a practical point of view means that there should be no fresh cases. No licensee can lawfully do what was done here, namely preserve sperm in this country without written consent. If the authority had appreciated this, it could well have influenced its decision and, in particular, overcome its reluctance to identify Mr Blood's wishes on the basis of Mrs Blood's evidence and the material which she can produce to support that evidence. It would be understandable for the authority not to wish to engage on an inquiry of this nature where there can be other cases where the evidence is not so credible since it could lead to invidious comparisons. However, the position is different if this case will not create an undesirable precedent.
>
> If the authority had taken into account that Mrs Blood was entitled to receive treatment in Belgium unless there is some good reason why she should not be allowed to receive

that treatment, the authority may well have taken the view that as the 1990 Act did not prohibit this, they should give their consent. The authority could well conclude that as this is a problem which will not reoccur there is not any good reason for them not to give their consent. If treated in Belgium, Mrs Blood is proposing to use a clinic which in general terms adopts the same standards as this country. The one difference being that they do not insist upon the formal requirements as to written consent which are required in this country. The need for formal requirements is not obvious in this situation.

Apart from the effect of Community law, the authority's view of the law was correct. It is not possible to say even taking into account Community law that the authority are bound to come to a decision in Mrs Blood's favour. What can be said is that the legal position having received further clarification, the case for their doing so is much stronger than it was when they last considered the matter.'

Comment

The growth of judicial review as a mechanism for scrutinising the legality of administrative decisions appears to allow greater scope for judicial creativity than any other branch of English Law, with the possible exception of equity. What is extraordinary about this decision is that judicial review was granted not on the basis of an unlawful administrative decision but rather on the basis that 'justice' required it. The case had received considerable publicity and the media had been overwhelmingly sympathetic towards Mrs Diane Blood, the applicant. It is possible that this background affected the reasoning of the judges. The decision of the Court of Appeal may be regarded as a remarkably creative use of adjudicatory powers which, whilst recognising the force of law, took a compassionate view in exceptional circumstances.

Shaw* v *Director of Public Prosecutions [1962] AC 220 House of Lords (Viscount Simonds, Lords Reid, Tucker, Morris and Hodson)

- *Judicial law making*

Facts

A conspiracy to corrupt public morals was an offence. The defendant had agreed to publish a 'Ladies Directory' containing names, addresses, photographs and other details of prostitutes.

Held

He had been rightly convicted of conspiracy to corrupt public morals.

Viscount Simonds:

> 'In the sphere of criminal law, I entertain no doubt that there remains in the courts of law a residual power to enforce the supreme and fundamental purpose of the law, to conserve not only the safety and the order but also the moral welfare of the state, and that it is their duty to guard it against attacks which may be the more insidious because they are novel and unprepared for.'

Comment

A very controversial decision showing perhaps the extremes to which judges can go in developing the common law. The generally hostile reaction to the decision from politicians and academics may have led to a more cautious and restrained attitude on the part of the judges to innovations in criminal law.

Sirros* v *Moore [1974] 3 WLR 459 Court of Appeal (Civil Division) (Lord Denning MR, Buckley and Ormrod LJJ)

- *Immunity of judges*

Facts

The plaintiff was a Turk and had overstayed his leave in England. He was brought before the magistrate who fined him and recommended that he be deported but directed that he should not be detained pending the Home Secretary's decision. The plaintiff appealed to the Crown Court against the recommendation. The appeal was heard by a circuit judge and two magistrates and was dismissed on the ground of lack of jurisdiction to hear the appeal. As the plaintiff was leaving the court the judge called out 'stop him' and sent police officers after him. They took him to the cells and he appeared before the judge again after lunch. Counsel on his behalf applied for bail but this was refused and he was put in custody. The next day the plaintiff applied to the Divisional Court for leave to move for a writ of habeus corpus. This was granted and he was released on bail. He was later granted a writ of habeus corpus on the grounds that the judge was functus officio when ordering the plaintiff to be taken into custody. The plaintiff then brought an action for damages against the judge and the police officers for assault and false imprisonment.

Held

1 The Crown Court did have jurisdiction to entertain the appeal but as it had not done so the magistrate's order remained in force and therefore the judge was not entitled to make the order detaining the plaintiff and his detention was unlawful.
2 The plaintiff had no cause of action against the judge.
3 The plaintiff had no action against the police who were acting on the judge's orders.

Lord Denning MR:

> 'Ever since the year 1613, if not before, it has been accepted in our law that no action is maintainable against a judge for anything said or done by him in the exercise of a jurisdiction which belongs to him. The words which he speaks are protected by an absolute privilege.
>
> The orders which he gives, and the sentences which he imposes, cannot be made the subject of civil proceedings against him. No matter that the judge was under some gross error or ignorance, or was actuated by envy, hatred and malice, and all uncharitableness, he is not liable to an action. The remedy of the party aggrieved is to appeal to a court of appeal or to apply for habeas corpus, or a writ of error or certiorari, or take some such step to reverse his ruling. Of course if the judge has accepted bribes or been in the least degree corrupt, or has perverted the course of justice, he can be punished in the criminal courts.
>
> That apart, however, a judge is not liable to an action for damages. The reason is not because the judge has any privilege to make mistakes or to do wrong. It is so that he should be able to do his duty with complete independence and free from fear. ...
>
> ... As a matter of principle the judges of superior courts have no greater claim to immunity than the judges of the lower courts. Every judge of the courts of this land – from the highest to the lowest – should be protected to the same degree, and liable to the same degree. If the reason underlying the immunity is to ensure "that they may be free in thought and independent in judgment", it applies to every judge, whatever his rank. Each should be protected from liability to damages when he is acting judicially. Each should be able to do his work in complete independence and free from fear. He should not have to turn the pages of his books with trembling fingers, asking himself: "If I do this, shall I be liable in damages?" So long as he does his work in the honest belief that it is within his jurisdiction, then he is not liable to an action. He may be mistaken in fact. He may be ignorant in law. What he does may be outside his jurisdiction – in fact or in law – but so long as he honestly believes it to be within his jurisdiction, he should not be liable. Once he maintains this belief, nothing else will make him liable. He is not to be plagued with allegations of malice or ill-will or bias or anything of the kind. Actions based on such allegations have been struck out and will

continue to be struck out. Nothing will make him liable except it will be shown that he was not acting judicially, knowing that he had no jurisdiction to do it.'

Comment

A case setting out the general principles of judicial immunity. The full speech of Lord Denning MR contained comments which applied the same principles to magistrates but this area has been affected by statutory regulation. The effect is that no action will lie against a magistrate in respect of any act or omission when acting in the execution of his duty and with respect to any matter within his jurisdiction. But an action will lie if the matter was not within his jurisdiction and it is proved that he acted in bad faith. See, further, Justices of the Peace Act 1997, which consolidates previous legislation in this field.

3 The Doctrine of Precedent

Ashville Investments Ltd v *Elmer Contractors Ltd* [1988] 3 WLR 867 Court of Appeal (May, Balcombe and Bingham LJJ)

- *Precedent – principles only binding*

Facts

There was a contract for the building of six warehouses and it provided that any dispute 'as to the construction of this contract ...' was to be referred to arbitration. The contractor commenced arbitration proceedings alleging mistake and misrepresentation; the owner sought a declaration that the arbitrator had no jurisdiction, inter alia, to hear and determine such issues. The judge upheld the arbitrator's jurisdiction; the owner appealed.

Held

The appeal would be dismissed, in the light of the true construction of the arbitration clause.

May LJ:

'In these circumstances I think that it is necessary carefully to consider the role of precedent and the doctrine of stare decisis in a case such as this, in which a question of construction is in truth the fundamental issue between the parties. In my opinion the doctrine of precedent only involves this: that when a case has been decided in a court it is only the legal principle or principles on which that court has so decided that bind courts of concurrent or lower jurisdictions and require them to follow and adopt them when they are relevant to the decision in later cases before those courts. The ratio decidendi of a prior case, the reason why it was decided as it was, is in my view only to be understood in this somewhat limited sense.

Thus, in the present context it has been decided and is a principle of law that an arbitrator does not have jurisdiction, nor can the arbitration agreement be construed to give him jurisdiction to rule on the initial existence of the contract. On the other hand, given an appropriate arbitration clause, an arbitrator does in general have jurisdiction to rule on the continued existence of the contract ...

Similarly it is a principle of law that the scope of an arbitrator's jurisdiction and powers in a given case depend fundamentally on the terms of the arbitration agreement, that is to say on its proper construction in all the circumstances.

However, I do not think that there is any principle of law to the effect that the meaning of certain specific words in one arbitration clause in one contract is immutable and that those same specific words in another arbitration clause in other circumstances in another contract must be construed in the same way. This is not to say that the earlier decision on a given form of words will not be persuasive, to a degree dependent on the extent of the similarity between the contracts and surrounding circumstances in the two cases. In the interests of certainty and clarity a court may well think it right to construe words in an arbitration agreement, or indeed in a particular type of contract, in the same way as those same words have earlier been construed in another case involving an arbitration clause by another court. But in my opinion the subsequent court is not bound by the doctrine of stare decisis to do so.

If I were wrong, then in any event it must be necessary to compare the surrounding circumstances in each case to ensure that

those in the later case did not require one to construe albeit the same words differently when used in the different context.'

Comment

The decision shows that it is only the principles of law which are binding under the doctrine of precedent. Other issues decided in a case which do not form part of these principles will not be binding, eg the way in which words are construed in a particular contract.

C v *DPP* [1995] 2 All ER 43 House of Lords (Lords Jauncey, Bridge, Ackner, Lowry and Browne-Wilkinson)

• *Judicial law reform and the doctrine of precedent*

Facts

A boy aged 12 was charged with interfering with a motor vehicle with intent to commit theft, contrary to s9(1) of the Criminal Attempts Act 1981. The defence relied on the common law presumption of doli incapax, ie that a child aged between 10 and 14 who was charged with a criminal offence was presumed not to know that his act was seriously wrong unless the prosecution could rely on positive proof that in fact the child knew that what he did was seriously wrong. Following the boy's conviction by a magistrates' court the defence appealed by way of case stated to the Divisional Court which held that the presumption of doli incapax was outdated and should be treated as being no longer good law. The appellant then appealed to the House of Lords, contending that the Divisional Court had indulged in unjustified law-making and was bound by authority to recognise and apply the presumption.

Held

The appeal would be allowed. The presumption of doli incapax was still part of English Law. The Divisional Court was bound by authority to recognise and apply the presumption. It was not an appropriate case for the House of Lords in its judicial capacity to reform the law.

Lord Lowry:

> 'My Lords, Mr Robertson QC for the appellant has argued cogently that the Divisional Court was not justified in holding that the presumption is "no longer part of the law of England"...
>
> The material which Mr Robertson put before your Lordships convinces me that the presumption is still universally recognised as an effective doctrine which the government has recently reaffirmed to be, in the government's view, part of the criminal law. The imperfections which have been attributed to that doctrine cannot, in my view, provide a justification for saying that the presumption is no longer part of our law. To sweep it away under the doubtful auspices of judicial legislation is to my mind, quite impracticable. ...
>
> The distinction between the treatment and the punishment of child "offenders" has popular and political overtones, a fact which shows that we have been discussing not so much a legal as a social problem, with a dash of politics thrown in, and emphasis that it should be within the exclusive remit of Parliament. There is need to study other systems, including that which holds sway in Scotland, a task for which the courts are not equipped. Whatever change is made, it should come only after collating and considering the evidence and after taking account of the effect which a change would have on the whole law relating to children's antisocial behaviour. This is a classic case for Parliamentary investigation, deliberation and legislation.'

Lords Jauncey, Bridge, Ackner and Browne-Wilkinson agreed with Lord Lowry.

Comment

A very interesting case showing a reluctance on the part of the Law Lords to reform the law in a controversial area. Lord Lowry's judgment is based on the 'leave it to Parliament'

argument on the ground that the issue in the case (the treatment and punishment of child offenders) was a classic one for parliamentary debate and resolution. A clause in the Crime and Disorder Bill 1998 proposes the abolition of the presumption of doli incapax, so it could be argued that the activism of the Divisional Court has helped to provoke this potential change in the law.

Colchester Estates (Cardiff)* v *Carlton Industries plc [1984] 2 All ER 601 High Court (Nourse J)

- *High Court – conflicting decisions*

Facts

The plaintiff owned leasehold property, and wished to bring an action to reclaim from the tenant thereof the cost of executing repairs to maintain the property. According to a 1981 decision of the High Court such a claim could not be started (by issue of a writ) without leave of the court. However, a 1984 decision of the High Court in another case, but on identical facts, had decided that no such leave was necessary before commencing the action. The 1981 decision had been cited to the court which reached the 1984 one, so that it was not open to the court in the present case to rely upon the per incuriam exception contained in Lord Greene MR's judgment in *Young* v *Bristol Aeroplane Co Ltd*: see below.

Held

The court would follow the later, 1984, decision holding as a general rule that where two decisions of the High Court are in conflict, the more recent decision should be followed, and the earlier one not followed, provided that the earlier was considered in the latter, but that it was still open to a judge faced with the inconsistent decisions to apply the earlier and not the later if he is convinced that the later is wrong.

Nourse J:

'... Since this is a question on which the court has an interest of its own, I thought it right to make an independent research. That led me to the decision of Denning J in *Minister of Pensions* v *Higham* [1948] 1 All ER 863, [1948] 2 KB 153. I put that case to counsel during the course of argument yesterday afternoon and I hope and believe that they both had an opportunity of saying what they wanted to say about it.

Minister of Pensions v *Higham* was a case where Denning J, who was then the judge nominated to hear appeals from the pensions appeal tribunals in England, was faced with a conflict between a dictum in an earlier case of his own and a decision of the Court of Session on an appeal from one of the pensions appeal tribunals in Scotland. In the later case the Court of Session, having considered the dictum in the earlier one and having no doubt considered it fully, said that it was unable to agree with it. Denning J, having stated the special position in which he was there placed, said ([1948] 1 All ER 863 at 865, [1948] 2 KB 153 at 155):

> "I lay down for myself, therefore, the rule that, where the Court of Session have felt compelled to depart from a previous decision of this court, that is a strong reason for my reconsidering the matter, and if, on reconsideration, I am left in no doubt of the correctness of my own decision, then I shall be prepared to follow the decision of the Court of Session, at any rate in those cases when it is in favour of the claimant because he should be given the benefit of the doubt."

Had the judge stopped there, I might well have agreed with counsel that the case could not, by reason of its special features, be treated as being of any general value. However, he went on to say this:

> "In this respect I follow the general rule that where there are conflicting decisions of courts of co-ordinate jurisdiction, the later decision is to be preferred if it is reached after full consideration of the earlier decisions."

That unqualified statement of a general rule comes from a source to which the greatest possible respect is due. It is fortuitous that

my own instinct should have coincided with it. However diffident I might have been in relying on instinct alone, the coincidence encourages me me to suggest a reason for the rule. It is that it is desirable that the law, at whatever level it is declared, should generally be certain. If a decision of this court, reached after full consideration of an earlier one which went the other way, is normally to be open to review on a third occasion when the same point arises for decision at the same level, there will be no end of it. Why not in a fourth, fifth or sixth case as well? Counsel for the defendant had to face that prospect with equanimity or, perhaps to be fairer to him, with resignation. I decline to join him, especially in times when the cost of litigation and the pressure of work on the courts are so great. There must come a time when a point is normally to be treated as having been settled at first instance. I think that that should be when the earlier decision has been fully considered, but not followed, in a later one. Consistently with the modern approach of the judges of this court to an earlier decision of one of their number (see eg *Huddersfield Police Authority* v *Watson* [1947] 2 All ER 193 at 196, [1947] KB 842 at 848 per Lord Goddard CJ), I would make an exception only in the case, which must be rare, where the third judge is convinced that the second was wrong in not following the first. An obvious example is where some binding or persuasive authority has not been cited in either of the first two cases. If that is the rule then, unless the party interested seriously intends to submit that it falls within the exception, the hearing at first instance in the third case will, so far as the point in question is concerned, be a formality, with any argument on it reserved to the Court of Appeal.'

Comment

A helpful decision on the mechanical operation of the rules of precedent in the High Court.

Davis* v *Johnson [1978] 2 WLR 553 House of Lords (Lords Diplock, Dilhorne, Kilbrandon, Salmon and Scarman)

- *Judicial precedent – Court of Appeal (Civil Division)*

Facts

The respondent, a young unmarried mother, who had a joint tenancy of a council flat with the appellant, the father of her child, left the home with the child because of his violent behaviour to her. She applied to the county court for injunctions under the Domestic Violence and Matrimonial Proceedings Act 1976 to restrain him from molesting her or the child and to exclude him from the home. The injunctions were granted by the county court, the appellant left the flat and the woman and child returned to it. Within a few days of this decision two other cases (*B* v *B* [1978] 2 WLR 160 and *Cantliff* v *Jenkins* [1978] 2 WLR 177) were decided by the Court of Appeal in which the Act was construed as not allowing an injunction to be granted in similar circumstances where a person had a right of property in the home. As a result the county court judge in the present case rescinded the injunction and the man returned to the flat while the woman and child found shelter in an overcrowded home for battered wives. The woman appealed to the Court of Appeal which decided to ignore their earlier decisions and allow the appeal. The man then appealed to the House of Lords.

Held

The two earlier decisions were wrong. The act was expressly intended to protect unmarried women who were subjected to domestic violence and who had minimal rights in a shared home. The court affirmed that the rules laid down in *Young* v *Bristol Aeroplane Co Ltd* [1944] KB 718 were still binding on the Court of Appeal.

Lord Diplock:

> 'In an appellate court of last resort a balance must be struck between the need on the one side for the legal certainty resulting from the binding effect of previous decisions and, on the other side, the avoidance of undue restriction on the proper development of the law. In the case of an intermediate appellate court, however, the second desideratum can be taken care of by appeal to a superior appellate court, if reasonable means of access to it are available; while the risk to the first desideratum, legal certainty, if the court is not bound by its own previous decisions grows ever greater. So the balance does not lie in the same place as in the case of a court of last resort.'

Lord Diplock then quoted Scarman LJ in *Tiverton Estates Ltd* v *Wearwell Ltd* [1975] Ch 172:

> ' "The Court of Appeal occupies a central but, save for a few exceptions, an intermediate position in our legal system. To a large extent, the consistency and certainty of the law depend upon it. It sits almost always in divisions of three: more judges can sit to hear a case, but their decision enjoys no greater authority than a court composed of three. If, therefore, throwing aside the restraints of *Young* v *Bristol Aeroplane Co Ltd*, one division of the court should refuse to follow another because it believed the other's decision to be wrong, there would be a risk of confusion and doubt arising where there should be consistency and certainty. The appropriate forum for the correction of the Court of Appeal's errors is the House of Lords." '

Comment

An important decision reaffirming the rules of precedent for the Court of Appeal (Civil Division). Lord Denning had attempted to avoid those rules in order to do 'justice' but was firmly rebuked by Lord Diplock. Consider whether Lord Diplock's reasoning is cogent bearing in mind that comparatively few cases reach the House of Lords, so that the opportunities to develop the law in a rational and humane way may be very limited.

Donoghue* v *Stevenson [1932] AC 562 House of Lords (Lords Buckmaster, Atkin, Tomlin, Thankerton and Macmillan)

- *Judicial activism – influential obiter dicta*

Facts

The appellant, a shop assistant, sued a drinks manufacturer for injuries she suffered as the result of consuming part of the contents of a ginger-beer bottle which contained the decomposed remains of a snail. The bottle was made of dark opaque glass and had been purchased by a friend from a shop in Paisley.

Held

The manufacturer of an article of food, medicine or the like, who sells it to a distributor in circumstances which prevent the distributor or ultimate purchaser or consumer from inspecting the contents, is under a legal duty to the consumer to take reasonable care that the goods are free from any defect likely to cause injury.

Lord Atkin:

> 'It is said that the law of England and Scotland is that the poisoned consumer has no remedy against the negligent manufacturer. If this were the result of the authorities, I should consider the result a grave defect in the law, and so contrary to principle that I should hesitate long before following any decision to that effect which had not the authority of this House. I would point out that, in the assumed state of the authorities, not only would the consumer have no remedy against the manufacturer, he would have none against anyone else, for in the circumstance alleged there would be no evidence of negligence against anyone other than the manufacturer; and, except in the case of a consumer who was also a pur-

chaser, no contract and no warranty of fitness ... The doctrine supported by the decision below would not only deny a remedy to the consumer who was injured by consuming bottled beer or chocolates poisoned by the negligence of the manufacturer, but also to the use of what should be a harmless proprietary medicine, an ointment, a soap, a cleaning fluid or cleaning powder ... I do not think so ill of our jurisprudence as to suppose that its principles are so remote from the ordinary needs of civilised society and the ordinary claims it makes upon its members as to deny a legal remedy where there is so obviously a social wrong.'

Comment

A famous case in the tort of negligence which shows how observations (obiter dicta) can prove to be so influential that they are eventually elevated into a binding principle, in this case the 'neighbour principle' which establishes the duty of care in the tort of negligence for acts and omissions.

Gallie v *Lee* [1969] 2 Ch 17 Court of Appeal (Lord Denning MR, Russell and Salmon LJJ)

- *Court of Appeal – bound by its own previous decisions?*

(The facts and decision are not important in this context. It is the views of the judges on the operation of precedent which is of significance here. For the ultimate decision see *Saunders* v *Anglia Building Society* [1971] AC 1004 (on the issue of non est factum in contract law).)

Lord Denning:

'We are of course, bound by the decisions of the House (of Lords) but I do not think we are bound by prior decisions of our own, or at any rate, not absolutely bound. We are not fettered as it was once thought. It was a self-imposed limitation: and we who imposed it can also remove it. The House of Lords have done it. So why should not we do likewise? We should be just as free, no more and no less, to depart from a prior precedent of our own, as in like case is the House of Lords or a judge of first instance. It is very, very rarely that we will go against a previous decision of our own, but if it is clearly shown to be erroneous, we should be able to put it right.'

Russell LJ:

'... I do not support the suggestion that this court is free to override its own decisions now that the House of Lords has given itself ability to override its own decisions. I am a firm believer in a system by which citizens and their advisers can have as much certainty as possible in the ordering of their affairs. Litigation is an activity that does not markedly contribute to the happiness of mankind, though it is sometimes unavoidable. An abandonment of the principle that this court follows its own decisions on the law would I think lead to greater uncertainty and tend to produce more litigation. In the case of decisions of the House of Lords error, or what is later considered to be error, could only previously be corrected by statute: and the other demands on parliamentary time made this possibility so remote that the decision of the House of Lords not necessarily to be bound by a previous decision was justifiable at the expense of some loss of certainty. But the availability of the House of Lords to correct error in the Court of Appeal makes it in my view unnecessary for this court to depart from its existing discipline.'

Salmon LJ:

'As I have already indicated, the law certainly ought, in my view to be as stated by the Master of the Rolls in his conclusions. I am confident that it would be so stated by the House of Lords were this question to come before it for decision ... I am, however, convinced that so long as this court considers itself absolutely bound by its own decisions I have no power to adopt the Master of the Rolls' conclusions; I must accept the law as stated in the authorities to

which I have referred in spite of the fact that it results too often in inconsistency, injustice, and an affront to commonsense. The dicta to the effect that this court is absolutely bound by its own decisions are very strong; see for example, *Young* v *Bristol Aeroplane Co Ltd* [1944] 1 KB 718; [1946] AC 163; *Bonsor* v *Musicians' Union* [1956] AC 104, but no stronger than those by virtue of which the House of Lords until recently treated itself as similarly bound by its own decisions.

The point about the authority of this court has never been decided by the House of Lords. In the nature of things it is not a point that could ever come before the House for decision. Nor does it depend upon any statutory or common law rule. This practice of ours apparently rests solely upon a concept of judicial comity laid down many years ago and automatically followed ever since: see *The Vera Cruz (No 2)* (1884) 9 PD 96 per Lord Brett at p98. Surely today judicial comity would be amply satisfied if we were to adopt the same principle in relation to our decisions as the House of Lords has recently laid down for itself by a pronouncement of the whole House. It may be that one day we shall make a similar pronouncement. I can see no valid reason why we should not do so and many why we should. But that day is not yet. It is, I think, only by a pronouncement of the whole court that we could effectively alter a practice which is so deeply rooted. In the meantime I find myself reluctantly obliged to accept the old authorities, however much I disagree with them. My only consolation is that in spite of the present unsatisfactory state of this branch of the law, it enables us, on the facts of this case, to reach a decision which accords with reason and justice.'

Comment

The judicial observations on the rules of precedent for the Court of Appeal are fascinating because they illustrate the classic conflict of opinion over the functions of a judge. Lord Denning's passionate belief that the duty of a judge is to do justice in each case, if necessary by removing traditional limitations on judicial law reform, should be contrasted with the colder and more logical opinions of Russell and Salmon LJJ as to the need to preserve certainty and consistency in judicial decision-making. The actual decision in the case was affirmed by the House of Lords: *Saunders* v *Anglia Building Society* [1971] AC 1004.

Hedley Byrne & Co Ltd v *Heller & Partners Ltd* [1963] 3 WLR 101 House of Lords (Lords Reid, Morris, Hodson, Devlin and Pearce)

- *Professional negligence – influential obiter dicta*

Facts

The appellants were advertising agents who had placed substantial forward advertising orders for a client company, the appellants being liable for the cost. They asked their bankers to inquire into the company's financial stability and their bankers made inquiries of the respondents, who were the company's bankers. The respondents gave favourable references but stipulated that these were 'without responsibility'. In reliance on these references the appellants placed orders which resulted in a loss of £17,000. They brought an action against the respondents for damages for negligence.

Held

A negligent misrepresentation, even though it might be made honestly, may give rise to an action for damages for consequential financial loss even though there is no contract or fiduciary relationship. The law will imply a duty of care by a person with a special skill towards another person who seeks information from him in circumstances where the former person knew or ought to have known that reliance was being placed on his skill and judgment. However, since in this case there was an express disclaimer of responsibility, no such duty was implied.

Lord Devlin:

> 'I think … that there is ample authority to justify your Lordships in saying now that the categories of special relationships which may give rise to a duty to take care in word as well as in deed are not limited to contractual relationships or to relationships of fiduciary duty, but include also relationships which in the words of Lord Shaw in *Nocton* v *Lord Ashburton* [1914] AC 932 are "equivalent to contract", that is, where there is an assumption of responsibility in circumstances in which, but for the absence of consideration, there would be a contract. Where there is an express undertaking, an express warranty as distinct from mere representation, there can be little difficulty. The difficulty arises in discerning those cases in which the undertaking is to be implied. In this respect the absence of consideration is not irrelevant. Payment for information or advice is very good evidence that it is being relied upon and that the informer or adviser knows that it is. Where there is no consideration, it will be necessary to exercise greater care in distinguishing between social and professional relationships and between those which are of a contractual character and those which are not. It may often be material to consider whether the adviser is acting purely out of a good nature or whether he is getting his reward in some indirect form. The service that a bank performs in giving a reference is not done simply out of a desire to assist commerce. It would discourage customers of the bank if their deals fell through because the bank had refused to testify to their credit when it was good.'

Comment

A famous case in the tort of negligence which shows how the common law can be continually extended by influential obiter dicta, in this case by extending the 'neighbour principle' of *Donoghue* v *Stevenson* (above) to negligent misstatements.

Johnson v *Agnew* [1979] 2 WLR 487 House of Lords (Lords Wilberforce, Salmon, Fraser, Keith and Scarman)

- *Overruling*

Facts

The plaintiff owned property which had been mortgaged to the defendants, but was in arrears with his repayments. He agreed to sell the property to a purchaser for a sum well in excess of the mortgage but, when the purchaser failed to complete, obtained an order for specific performance. Nine months later, the order for specific performance not having been carried out, the defendant mortgagees enforced their security by selling the property. The proceeds realised by the mortgage were insufficient to discharge the mortgage in full, and the plaintiff applied for an order that the purchaser should pay the balance of the purchase price to him.

Held

Although a vendor had to elect at the trial whether to pursue the remedy of specific performance or that of damages, if specific performance was ordered the contract remained in effect and was not merged in the judgment so that, if the order was not complied with, he might apply to the court to put an end to the contract and, if he did so, he was entitled to damages appropriate to the breach of contract.

Lord Wilberforce:

> 'In my opinion *Henty* v *Schroder* (1879) 12 Ch D 666 cannot stand against the powerful tide of logical objection and judicial reasoning. It should no longer be regarded as of authority: the cases following it should be overruled. In particular *Barber* v *Wolfe* and *Horsler* v *Zorro* cannot stand so far as they are based on the theory of "rescission ab initio" which has no application to the termination of a contract on accepted repudiation.'

Comment

A simple case showing the effect of overruling an earlier decision which had incorrectly interpreted the law: the effect is to deprive the earlier decision of all authority as precedent.

Jones* v *Secretary of State for Social Services [1972] 2 WLR 210 House of Lords (Lords Reid, Morris, Dilhorne, Wilberforce, Pearson, Diplock and Simon)

- *Departure from previous decision*

Facts

This case involved the construction of the National Insurance (Industrial Injuries) Act 1946. Their Lordships were asked to depart from one of their previous decisions (*Re Dowling*) which they declined to do. (The courts below had both distinguished the case.)

Held

The majority of the House considered the ratio of the precedent to be wrongly decided but on a majority their Lordships refused to overrule the case. The majority expressed the view that the power of the House of Lords to depart from its previous decisions should only be 'sparingly exercised' to ensure certainty. They considered that a matter of statutory construction would rarely of itself provide a suitable occasion for such a departure. They added that there was no broad principle of justice or public policy involved in the instant case nor any question of legal principle.

Lord Reid gave his view of the purpose of the Law Lords' 1966 *Practice Statement* (see [1966] 1 WLR 1234):

> 'My understanding of the position when this resolution was adopted was and is that there was a comparatively small number of reported decisions of this House which were generally thought to be impeding the proper development of the law or to have led to results which were unjust or contrary to public policy and that such decisions should be reconsidered as opportunities arose. But this practice was not to be used to weaken existing certainty in the law. The old view was that any departure from rigid adherence to precedent would weaken that certainty. I did not and do not accept that view. It is notorious that where an existing decision is disapproved but cannot be overruled courts tend to distinguish it on inadequate grounds. I do not think that they act wrongly in so doing; they are adopting the less bad of the only alternatives open to them. But this is bound to lead to uncertainty for no one can say in advance whether in a particular case the court will or will not feel bound to follow the old unsatisfactory decision. On balance it seems to me that overruling such a decision will promote and not impair the certainty of the law.
>
> But that certainty will be impaired unless this practice is used sparingly. I would not seek to categorise cases in which it should or cases in which it should not be used. As time passes experience will supply some guide. But I would venture the opinion that the typical case for reconsidering an old decision is where some broad issue is involved, and that it should only be in rare cases that we should reconsider questions of construction of statutes or other documents. In very many cases it cannot be said positively that one construction is right and the other is wrong. Construction so often depends on weighing one consideration against another. Much may depend on one's approach. If more attention is paid to meticulous examination of the language used in the statute the result may be different from that reached by paying more attention to the apparent object of the statute so as to adopt the meaning of the words under consideration which best accord with it.'

Lord Simon, after concluding his judgment, gave his opinion of prospective overruling:

> 'I am left with the feeling that, theoretically, in some way the most satisfactory outcome of these appeals would have been to have allowed them on the basis that they were governed by the decision in Dowling's case,

but to have overruled that decision prospectively. Such a power – to overrule prospectively a previous decision, but so as not necessarily to affect the parties before the court – is exercisable by the Supreme Court of the United States, which has held it to be based on the common law: see *Linkletter* v *Walker* (1965) 381 US 618.

It might be argued that a further step to invest your Lordships with the ampler and more flexible powers of the Supreme Court of the United States would be no more than a logical extension of present realities and of powers already claimed without evoking objection from other organs of the constitution. But my own view is that, although such extension should be seriously considered, it would preferably be the subject matter of Parliamentary enactment. In the first place, informed professional opinion is probably to the effect that your Lordships have no power to overrule decisions with prospective effect only; such opinion is itself a source of law; and your Lordships sitting judicially, are bound by any rule of law arising extra-judicially. Secondly, to proceed by Act of Parliament would obviate any suspicion of endeavouring to upset one-sidedly the constitutional balance between executive, legislature and judiciary. Thirdly, concomitant problems could receive consideration – for example, whether other courts supreme within their own jurisdictions should have similar powers as regards the rule of precedent; whether machinery could and should be devised to apprise the courts of the potential repercussions of any particular decisions; and whether any court (including the appellate committee of your Lordships' House) should sit in banc when invited to review a previous decision.'

Comment

This is an important case because of the explanation given by Lord Reid for the need for sparing use of the 1966 *Practice Statement.* In addition, Lord Simon's judgment contains interesting observations on the advantages of prospective overruling. Note his view that it is for Parliament, not the judges, to authorise any fundamental changes in the practice of overruling decisions.

London Street Tramways Co* v *London County Council [1898] AC 375 House of Lords (Earl of Halsbury LC, Lords Macnaughten, Morris and James of Hereford)

- *House of Lords – previous decisions*

(The facts and decision are not important in this context. It is the statement on the operation of precedent in the House of Lords which is of significance here, if only from an historical viewpoint.)

Earl of Halsbury LC:

> 'My Lords it is totally impossible, as it appears to me, to disregard the whole current of authority upon this subject, and to suppose that what some people call an "extraordinary case", an "unusual case", a case somewhat different from the common, in the opinion of each litigant in turn, is sufficient to justify the rehearing and rearguing before the final Court of Appeal of a question which has already been decided. Of course I do not deny that cases of individual hardship may arise, and there may be a current of opinion in the profession that such and such a judgment was erroneous; but what is that occasional interference with what is perhaps abstract justice as compared with the inconvenience – the disastrous inconvenience – of having each question subject to being reargued and the dealings of mankind rendered doubtful by reason of different decisions, so that in truth and in fact there would be no real final Court of Appeal? My Lords, "interest rei publicae" demands that there should be "finis litium" at some time, and there could be no "finis litium" if it were possible to suggest in each case that it might be reargued, because it is "not an ordinary case", whatever that may mean. Under these circumstances I am of opinion that we ought not to allow this question to be reargued.'

Comment

The case remains of historic importance in showing the practice of the House of Lords prior to the 1966 *Practice Statement.* Consider whether the old practice of regarding previous decisions as absolutely binding was preferable on constitutional grounds to the change authorised by the 1966 *Practice Statement.*

Miliangos v *George Frank (Textiles) Ltd* [1975] 3 WLR 758 House of Lords (Lords Wilberforce, Simon, Cross, Edmund-Davies and Fraser)

- *House of Lords – previous decisions*

Facts

The plaintiff, a Swiss national, supplied yarn to an English company under a contract which provided that payment was to be in Swiss francs to a Swiss bank account. The defendants failed to pay and the plaintiff brought an action claiming the equivalent amount due in sterling. Between the issuing of the writ and the hearing, sterling fell in value as against the Swiss franc and the plaintiff sought to claim the sum in francs. The defendant admitted liability but contended that the plaintiffs were not entitled to a judgment expressed in a foreign currency, there being a House of Lords case *Re United Railways of the Havana and Regla Warehouses Ltd* [1960] 2 All ER 332 stating that judgments can only be expressed in sterling.

Held

Where a plaintiff brought an action for money due under a contract he could claim and obtain judgment of the debt expressed in foreign currency if the law of the contract was the law of that country and the money of account and payment was also of that country. Their Lordships therefore departed from their previous decision.

Lord Simon:

> 'Courts which are bound by the rule of precedent are not free to disregard an otherwise binding precedent on the ground that the reason which led to the formulation of the rule embodied in such precedent seems to the court to have lost cogency.'

Comment

A useful illustration of the mechanical operation of the rules of precedent. The fact that an earlier precedent appears to have lost its rational basis may still be a factor in deciding whether to overrule it under the 1966 *Practice Statement.*

Moodie v *Inland Revenue Commissioners* [1993] 1 WLR 266 House of Lords (Lords Keith of Kinkel, Templeman, Goff of Chieveley, Browne-Wilkinson and Mustill)

- *House of Lords – conflicting decisions*

Facts

In relation to tax avoidance schemes, it appeared that there were conflicting House of Lords' decisions (*Inland Revenue Commissioners* v *Plummer* [1979] 3 WLR 689 and *WT Ramsay Ltd* v *Inland Revenue Commissioners* [1981] 2 WLR 449) as to the construction of the relevant statutory provisions.

Held

The later decision would now be followed.

Lord Templeman:

> '[Counsel] on behalf of the taxpayers made a number of gallant attempts to argue that *Plummer*'s case and the present appeals were distinguishable from *Ramsay* but all these attempts foundered ... If *Plummer*'s case had been decided after *Ramsay*, the Crown would have succeeded, though not on any of the grounds advanced in *Plummer.* The present appeals are heard after *Ramsay* and this House is bound to give effect to the principle of *Ramsay.* I do not consider that it is necessary to invoke the 1966 practice state-

ment which allows the House "to depart from a previous decision when it appears right to do so" (see Note [1966] 1 WLR 1234). The result in *Plummer*'s case (which is a decision of this House) is inconsistent with the later decision in *Ramsay* (which is also a decision of the House). Faced with conflicting decisions, the courts are entitled and bound to follow *Ramsay* because in *Plummer*'s case this House was never asked to consider the effect of a [particular] scheme and because the *Ramsay* principle restores justice between individual taxpayers and the general body of taxpayers ... If it were necessary to invoke the 1966 practice statement I have no doubt that this would be an appropriate course to take but in my opinion it is sufficient to state that the decision in *Plummer*'s case would have been different if the appeal had been heard after the enunciation by this House of the *Ramsay* principle ...

The Crown failed against Mr Plummer because the *Ramsay* principle had not been adumbrated by the House at that time. The Crown succeeds now because the *Ramsay* principle applies.'

Comment

Note the reasons why the 1966 *Practice Statement* was not used in this case. The decision illustrates an important rule of precedent: that a later decision should be followed in regard to the construction of a statute on the ground that any conflicting earlier decision might have been different had the earlier decision been informed of the principles set out in the later decision.

Murphy v *Brentwood District Council* [1990] 3 WLR 414 House of Lords (Lords Mackay of Clashfern, Keith of Kinkel, Bridge of Harwich, Brandon of Oakbrook, Ackner, Oliver of Aylmerton and Jauncey of Tullichettle)

• *House of Lords – overruling previous decision*

Facts

In *Anns* v *Merton London Borough Council* [1977] 2 WLR 1024 the House of Lords decided that a local authority which exercises statutory control over building operations is liable in tort to a building owner or occupier for the cost of remedying a dangerous defect in a building which results from the negligent failure by the authority to ensure that the building was erected in conformity with applicable standards prescribed by building byelaws or regulations.

Held

Anns v *Merton London Borough Council* would be overruled.

Lord Keith of Kinkel:

'In my opinion there can be no doubt that *Anns* has for long been widely regarded as an unsatisfactory decision. It relation to the scope of the duty owed by a local authority it proceeded on what must, with due respect to its source, be regarded as a somewhat superficial examination of principle and there has been extreme difficulty ... in ascertaining on exactly what basis of principle it did proceed. I think it must now be recognised that it did not proceed on any basis of principle at all, but constituted a remarkable example of judicial legislation. It has engendered a vast spate of litigation, and each of the cases in the field which have reached this House has been distinguished. Others have been distinguished in the Court of Appeal. The result has been to keep the effect of the decision within reasonable bounds, but that has been achieved only by applying strictly the words of Lord Wilberforce [in *Anns*] and by refusing to accept the logical implications of the decision itself. These logical implications show that the case properly considered has potentiality for collision with long-established principles regarding liability in the tort of negligence for economic loss. There can be no doubt that to depart from the decision would re-establish a degree of certainty in this field of law which it has done a remarkable amount to upset ...

It must, of course, be kept in mind that the decision has stood for some 13 years. On the other hand, it is not a decision of the type that is to a significant extent taken into account by citizens or indeed local authorities in ordering their affairs. No doubt its existence results in local authorities having to pay increased insurance premiums, but to be relieved of that necessity would be to their advantage, not to their detriment. To overrule it is unlikely to result in significantly increased insurance premiums for householders. It is perhaps of some significance that most litigation involving the decision consists in contests between insurance companies, as is largely the position in the present case. The decision is capable of being regarded as affording a measure of justice, but as against that the impossibility of finding any coherent and logically based doctrine behind it is calculated to put the law of negligence into a state of confusion defying rational analysis. It is also material that *Anns* has the effect of imposing on builders generally a liability going far beyond that which Parliament thought fit to impose on house builders alone by the Defective Premises Act 1972, a statute very material to the policy of the decision but not adverted to in it. There is much to be said for the view that in what is essentially a consumer protection field … the precise extent and limits of the liabilities which in the public interest should be imposed on builders and local authorities are best left to the legislature.'

Comment

A famous case from the tort of negligence illustrating a comparatively rare use of the 1966 *Practice Statement.* Note the reasons given to justify departing from a decision which had stood for some 13 years.

R* v *Clegg [1995] 1 All ER 334 House of Lords (Lords Keith, Browne-Wilkinson, Slynn, Lloyd and Nicholls)

- *Judicial law reform and the doctrine of precedent*

Facts

A British soldier in Northern Ireland at a vehicle checkpoint opened fire at a car which had accelerated away in a suspicious manner from the checkpoint. The rear-seat passenger in the car was killed by a bullet fired from the soldier's rifle. The soldier was convicted of murder. His appeal to the Court of Appeal in Northern Ireland was dismissed, but the Court observed that in the circumstances a conviction for manslaughter had it been permitted, would have reflected more clearly the nature of the offence which he had committed. The appellant then appealed to the House of Lords.

Held

The appeal would be dismissed. It was a well settled principle that a plea of self-defence could not reduce a culpable homicide from murder to manslaughter, where a plea of self-defence to a charge of murder failed because the force used was excessive and unreasonable the homicide could not be reduced to manslaughter. The issue of whether there should be a qualified defence available to a police officer or soldier acting in the course of his duty of using excessive force in self-defence or to prevent crime or to effect a lawful arrest which reduces what would otherwise be murder to manslaughter was part of the wider issue of whether the mandatory life sentence for murder should be retained. This wider issue, and hence the issue in the present case, was a matter for Parliament, not the House of Lords in its judicial capacity.

Lord Lloyd:

'I am not averse to judges developing law, or indeed making new law, when they can see their way clearly, even where questions

of social policy are involved. A good recent example would be the affirmation by this House of the decision of the Court of Appeal (Criminal Division) that a man can be guilty of raping his wife (*R* v *R – (rape: marital exemption)* [1991] 4 All ER 481, [1992] 1 AC 599; *affg* [1991] 2 All ER 257, [1991] 2 WLR 1065). But in the present case I am in no doubt that your Lordships should abstain from law-making. The reduction of what would otherwise be murder to manslaughter in a particular class of case seems to me essentially a matter for decision by the legislature, and not by this House in its judicial capacity. For the point in issue is, in truth, part of the wider issue whether the mandatory life sentence for murder should still be maintained. That wider issue can only be decided by Parliament. I would say the same for the point at issue in this case. Accordingly I would answer the certified question of law as follows. On the facts stated, and assuming no other defence is available, the soldier or police officer will be guilty of murder, and not manslaughter. It follows that the appeal must be dismissed.'

Lords Keith, Browne-Wilkinson, Slynn and Nicholls agreed with Lord Lloyd.

Comment

An interesting recent case showing the limits to the scope of judicial law reform. Once again the 'leave it to Parliament' argument prevailed. Note the reasons given by Lord Lloyd for distinguishing the case from *R* v *R (Rape: Marital Exemption)* (1991) (below), where significant judicial law reform took place. Are the reasons cogent? Both cases involve contentious issues of public and political debate.

R* v *Gould [1968] 2 WLR 643 Court of Appeal (Criminal Division) (Diplock LJ, Widgery and Blain JJ)

- *Court of Appeal (Criminal Division) – previous decisions*

Facts

The appellant was convicted of committing bigamy and the issue was whether an honest belief on reasonable grounds on the date of the second marriage that the former marriage was dissolved was a good defence. There was a Court of Appeal precedent to the effect that it was not (*R* v *Wheat*, *R* v *Stocks* [1921] 2 KB 119).

Held

The defence was good, accordingly the conviction would be quashed.

Diplock LJ:

> 'In its criminal jurisdiction which it has inherited from the Court of Criminal Appeal, the Court of Appeal does not apply the doctrine of stare decisis with the same rigidity as in its civil jurisdiction. If on due consideration we were to be of opinion that the law had been either misapplied or misunderstood in an earlier decision of this court, or its predecessor the Court of Appeal, we should be entitled to depart from the view as to the law expressed in the earlier decision notwithstanding that the case could not be brought within any of the exceptions laid down in *Young* v *Bristol Aeroplane Co Ltd* as justifying the Court of Appeal in refusing to follow one of its own decisions in a civil case (*R* v *Taylor*). A fortiori we are bound to give effect to the law as we think it is if the previous decision to the contrary effect is one of which the ratio decidendi conflicts with that of other decisions of this court or its predecessors of co-ordinate jurisdiction.'

Comment

An important decision which illustrates the flexibility adopted by the Court of Appeal (Criminal Division) in cases where liberty is at stake. Contrast the more limited room for manoeuvre granted to the Civil Division by *Young* v *Bristol Aeroplane Co Ltd* (1944) (below).

R* v *Governor of Brockhill Prison, ex parte Evans [1997] 1 All ER 439 Queen's Bench Division (Bingham LCJ, Rose LJ and Blofeld J)

• *Operation of precedent in the Divisional Court*

Facts

The applicant had been sentenced to four concurrent terms of imprisonment for various offences, the longest term of imprisonment (and therefore the total sentence) being two years. The governor of the prison where the applicant was detained took the view that the two years was to be reduced only by the period spent in custody for the offence for which the longest term of imprisonment had been imposed, and that no discount should be made for the time spent in custody for the other offences. The applicant sought judicial review of the governor's decision.

Held

Judicial review would be granted to quash the governor's decision because, upon a correct interpretation of the relevant statute law, the period by which the sentence is to be reduced in such a case is the total period that the defendant spent in custody before sentence. In reaching this decision the Divisional Court departed from several of its own previous decisions which were accordingly disapproved.

Bingham LCJ:

> 'It has been urged upon us, and we unreservedly accept, that we should not depart from previous decisions of this court unless we are satisfied that they are wrong. Our reluctance must be the greater when, as in this case, the authorities have quite rightly founded their practice on these decisions. We are, however, of the clear opinion that the construction previously put upon the legislative provisions we have reviewed was wrong. We are moreover of opinion that that construction is capable of producing, and has in some of the decided cases produced, injustice.'

Comment

A useful illustration of the doctrine of precedent in the Divisional Court.

R* v *Greater Manchester Coroner, ex parte Tal [1984] 3 WLR 643 High Court (Robert Goff LJ, McCullough and Mann JJ)

• *Divisional court – bound to follow earlier decisions of another divisional court?*

(The facts and decision of this case are not important in this context. It is the statement on the operation of precedent which is of significance here.)

Robert Goff LJ:

> '... every Divisional Court is simply a court, constituted of not less than two judges, held for the transaction of business of the High Court, which is (by rules of court or by statute) required to be heard by a Divisional Court. Among the business of the High Court required to be so heard are to be found applications for judicial review in any criminal cause or matter, or in other causes or matters where the court so directs ... It is however, also to be observed that, when a Divisional Court is constituted to hear an application for judicial review, it is not sitting in an appellate capacity. It is not hearing an appeal from another court, nor is it considering a question of law on a case stated by another court, as in the case of appeals by way of cases stated by magistrates' courts. It is exercising what is often called a supervisory jurisdiction. That jurisdiction is exercised by the High Court over inferior courts and tribunals. It is only exercised by a Divisional Court when required to do so by statute or by rules of court, and any decision made in the exercise of that jurisdiction may be the subject of appeal, either to the Court of Appeal in civil cases,

or to the House of Lords (under the requisite conditions) in criminal cases. If a judge of the High Court sits exercising the supervisory jurisdiction of the High Court then it is, in our judgment, plain that the relevant principle of stare decisis is the principle applicable in the case of a judge of first instance exercising the jurisdiction of the High Court, viz that he will follow a decision of another judge of first instance, unless he is convinced that that judgment is wrong, as a matter of judicial comity; but he is not bound to follow the decision of a judge of equal jurisdiction (see *Huddersfield Police Authority* v *Watson* [1947] KB 842 at 848 per Lord Goddard CJ), for either the judge exercising such supervisory jurisdiction is (as we think) sitting as a judge of first instance, or his position is so closely analogous that the principle of stare decisis applicable in the case of a judge of first instance is applicable to him.

In our judgment, the same principle is applicable when the supervisory jurisdiction of the High Court is exercised not by a single judge but by a Divisional Court, where two or three judges are exercising precisely the same jurisdiction as the single judge. We have no doubt that it will be only in rare cases that a Divisional Court will think it fit to depart from a decision of another Divisional Court exercising this jurisdiction. Furthermore, we find it difficult to imagine that a single judge exercising this jurisdiction would ever depart from a decision of a Divisional Court. If any question of such a departure should arise before a single judge, a direction can be made … that the relevant application should be made before a Divisional Court. These are, therefore, the principles which we propose to apply in the present case …'

Comment

A useful decision on the mechanical operation of the doctrine of precedent and illustrating the discretion of the Divisional Court to depart from an earlier decision of its own if convinced it was wrongly decided.

R* v *Newsome, R* v *Browne [1970] 2 QB 711 Court of Appeal (Criminal Division) (Widgery and Fenton Atkinson LJJ, Melford Stevenson, O'Connor and Eveleigh JJ)

- *Court of Appeal (Criminal Division) – previous decisions*

Facts

The defendants appealed against sentence. The trial judge had imposed immediate custodial sentences of six months on each and immediately afterwards had altered it to a period exceeding six months so as to avoid a mandatory suspension of the imprisonment in accordance with s39 of the Criminal Justice Act 1967. It was contended that the length of the sentences was wrong in principle and not allowable when motivated by the desire to avoid a mandatory suspension. Reliance was placed on previous Court of Appeal decisions when the court had sat with only three members and in similar cases had substituted suspended sentences.

Held

A five judge court duly constituted to consider an issue and principles of exercise of discretion in imposing sentence could depart from a previous decision and should do so if it took the view that the earlier decision was wrong.

Widgery LJ:

> 'We do not in this case have to go to extremes in this matter, and in particular, we do not have to consider to what extent a court of five can properly depart from an earlier decision of a court of three when the issue goes to guilt or innocence … Where the question at issue determined whether an act was criminal or not, then even a court of five should at the very least have far greater reluctance in departing from an earlier decision than it would where such a fundamental issue did not arise.'

Comment

A simple case on the authority of courts composed of different numbers of judges.

R v *R (Rape: Marital Exemption)* [1991] 4 All ER 481 House of Lords (Lords Keith, Brandon, Griffiths, Ackner and Lowry)

- *Judicial law reform and the doctrine of precedent*

Facts

The appellant had pleaded guilty to attempted rape of his wife. It was not disputed that the attempt to have sexual intercourse was without his wife's consent. He appealed against the conviction on the ground that an ancient principle of English common law provided that a husband cannot be criminally liable for raping his wife if he has sexual intercourse with her without her consent. The Court of Appeal dismissed his appeal on the ground that the principle no longer formed part of Englishlaw. He appealed to the House of Lords.

Held

The appeal would be dismissed and decision of the Court of Appeal would be affirmed.

Lord Keith:

> 'Sir Matthew Hale in his *History of the Pleas of the Crown* wrote (1 Hale PC (1736) 629):
>
> > "But the husband cannot be guilty of a rape committed by himself upon his lawful wife, for by their mutual matrimonial consent and contract the wife hath given herself up in this kind unto her husband which she cannot retract." ...
>
> ... It may be taken that the proposition was generally regarded as an accurate statement of the common law of England. The common law is, however, capable of evolving in the light of changing social, economic and cultural developments. Hale's proposition reflected the state of affairs in these respects at the time it was enunciated. Since then the status of women, and particularly of married women, has changed out of all recognition in various ways which are very familiar and upon which it is unnecessary to go into detail. Apart from property matters and the availability of matrimonial remedies, one of the most important changes is that marriage is in modern times regarded as a partnership of equals, and no longer one in which the wife must be the subservient chattel of the husband. Hale's proposition involves that by marriage a wife gives her irrevocable consent to sexual intercourse with her husband under all circumstances and irrespective of the state of her health or how she happens to be feeling at the time. In modern times any reasonable person must regard that conception as quite unacceptable.'

Lord Keith then reviewed relevant authorities and found that Sir Matthew Hale's proposition had been departed from in a series of decided cases. Lord Keith then concluded that on grounds of principle there was no good reason why Sir Matthew Hale's proposition should not be held inapplicable in modern times. Lord Keith was not convinced by an argument that Parliament had intended to preserve the Hale proposition when enacting s1(1) of the Sexual Offences (Amendment) Act 1976, which defines rape as having 'unlawful' intercourse with a woman without her consent. Lord Keith thought that the word 'unlawful' in this context was mere surplusage and was not to be taken as meaning 'outside marriage', since it was clearly unlawful to have sexual intercourse with any woman without her consent. He continued:

> 'I am therefore of the opinion that s1(1) of the 1976 Act prevents no obstacle to this House declaring that in modern times the supposed marital exception in rape forms no part of the law of England. The Court of Appeal, Criminal Division took a similar view. Towards the end of the judgment of that court Lord Lane CJ said ([1991] 2 All ER 257 at 266, [1991] 2 WLR 1965 at 1074):

> "The remaining and no less difficult question is whether, despite that view, this is an area where the court should step aside to leave the matter to the parliamentary process. This is not the creation of a new offence, it is the removal of a common law fiction which has become anachronistic and offensive and we consider that it is our duty having reached that conclusion to act upon it."

I respectfully agree.'

Comment

An important and controversial decision raising issues as to the legitimacy of judicial law reform in a contentious area of criminal law. The decision illustrates the problems caused by the practice of retrospective overruling. Nevertheless, this practice did not in this case infringe the right of the accused to a fair trial: *CR* v *UK* (1995) The Times 5 December (European Court of Human Rights).

R* v *Shivpuri [1986] 2 WLR 988 House of Lords (Lords Hailsham LC, Elwyn-Jones, Scarman, Bridge and Mackay)

- *House of Lords – previous decisions*

Facts

The defendant was convicted of attempting to deal in prohibited drugs because of his confession. On analysis, however, it was shown that the defendant's suitcase had contained only snuff or some similar harmless vegetable matter. Shivpuri appealed on the ground that he had not committed 'an act which is more than merely preparatory to the commission of the offence'. *Shivpuri* relied on *Anderton* v *Ryan* [1985] 2 All ER 355 (HL).

Held

His appeal would be dismissed. *Anderton* v *Ryan* was overruled.

Lord Bridge of Harwich:

'I am ... led to the conclusion that there is no valid ground on which *Anderton* v *Ryan* can be distinguished. I have made clear my own conviction, which as a party to the decision (and craving the indulgence of my noble and learned friends who agreed in it) I am the readier to express, that the decision was wrong. What then is to be done? If the case is indistinguishable, the application of the strict doctrine of precedent would require that the present appeal be allowed. Is it permissible to depart from precedent under the 1966 *Practice Statement* ([1966] 3 All ER 77, [1966] 1 WLR 1234) notwithstanding the especial need for certainty in the criminal law? The following considerations lead me to answer that question affirmatively. Firstly, I am undeterred by the consideration that the decision in *Anderton* v *Ryan* was so recent. The 1966 *Practice Statement* is an effective abandonment of our pretention to infallibility. If a serious error embodied in a decision of this House has distorted the law, the sooner it is corrected the better. Secondly, I cannot see how, in the very nature of the case, anyone could have acted in reliance on the law as propounded in *Anderton* v *Ryan* in the belief that he was acting innocently and now find that, after all, he is to be held to have committed a criminal offence. Thirdly, to hold the House bound to follow *Anderton* v *Ryan* because it cannot be distinguished and to allow the appeal in this case would, it seems to me, be tantamount to a declaration that the 1981 Act left the law of criminal attempts unchanged following the decision in *Houghton* v *Smith* [1973] 3 All ER 1109, [1975] AC 476. Finally, if, contrary to my present view, there is a valid ground on which it would be proper to distinguish cases similar to that considered in *Anderton* v *Ryan* my present opinion on that point would not foreclose the option of making such a distinction in some future case.

I cannot conclude this opinion without disclosing that I have had the advantage, since the conclusion of the argument in this appeal, of reading an article by Professor

Glanville Williams entitled The Lords and Impossible Attempts, or Quis Custodet Ipsos Custodies? [1986] CLJ 33. The language in which he criticises the decision in *Anderton* v *Ryan* is not conspicuous for its moderation, but it would be foolish, on that account, not to recognise the force of the criticism and churlish not to acknowledge the assistance I have derived from it.'

Comment

An important decision illustrating a comparatively rare use of the 1966 *Practice Statement* in criminal law. Note the reasons given for departing from a decision made only a year earlier. What happened to the usual cautious 'leave it to Parliament' argument?

R* v *Taylor [1950] 2 KB 368 Court of Appeal (Criminal Division) (Goddard LCJ, Humphreys, Stable, Cassels, Hallett, Morris and Parker JJ)

- *Court of Appeal (Criminal Division) – previous decisions*

Facts

On a charge of bigamy, the issue was whether the defence of absence of the spouse for seven years was available in the case of a second marriage only or on any subsequent marriage. There was a Court of Criminal Appeal precedent supporting the former view, *R* v *Treanor* (1939).

Held

The decision in *R* v *Treanor* would be overruled and therefore the defence was open to the appellant.

Goddard LCJ:

> 'This court, however, has to deal with questions involving the liberty of the subject, and it finds on reconsideration, that, in the opinion of a full court assembled for that purpose, the law has either been misapplied or misunderstood in a decision which it has previously given, and that, on the strength of that decision, an accused person has been sentenced and imprisoned, it is the bounden duty of the court to reconsider the earlier decision with a view to seeing whether that person had been properly convicted. The exceptions which apply in civil cases ought not to be the only ones applied in such a case as the present.'

Comment

A simple case showing the greater flexibility of the Court of Appeal (Criminal Division) to depart from a previous decision if the liberty of the individual is at stake.

Rickards* v *Rickards [1989] 3 WLR 748 Court of Appeal (Lord Donaldson of Lymington MR, Balcombe and Nicholls LJJ)

- *Court of Appeal – bound by previous decision?*

Facts

Following a divorce, the registrar made a 'clean break' financial order against the former husband. Under the relevant rules, he had five days within which to appeal: he failed to do so, but later applied to the county court judge for an extension of time. The judge refused this application and the former husband appealed to the Court of Appeal against this decision. There was a previous Court of Appeal decision that such an appeal could not be entertained, notwithstanding a statutory provision apparently to the contrary.

Held

The appeal could be heard but, in all the circumstances, it would be dismissed.

Lord Donaldson of Lymington MR:

> 'I am satisfied that this court erred in (the previous case) *Podbery* v *Peak* [1981] 2 WLR 686 ... Accordingly, I am confronted with the question of whether we are bound to, or should, follow it and thereby decline to exercise an appellate jurisdiction which I

have no doubt that we have. The importance of the rule of stare decisis in relation to the Court of Appeal's own decisions can hardly be overstated. We now sometimes sit in eight divisions and, in the absence of such a rule, the law would quickly become wholly uncertain. However, the rule is not without exceptions, albeit very limited. These exceptions were considered in *Young* v *Bristol Aeroplane Co Ltd* [1944] KB 718, *Morelle Ltd* v *Wakeling* [1955] 2 WLR 672 and more recently, in *Williams* v *Fawcett* [1985] 1 WLR 787, where relevant extracts from the two earlier decisions are set out. These decisions show that this court is justified in refusing to follow one of its own previous decisions not only where that decision is given in ignorance or forgetfulness of some inconsistent statutory provision or some authority binding on it, but also, in rare and exceptional cases, if it is satisfied that the decision involved a manifest slip or error.

In previous cases the judges of this court have always refrained from defining this exceptional category and I have no intention of departing from that approach save to echo the words of Lord Greene MR (in *Young's* case) and Evershed MR (in *Morelle's* case) and to say that they will be of the rarest occurrence. Nevertheless, some general considerations are relevant. First, the preferred course must always be to follow the previous decision, but to give leave to appeal in order that the House of Lords may remedy the error. ... Second, certainty in relation to substantive law is usually to be preferred to correctness, since this at least enables the public to order their affairs with confidence. Erroneous decisions as to procedural rules affect only the parties engaged in the relevant litigation. This is a much less extensive group and, accordingly, a departure from established practice is to that extent less undesirable. Third, an erroneous decision which involves the jurisdiction of the court is particularly objectionable, either because it will involve an abuse of power if the true view is that the court has no jurisdiction or a breach of the court's statutory duty if the true view is that the court is wrongly declining jurisdiction. Such a decision, of which this case provides an example, is thus in a special category. Nevertheless, this court must have very strong reasons if any departure from its own previous decisions is to be justifiable. Indeed, it has only done so on one previous occasion of which I am aware (see *Williams* v *Fawcett*).

In the instant case, I am fully satisfied that we are justified in treating *Podbery* v *Peak* as a decision given per incuriam. It involves a wrongful rejection of the jurisdiction of this court and, if we follow it, there is no possibility of an appeal to the House of Lords in the instant case. In the light of our decision on the merits of the husband's appeal, he has no incentive to appeal and the wife, having succeeded, cannot do so. The decision in *Podbery* v *Peak* is likely to affect a large number of decisions in matrimonial causes which, although of vital importance to the parties, arise in circumstances in which neither party can be expected to pursue the matter to the House of Lords because of the cost which, in the case of legally aided appeals, may still ultimately fall on the parties because of the legal aid fund's charge. It is therefore unlikely to be considered by the House of Lords in any other case and mean while we should be in continuing breach of our statutory duty.

I would therefore hold that we have jurisdiction to entertain the husband's appeal.'

Comment

A useful illustration of the application of the 'per incuriam' rule – the third 'escape route' from an otherwise binding precedent listed in *Young* v *Bristol Aeroplane Co Ltd* (1944) (below).

Roberts Petroleum Ltd* v *Bernard Kenny Ltd [1983] 2 WLR 305 House of Lords (Lords Diplock, Edmund-Davies, Keith, Roskill and Brightman)

- *Case law reporting – citation of unreported precedents*

(The facts and decision are not important in this context. It is the statement on the citation of unreported cases which is of significance here.)

Per curiam. The House of Lords would in future adopt the practice of declining to allow transcripts of unreported judgments of the Court of Appeal (Civil Division) to be cited on the hearing of appeals to the House unless leave were given to do so; such leave would only be granted on counsel's giving an assurance that the transcript contained a statement of some principle of law relevant to an issue in the appeal to the House, that it was binding on the Court of Appeal and of which the substance, as distinct from the mere choice of phraseology, was not to be found in any judgment of that court that had appeared in one of the generalised or specialised series of reports.

Lord Diplock:

> 'If a civil judgment of the Court of Appeal (which has a heavy caseload and sits concurrently in several civil divisions) has not found its way into the generalised series of law reports or even into one of the specialised series, it is most unlikely to be of any assistance to your Lordships on an appeal which is sufficiently important to reach this House.'

Comment

A significant and controversial piece of judicial law reform in the area of procedure and practice. Whilst the reasons given by Lord Diplock for limiting the citation of unreported cases are cogent on practical grounds, do they offend the basic principle that a precedent is created because judges so decided rather than because someone chose to report it?

Scruttons Ltd* v *Midland Silicones Ltd [1962] 2 WLR 186 House of Lords (Lords Simonds, Reid, Keith, Denning and Morris)

- *Distinguishing earlier decisions*

(The facts and decision are not important in this context. It is the statement on the practice of distinguishing decisions which is of significance here.)

Lord Reid:

> 'I would certainly not lightly disregard or depart from any ratio decidendi of this House. But there are at least three classes of case where I think we are entitled to question or limit it: first, where it is obscure, secondly, where the decision itself is out of line with other authorities or established principles, and thirdly, where it is much wider than was necessary for the decision so that it becomes a question of how far it is proper to distinguish the earlier decision.'

Comment

A useful summary by Lord Reid of three situations in which it would be appropriate to distinguish a decision and depart from its normally binding authority.

Westdeutsche Landesbank Girozentrale* v *Islington London Borough Council [1996] 2 All ER 961 House of Lords (Lords Goff, Browne-Wilkinson, Slynn, Woolf and Lloyd)

- *Judicial reform and the doctrine of precedent*

Facts

The plaintiff bank had entered into an interest rate swap agreement with the defendant local authority. Subsequently in *Hazell* v *Hammersmith and Fulham London Borough Council* [1991] 1 All ER 545 the House of Lords held that such a transaction was beyond the powers of a local authority and was void ab initio. The House left open the question of whether payments made pursuant to such an agreement were recoverable. The bank brought an action claiming repayment of monies already paid under the agreement, plus interest.

The trial judge ordered repayment of the principal sum, plus compound interest. The Court of Appeal dismissed the local authority's appeal. The local authority then appealed to the House of Lords solely against the award of compound interest.

Held (Lords Goff and Woolf dissenting) The appeal was allowed on the ground that the judge had no jurisdiction under statute or at common law to award compound interest. In a common law action for money had and received P bank was entitled to recover only simple interest under s35A Supreme Court Act 1981.

There was no basis for awarding compound interest under the existing rules of equity and even though the bank had a strong moral claim to receive full restitution it would not be appropriate to develop the law of equity so as to justify an award of compound interest. Parliament had twice considered the issue (in 1934 and 1981 legislation) and each time had declined to authorise the award of compound interest.

Lord Browne-Wilkinson:

> '... in my judgment, your Lordships would be usurping the function of Parliament if, by expanding the equitable rules for the award of compound interest, this House were now to hold that the court exercising its equitable jurisdiction in aid of the common law can award compound interest which the statutes have expressly not authorised the court to award in exercise of its common law jurisdiction.'

Lord Browne-Wilkinson also refused to develop the law because the argument for doing so had not been advanced at the hearing and the local authority had had no chance to address it. In any event he saw difficulties with the proposed change:

> 'Although I express no concluded view on the points raised, the proposed development of the law bristles with unresolved questions. For example, given that the right to interest is not a right which existed at common law but is solely the creation of statute, would equity in fact be acting in aid of the common law or would it be acting in aid of the legislature? Does the principle that equity acts in aid of the common law apply where there is no concurrent right of action in equity? If not, in the absence of any trust or fiduciary relationship what is the equitable cause of action in this case? What were the policy reasons which led Parliament to provide expressly that only the award of simple interest was authorised? In what circumstances should compound interest be awarded under the proposed expansion of the equitable rules? In the absence of argument on these points it would in my view be imprudent to change the law. Rather, the whole question of the award of compound interest should be looked at again by Parliament so that it can make such changes, if any, as are appropriate.'

Lords Slynn and Lloyd agreed (Lord Lloyd emphasised that the need for certainty in commercial transactions should be paramount).

Lords Goff and Woolf (dissenting) took a more generous view of their function and were prepared to develop the law of restitution so as to provide the remedy of compound interest in this case. Both Law Lords made interesting observations on the creative role of judges.

Lord Goff:

> '... it is the great advantage of a supreme court that, not only does it have the great benefit of assistance from the judgments of the courts below, but also it has a greater freedom to mould, and remould, the authorities to ensure that practical justice is done within a framework of principle. The present case provides an excellent example of a case in which this House should take full advantage of that freedom ...
>
> ... where the jurisdiction of the court derives from common law or equity, and is designed to do justice in cases which come before the courts, it is startling to be faced by an argument that the jurisdiction is so restricted as to prevent the courts from doing justice. Jurisdiction of that kind

should as a matter of principle be as broad as possible, to enable justice to be done wherever necessary; and the relevant limits should be found, not in the scope of the jurisdiction, but in the manner of its exercise as the principles are worked out from case to case. Second, I find it equally startling to find that the jurisdiction is said to be limited to certain specific categories of case. Where jurisdiction is founded on a principle of justice, I would expect that the categories of the case where it is exercised should be regarded not as occupying the whole field but rather as emanations of the principle, so that the possibility of the jurisdiction being extended to other categories of case is not foreclosed.

... I conclude that the equitable jurisdiction to award compound interest may be exercised in the case of personal claims at common law, as it is in equity ...

I recognise that, in so holding, the courts would be breaking new ground, and would be extending the equitable jurisdiction to a field where it has not hitherto been exercised. But that cannot of itself be enough to prevent what I see to be a thoroughly desirable extension of the jurisdiction, consistent with its underlying basis that it exists to meet the demands of justice. An action of restitution appears to me to provide an almost classic case in which the jurisdiction should be available to enable the courts to do full justice. Claims in restitution are founded upon a principle of justice, being designed to prevent the unjust enrichment of the defendant ...

... It would be strange indeed if the courts lacked jurisdiction in such a case to ensure that justice could be fully achieved by means of an award of compound interest, where it is appropriate to make such an award, despite the fact that the jurisdiction to award such interest is itself said to rest upon the demands of justice. I am glad not to be forced to hold that English law is so inadequate as to be incapable of achieving such a result. In my opinion the jurisdiction should now be made available, as justice requires, in cases of restitution, to ensure that full justice can be done. The seed is there, but the growth has hitherto been confined within a small area. That growth should now be permitted to spread naturally elsewhere within this newly recognised branch of the law. No genetic engineering is required, only that the warm sun of judicial creativity should exercise its benign influence rather than remain hidden behind the dark clouds of legal history.'

Lord Woolf:

'What is more important than the absence of clear support in the authorities for the grant of compound interest is the absence from the existing authorities of any statement of principle preventing the natural development of a salutary equitable jurisdiction enabling compound interest to be awarded. The jurisdiction is clearly desirable if full restitution in some cases is to be achieved ...

Restitution is an area of the law which is still in the process of being evolved by the courts. In relation to restitution there are still questions remaining to be authoritatively decided ...

The fact that, until the law was clarified by the decision in this case, the local authority may reasonably not have appreciated that it should make restitution is not critical. What is critical is that the payment of compound interest is required to achieve restitution. A defendant may perfectly reasonably not regard himself as having been a trustee until the court so decides but this does not affect the remedies which the court has jurisdiction to grant. The jurisdiction of the court to grant remedies has to be judged in the light of what the court decides.'

Comment

The case gives a fascinating insight into the differences of opinion between senior judges on the scope for judicial law reform.

Young* v *Bristol Aeroplane Co Ltd [1944] KB 718 Court of Appeal (Lord Greene MR, Scott, MacKinnon and Luxmore LJJ, Lord Goddard and du Parcq LJ)

• *Court of Appeal – bound by its own decisions?*

(The facts and decisions are not important in this context. It is the statement on the operation of precedent in the Court of Appeal which is of significance here.)

Lord Greene MR:

> 'The Court of Appeal is a creature of statute and its powers are statutory. It is one court though it usually sits in two or three divisions. Each division has co-ordinate jurisdiction, but the full has no greater powers of jurisdiction than any division ... (W)hat cannot be done by a division of the court cannot be done by the full court.
>
> In considering the question whether or not this court is bound by its previous decisions and those of courts of co-ordinate jurisdiction, it is necessary to distinguish four classes of case. The first is that with which we are now concerned, namely, cases where this court finds itself confronted with one or more decisions of its own or of a court of co-ordinate jurisdiction which cover the question before it and there is no conflicting decision of this court or of a court of co-ordinate jurisdiction. The second is where there is such a conflicting decision. The third is where this court comes to the conclusion that a previous decision, although not expressly overruled, cannot stand with a subsequent decision of the House of Lords. The fourth (a special case) is where this court comes to the conclusion that a previous decision was given per incuriam. In the second and third classes of case it is beyond question that the previous decision is open to examination. In the second class, the court is unquestionably entitled to choose between the two conflicting decisions.
>
> In the third class of case the court is merely giving effect to what it considers to have been a decision of the House of Lords by which it is bound. The fourth class requires more detailed examination ... Where the court has construed a statute or a rule having the force of a statute its decision stands on the same footing as any other decision on a question of law, but where the court is satisfied that an earlier decision was given in ignorance of the terms of a statute or a rule having the force of a statute the position is very different. It cannot, in our opinion, be right to say that in such a case the court is entitled to disregard the statutory provision and is bound to follow a decision of its own given when that provision was not present to its mind. Cases of this description are examples of decisions given per incuriam. We do not think that it would be right to say that there may not be other cases of decisions given per incuriam in which this court might properly consider itself entitled not to follow an earlier decision of its own. Such cases would obviously be of the rarest occurrence and must be dealt with in accordance with their special facts.
>
> Two classes of decisions per incuriam fall outside the scope of our inquiry, namely, those where the court has acted in ignorance of a previous decision of its own or of a court of co-ordinate jurisdiction which covers the case before it – in such a case a subsequent court must decide which of the two decisions it ought to follow; and those where it has acted in ignorance of a decision of the House of Lords which covers the point – in such a case a subsequent court is bound by the decision of the House of Lords.
>
> On a careful examination of the whole matter we have come to the clear conclusion that this court is bound to follow previous decisions of its own as well as those of courts of co-ordinate jurisdiction. The only exceptions to this rule (two of them apparent only) are those already mentioned.'

Comment

This is one of the leading cases on the doctrine of precedent. In this case the Court of

Appeal (Civil Division) imposed on itself a severely limited discretion to depart from its own previous decisions. Note the three 'escape routes' listed by Lord Greene MR. Although these have been reformulated and refined in later cases they have not been abandoned, despite the robust calls for greater flexibility made by Lord Denning when he was Master of the Rolls (1962–1982): see *Davis* v *Johnson* (1979) (above). The actual decision in the case was affirmed by the House of Lords: [1946] AC 163.

Younghusband* v *Luftig [1949] 2 All ER 72 High Court (Goddard LCJ, Oliver, Birkett, Lynskey and Sellers JJ)

- *Divisional court – bound by its own decisions?*

(The facts and decision are not important in this context. It is the statement on the operation of precedent in the Divisional Court which is of significance here.)

Goddard LCJ:

> 'Before considering the law applicable to the case, we think it well to emphasise that a Divisional Court of five judges has no greater powers than one of three or even two. This court is bound by its own decision as is the Court of Appeal, whatever the number of judges that may constitute it: see *Huddersfield Police Authority* v *Watson* (above). The principles of *Young* v *Bristol Aeroplane Co Ltd* (above), apply equally to this court. It was there held by the Court of Appeal ([1944] 2 All ER 300):
>
> > "The only exceptions to this rule ... are ... (i) The court is entitled and bound to decide which of two conflicting decisions of its own it will follow. (ii) The court is bound to refuse to follow a decision of its own which, though not expressly overruled, cannot in its opinion stand with a decision of the House of Lords. (iii) The court is not bound to follow a decision of its own if it is satisfied that the decision was given per incuriam."
>
> That is to say, the court is not bound by a decision of its own if a case or a statute had not been brought to the attention of the court and the decision had been given in ignorance or forgetfulness of the existence of that case or statute. The case most relied on by the appellant here was *Jutson* v *Barrow* [1936] 1 KB 236, and it was because the court before which the case which is now before us came in the first instance thought that there were certain dicta in *Jutson* v *Barrow* which might be in conflict with or go beyond certain earlier decisions, which were apparently not cited, that they directed a re-argument, and when re-argument is directed it is often desirable that it should take place before a full court.'

Comment

A simple case on the authority of a court containing different numbers of judges; see also *R* v *Greater Manchester Coroner, ex parte Tal* (1984) (above).

4 Statutory Interpretation

Allen v *Emerson* [1944] KB 362 High Court (Humphreys, Asquith and Cassels JJ)

- *Ejusdem generis rule*

Facts

Statute provided that 'no theatre or other place of public entertainment' could be used as such without a licence. Did funfairs require a licence?

Held

They did, as they were places of 'public entertainment' within the meaning of the Act.

Asquith J:

> 'Are the words "theatre or other place of public entertainment" ... to be read subject to the ejusdem generis rule or not? We are satisfied on the one hand that, if they have to be read subject to the restriction of this rule, a funfair of the kind involved in this case is not a kind of "public entertainment" of the same genus as a theatre. We are not, however, of opinion that the ejusdem generis rule applies to the words in question ...
>
> Words excepting a species from a genus are meaningless unless the species in question prima facie falls within the genus. "All hats other than top hats" makes sense. "All top hats other than bowler hats" does not. Equally little does "All top hats and other articles except gloves," if "other articles" are to be read as ejusdem generis with "top hats". Here the "places" covered by ... the ... Act – the places excepted – do not fall within the assumed genus "theatre or other" similar "place of public entertainment," although there may be an overlap between the two. ... No case was cited to us in which a genus has been held to be constituted, not by the enumeration of a number of classes followed by the words "or other," but by the mention of a single class (in this case "theatre") followed by those words. ... The tendency of the more modern authorities is to attenuate the application of the ejusdem generis rule: see *Anderson* v *Anderson* [1895] 1 QB 749.'

Comment

A straightforward illustration of the use of the 'ejusdem generis' rule of statutory construction.

Armah v *Government of Ghana* [1968] AC 192 House of Lords (Lords Reid, Morris of Borth-y-Gest, Pearce, Upjohn and Pearson)

- *Statutory antecedents*

Facts

By s5 of the Fugitive Offenders Act 1881, a Bow Street magistrate was bound to commit a fugitive (a former Minister of Trade in the government of Ghana) to prison if such evidence was produced as raised 'a strong or probable presumption' that the fugitive had committed the offence mentioned in the warrant. On the former minister's application for a write of habeas corpus, the Divisional Court, refusing the application, said that the words 'strong or probable presumption' required no more than that a prima facie case must be established.

Held (Lords Morris of Borth-y-Gest and Pearson dissenting)

The wrong test had been applied so the former minister would be discharged from prison.

Lord Reid:

> 'The evidence produced to the magistrate at Bow Street consisted of sworn statements … The appellant's case is that this evidence is insufficient to raise a strong or probable presumption that he committed the offence with which he is charged; and that no reasonable magistrate could, if he applied the proper test to this evidence, decide that it did raise such a presumption.
>
> I think it best first to deal with the … point of law stated by the Divisional Court and then to consider the nature and extent of the power or duty of the High Court to review the decision of the magistrate. In order to find the meaning of the phrase "strong or probable presumption" in s5 it is of course necessary to read the Act of 1881 as a whole, and I think that it is also proper to have regard to the statutory antecedents of that Act. The phrase occurs in a rather puzzling context in 1848 and we are indebted to the industry of counsel … for references to earlier statutes which I think supply an explanation … I am satisfied that … the court can and must interfere if there is insufficient evidence to satisfy the relevant test; and in the present case that test is whether a magistrate could reasonably have held that a strong or probable presumption had been made out.'

Comment

A case which shows how sometimes the historical development of particular statutory provisions may be referred to when construing the modern version of those provisions.

Attorney-General v *Jones* [1990] 1 WLR 859 Court of Appeal (Lord Donaldson of Lymington MR, Stuart-Smith and Staughton LJJ)

- *Statutory interpretation – vexatious proceedings – use of mischief rule*

Facts

Under s42 of the Supreme Court Act 1981, the High Court may make a 'civil proceedings order' forbidding the institution of proceedings or the making of applications without leave, where a person has instituted vexatious civil proceedings, or made vexatious applications in any civil proceedings, whether in the High Court or any inferior court.

Held

Such an order could cover the making of a counterclaim and proceedings in the Court of Appeal on appeal from the High Court or any inferior court.

Lord Donaldson MR:

> 'For my part, I consider that s42 is ambiguous. From this it follows that it is both permissible and necessary to have regard to its purpose, to the mischief at which it is directed. This is that the compulsive authority of the state vested in the courts and the judiciary shall not be invoked without reasonable cause to the detriment of other citizens and that, where someone takes this course habitually and persistently, that person shall be restrained from continuing to do so, but shall nevertheless be as free as any other citizen to use those processes if he has reasonable cause for so doing. Given that purpose, there is no obvious or indeed any reason why the section should have been intended by Parliament to have regard only to proceedings in the High Court or in an inferior court to the exclusion of proceedings in the Court of Appeal. Counsel for the Attorney-General submitted, correctly as I think, that the reference to the High Court and to inferior courts was intended to make it clear that, although the 1981 Act was primarily concerned with the powers, duties and procedures of the Supreme Court, this section was to extend to proceedings initiated in other courts, such as the county courts, but was not intended to extend to proceedings initiated in those tribunals which were not properly characterised as courts. Accordingly, I would reject this submission by Mr Jones and hold that "civil proceedings" in s42(1)(b) of the 1981 Act includes proceedings in the Court

> of Appeal on appeal from the High Court or any inferior court. It does not, however, extend to proceedings originating in the Court of Appeal, for example a renewed application for leave to apply for judicial review, or on appeal from decisions of bodies which are not courts.'

Comment
A straightforward illustration of the mischief rule when adopting a purposive approach to statutory construction.

Attorney-General v *Prince Ernest Augustus of Hanover* [1957] AC 436 House of Lords (Lords Simonds, Normand, Morton, Tucker and Somervell)

- *The literal rule – the relevance of the preamble*

Facts
The respondent was a great-great-grandson of a descendant of Princess Sophia, Electress of Hanover, who sought a declaration that he was a British subject so that he could claim on a fund put up by the Polish Government to compensate Britons who had lost property in Poland because of nationalisation. It was the task of the House to interpret an old statute, the Princess Sophia Naturalisation Act 1705. The case turned on whether the words 'and all persons descending from Her' were limited to persons born in Queen Anne's lifetime (the statute being passed in her reign). The effect of the preamble was considered. At first instance the golden rule was adopted to avoid the absurdity that could occur under the literal approach, for under the latter there was no limitation on who could be a descendant – even the Kaiser could have been a British subject. Regard was had to the preamble.

Held
The plain and ordinary meaning of the material words was to be adhered to and the class of descendants could not be limited. There was nothing in the preamble or any earlier Act capable of limiting or controlling the meaning of these words.

Viscount Simonds:

> 'The context of the preamble is not to influence the meaning otherwise ascribable to the enacting part unless there is a compelling reason for it ... and that is not to be found merely in the fact that the enacting words go further than the preamble has indicated. Still less can the preamble affect the meaning of the enacting words when its own meaning is in doubt.'

Comment
A straightforward decision showing that a statute must be read as a whole, that the literal rule must be applied to unambiguous words, and that the preamble cannot have an influence on a literal construction in such circumstances.

Bidie, Re [1948] 2 All ER 995 Court of Appeal (Lord Greene MR, Somervell and Evershed LJJ)

- *Principles of construction*

Facts
A husband, who had been separated from his wife for 23 years, died in 1945 having made a will. The will was not found and, assuming that he had died intestate, his widow applied for and was granted letters of administration. A few months later the will was found and the letters of administration revoked, a grant of probate being made instead to the executor named in the will. Since no provision had been made in the will for the widow, she claimed against the estate under the Inheritance (Family Provision) Act 1938. The judge at first instance rejected the claim and she appealed.

Held
The appeal should be allowed since, although

her application was made more than six months after the grant of letters of administration, it was made within six months of the grant of probate.

Lord Greene MR:

> 'If (the) will had been proved in the ordinary way, the widow unquestionably would have had a locus standi to apply for relief, and, subject to her being able to satisfy the court on the relevant matters, would have been entitled to an appropriate order. She is clearly a person who prima facie belongs to the class of dependants which the Act was designed to help. The Act is described in its title as "An Act to amend the law relating to testamentary dispositions ..." It is concerned, and concerned only, with testamentary dispositions. The Act does not seek to amend the law relating to the distribution of intestates' estates. The legislature obviously was of opinion that the class of dependants named in the Act was sufficiently provided for by the existing law in the case of an intestacy. It, therefore, set itself to deal only with the case where, by his testamentary disposition, a testator has displaced the succession which would have taken place if he had died intestate.
>
> I can well understand the good sense, in an Act of this kind, of putting a limitation section in the Act but, if this section has the effect contended for by the defendants, it would have what is, I think, the strange effect ... of making the period of limitation run during a time when a person intending to make an application cannot possibly make it. The right to make an application never arose during the six month period, and the result of the learned judge's construction would be to construe this limitation as applying not to a person who has been dilatory in enforcing a right but to a person who never had the chance of enforcing it. The legislature may intend such things, of course, and I give full weight to the sort of broad suggestion that certainty is a desirable thing and that it is not really fair to disturb people who have mapped out their lives, possibly, on a particular basis, but, giving full effect to that, it appears to me that one must remember that, talking of hardship, the whole Act is on the footing that a particular limited class of dependant has suffered hardship because a testator has not made the provision which the legislature thinks ought reasonably to be made.
>
> The learned judge found that the construction argued for by counsel for the widow lacked logic. He visualised the case where there was a will and probate and then more than six months afterwards another will was found and the probate of the first will was revoked, and he asked what happened to the six months limitation period in such a case. He formed the view, apparently, that in such a case the limitation period would run from the representation granted in respect of the first will, and he thought it illogical to say that where the earliest representation is not a will but letters of administration a similar result would not follow. With all respect to the learned judge, I do not agree with this reasoning.'

Comment

Note the stern rebuke issued to the trial judge by Lord Greene MR for treating particular provisions of a statute in complete isolation and divorced from their context. The basic rule that a statute must be read as a whole is strongly reaffirmed.

Black-Clawson International Ltd* v *Papierwerke Waldhof-Aschaffenburg AG [1975] AC 591 House of Lords (Lords Reid, Dilhorne, Wilberforce, Diplock and Simon)

- *Material aids – committee report – use of Hansard*

Facts

The dispute between the parties concerned the enforcement of a foreign judgment and thereby a conflict of laws. The case turned on the interpretation of s8(1) of the Foreign Judgments (Reciprocal Enforcement) Act

1933. The court had to decide whether it could refer to a report of a committee to use the mischief rule and also for a direct statement as to the meaning of the statute. The Foreign Judgments (Reciprocal Enforcement) Committee consisting of eminent lawyers was set up by the Lord Chancellor and submitted a report containing a statement of the present law relating to enforcement of foreign judgments in the UK and recommendations for proposed legislation. A draft Bill was annexed to the report. Following this report the Foreign Judgments (Reciprocal Enforcement) Act 1933 was passed and clause 8 of the draft Bill was enacted without alteration in the statute.

Held

Per curiam: if there was an ambiguity in a statute the court may have regard to the report of a committee presented by Parliament containing proposals for legislation which resulted in the enactment of the statute in order to ascertain the mischief which the act was intended to remedy. Lord Reid and Lord Wilberforce (Viscount Dilhorne and Lord Simon of Glaisdale dissenting) went on to say that reference could not be made to the report for a direct statement of what the enactment means, even though the report sets out a draft Bill which is subsequently enacted without alteration.

Lord Reid explained that the courts are 'seeking not what Parliament meant but the true meaning of what they said'. His reasons for contending that Hansard and committee reports should not be used as aids to constructions were as follows:

> 'Construction of the provision of an Act is for the court and no-one else. This may seem technical but it is good sense. Occasionally we can find clear evidence of what was intended, more often any such evidence if there is any, is vague and uncertain. If we are to take into account evidence of Parliament's intention the first thing we must do is reverse our present practice with regard to consulting Hansard. I have more than once drawn attention to the practical difficulties that would involve but the difficulty goes deeper. The question which gives rise to debate are rarely those which later have to be decided by the courts. One might take the views of the promoters of a Bill as an indication of the intention of Parliament but any view the promoters may have had about questions which later come before the court will not often appear in Hansard and often those questions have never occurred to the promoters.'

Comment

An important case which remains of some relevance as an illustration of what materials may be used when using the mischief rule of statutory construction, though the ban on the use of Hansard has since been lifted: see *Pepper* v *Hart* (1993) (below).

Bulmer (HP) Ltd v *J Bollinger SA* [1974] 3 WLR 202 Court of Appeal (Civil Division) (Lord Denning MR, Stamp and Stephenson LJJ)

• *Interpretation of European Community legislation*

(The facts and decision are not important in this context. It is Lord Denning's view on the interpretation of European Community law which is of significance here.)

Lord Denning MR:

> 'What then are the principles of interpretation to be applied? Beyond doubt the English courts must follow the same principles as the European Court, otherwise there would be differences between the countries of the nine. That would never do. All the courts of all nine countries should interpret the treaty in the same way. They should all apply the same principles. It is enjoined on the English courts by s3 of the European Communities Act 1972, which I have read.
>
> What a task is thus set before us! The treaty is quite unlike any of the enactments to which we have become accustomed. The draftsmen of our statutes have striven to

express themselves with the utmost exactness. They have tried to foresee all possible circumstances that may arise and to provide for them. They have sacrificed style and simplicity. They have foregone brevity. They have become long and involved. In consequence, the judges have followed suit. They interpret a statute as applying only to the circumstances covered by the very words. They give them a literal interpretation. If the words of the statute do not cover a new situation – which was not foreseen – the judges hold that they have no power to fill the gap. To do so would be a "naked usurpation of the legislative function": see *Magor and St Mellons Rural District Council* v *Newport Corporation*. The gap must remain open until Parliament finds time to fill it.

How different is this treaty. It lays down general principles. It expresses its aims and purposes. All in sentences of moderate length and commendable style. But it lacks precision. It uses words and phrases without defining what they mean. An English lawyer would look for an interpretation clause, but he would look in vain. There is none. All the way through the treaty there are gaps and lacunae. These have to be filled in by the judges, or by regulations or directives. It is the European way.'

Comment

Useful guidance is given in this case on the manner of construing European Community legislation. Whilst judges have moved toward adopting a purposive approach to the construction of domestic legislation (*Pepper* v *Hart* (1993) (below)), this still falls short of the kind of judicial activism permitted when interpreting the laws of the European Union.

Chief Adjudication Officer v *Foster* [1993] 2 WLR 292 House of Lords (Lords Templeman, Bridge of Harwich, Ackner, Browne-Wilkinson and Slynn of Hadley)

- *Statutory regulations – ultra vires – use of Hansard*

Facts

The question arose as to whether a severely disabled young woman, the appellant, was entitled to the severe disability premium, in addition to the statutory allowances, payable by virtue of the Social Security Act 1986 and regulations made under it. The social security commissioner had held that the regulation which would have defeated her claim was ultra vires but the Court of Appeal took the view that he had no jurisdiction to question the vires of the regulation and that in any case his decision as to vires had been mistaken.

Held

In exercising his appellate function the commissioner had been entitled to determine any challenge as to vires, but the regulation was indeed intra vires and the appellant's claim to the premium therefore failed.

Lord Bridge of Harwich:

'... the opinion I had formed at the conclusion of the oral arguments, which I understand all your Lordships shared, [was] that the appellant must fail on the vires issue. But since the oral argument on the appeal your Lordships' House has ruled in *Pepper* v *Hart* [1992] 3 WLR 1032 that in certain circumstances the parliamentary history of a provision in a Bill and references to it in Hansard may be considered when that provision reaches the statute book and falls to be construed. Since the delivery of that judgment the respondents have invited your Lordships to consider the circumstances in which [the relevant provisions] came to be enacted and certain passages from the debates in both Houses as satisfying the conditions of admissibility as aids to construction laid down in *Pepper* v *Hart* and your Lordships have had the benefit of submissions in writing by both parties directed to this issue ...

... the circumstances in which [the relevant provisions] came to be enacted and the statements made by the government spokesman moving the relevant amendment in both Houses seem to me to provide precisely the kind of material which was con-

sidered in *Pepper* v *Hart* to be available as an aid to statutory construction. [The relevant section] is undoubtedly ambiguous, as the difference of opinion in the courts below clearly shows. But it was made perfectly clear to both Houses that it was intended to use the regulation-making power ... so as to provide that a person was only to be treated as severely disabled [in certain specified circumstances] ... This is, of course, precisely what, in principle, [the relevant paragraph of the] 1987 regulations sets out to achieve. Parliament, having enacted the [provisions] with full knowledge of how the regulation-making power was proposed to be used, must clearly have intended that it should be effective to authorise such use. Thus the parliamentary material unequivocally indorses the conclusion I had reached as a matter of construction independently of that material.

The significance of this, following as it does two other cases decided by your Lordships' House since *Pepper* v *Hart* (*Stubbings* v *Webb* [1993] 2 WLR 120 and *Warwickshire CC* v *Johnson* [1993] 2 WLR 1) where the parliamentary material has been found decisive of a statutory ambiguity, is to illustrate how useful the relaxation of the former exclusionary rule may be in avoiding unnecessary litigation. Certainly in this case, if it had been possible to take account of the parliamentary material at the outset, it would have been clear that it refuted the appellant's contention and there would probably never have been any appeal to the commissioner, let alone beyond him. I doubt if any of us who were party to the decision in *Pepper* v *Hart* anticipated that within so short a time after it Hansard would be found to provide the answer in three other cases before the House. But this encourages the hope that as time passes the effect of the new rule will be to prevent or to curtail much litigation relating to ambiguous statutory provisions which would otherwise be fought through the courts.'

Comment

One of the first cases to make use of the freedom to consult Hansard when interpreting statutes – a freedom granted by *Pepper* v *Hart* (1993), below.

Eastman Photographic Materials Co Ltd* v *Comptroller-General of Patents, Designs and Trade-marks [1898] AC 571 House of Lords (Earl of Halsbury LC, Lords Herschell, Shand, Morris and Macnaughten)

• *The mischief rule – use of a commission's report*

(The facts and decision are not important in this context. It is Lord Halsbury's view as to the scope of the mischief rule which is of significance here.)

Lord Halsbury LC:

> 'Before dealing with the decision itself I feel it desirable ... to say something as to what sources of construction we are entitled to appeal in order to construe a statute. Among the things which have passed into canons of construction recorded in *Heydon*'s Case we are to see what was the law before the Act was passed, and what was the mischief or defect for which the law had not provided, what remedy Parliament appointed, and the reason for the remedy. Now the law before the Act now in question was passed was one which had given rise to considerable litigation ... and on February 24 1887, a commission was appointed to inquire into the duties, organisation and arrangements of the Patent Office under the Trade Mark Act so far as they related to trade-marks and design ... I think no more accurate source of information as to what the evil or defect which the Act ... now under consideration was intended to remedy could be imagined than the Report of that Commission (which had led to the particular enactment).'

Comment

A straightforward application of the mischief rule of statutory construction.

Fisher* v *Bell [1961] 1 QB 394 High Court (Lord Parker CJ, Ashworth and Elwes JJ)

- *The literal rule*

Facts
A knife was displayed in a shop window with a price ticket attached to it. The shopkeeper was charged with offering for sale a flick knife contrary to s1(1) of the Restriction of Offensive Weapons Act 1959 which provides:

> 'Any person who manufactures, sells or hires or offers for sale or hire, or lends or gives to any other person – (a) any knife which has a blade which opens automatically by hand pressure applied to a button or spring or other device in or attached to the handle of the knife, sometimes known as a "flick knife" ... shall be guilty of an offence ...'

Held
The displaying knife was merely an invitation to treat and therefore the shopkeeper was not guilty as he had not offered the knife for sale. (No extract from a judgment is necessary on this point.)

Comment
A famous little case illustrating the absurdity of an over-rigid literal interpretation of statutory language. It is unlikely to occur again because of the new purposive approach adopted by judges and their greater willingness to consult Hansard to discover what Parliament truly meant by the words in question (*Pepper* v *Hart* (1993) (below)). The problem caused by the decision was later rectified by statute: Registration of Offensive Weapons Act 1961.

Grey* v *Pearson (1857) 6 HL Cas 61 House of Lords (Lord Cranworth LC, Lords St Leonards and Wensleydale)

- *The golden rule*

(The facts and decision are not important in this context. It is Lord Wensleydale's definition of the golden rule which is of significance here.)

Lord Wensleydale:

> 'In construing wills, and indeed statutes, and all written instruments, the grammatical and ordinary sense of the words is to be adhered to, unless that would lead to some absurdity or some repugnance or inconsistency with the rest of the instrument, in which case the grammatical and ordinary sense of the words may be modified, so as to avoid that absurdity and inconsistency, but no further.'

Comment
A famous old case explaining the scope of the golden rule of statutory construction.

Heydon's Case (1584) 3 Co Rep 74; 76 ER 637

- *The mischief rule*

(The facts and decision are not important in this context. It is the proclamation of the Mischief Rule which is the significant factor here.)

It was unanimously agreed by the Barons of the Exchequer that four things were to be considered in the interpretation of statutes:

> '1st What was the common law before the making of the Act?
>
> 2nd What was the mischief and defect for which the common law did not provide?
>
> 3rd What remedy the Parliament has resolved and appointed to cure the disease of the Commonwealth?
>
> and 4th The true reason of the remedy.'

Comment
This is a celebrated ancient case which pronounced upon the mischief rule and gave birth to a purposive approach to statutory construction.

Inland Revenue Commissioners v *Hinchy* [1960] AC 748 House of Lords (Viscount Kilmuir LC, Lords Reid, Radcliffe, Cohen and Keith)

- *The literal rule*

Facts

The respondent failed to disclose the full amount of interest which had accrued on his Post Office savings account. The Inland Revenue later discovered this from another source and made a further assessment on him. Subsequently they brought an action against him under s25(3)(a) of the Income Tax Act 1952 claiming the fixed penalty of £20 and 'treble the tax which he ought to be charged under this Act'.

Held

The Crown was entitled to the full amount claimed because the literal meaning of the words was 'treble the whole tax which the taxpayer ought to be charged for the relevant year'.

The case turned on the proper construction of s25(3) Income Tax Act 1952 which provides:

> 'A person who neglects or refuses to deliver, within the time limited in any notice served on him, or wilfully makes delay in delivering, a true and correct list, declaration, statement or return which he is required under the preceding provisions of this Chapter to deliver shall – (a) if proceeded against by action in any court, forfeit the sum of £20 and treble the tax which he ought to be charged under this Act; or (b) if proceeded against before the General Commissioners, forfeit a sum not exceeding £20 and treble the tax which he ought to be charged under this Act, and where he is proceeded against before the General Commissioners, the penalty shall be recovered in the same manner as any other penalty under this Act, and the increased tax shall be added to the assessment.'

In the Court of Appeal Diplock J took the view that the interpretation put forward by the Crown was 'absurd and unjust'. The Court of Appeal found it possible to adopt a secondary meaning to the words and expressed itself as follows:

> 'So as a matter of English it seems to us at least a legitimate interpretation of the phrase "tax which he ought to be charged" to limit its significance to that amount of tax with which, at the present point of time, the taxpayer ought to be charged but with which he has not been charged by reason of his defective return; in other words, the tax appropriate to the undisclosed income.'

Commenting on their decision in his judgment Lord Reid made the following observations:

> 'What we must look for is the intention of Parliament, and I also find it difficult to believe that Parliament ever really intended the consequences which flow from the Crown's contention. But we can only take the intention of Parliament from the words which they have used in the Act, and therefore the question is whether these words are capable of a more limited construction. If not then we must apply them as they stand, however unjust and unreasonable the consequences and however strongly we may suspect that this was not the real intention of Parliament ... I agree with the Court of Appeal that if it is possible to infer the meaning which they attach to these words, that should be done.'

Comment

A chilling illustration of the hardship caused by a strict literal interpretation of statutory language. Whilst *Pepper* v *Hart* (1993) (below) encourages greater use of a purposive approach it must be remembered that this will only be permissible if the statutory language is ambiguous or obscure.

Kruhlak v *Kruhlak* [1958] 2 QB 32 High Court (Goddard LCJ, Devlin and Pearson JJ)

- *The mischief rule*

Facts

A married woman had been living apart from her husband for thirteen years. A child was born and after divorce proceedings she married the putative father. Four years later a separation order containing a non-cohabitation clause was made in favour of the appellant woman. She then applied as 'single woman' within s3 of the Bastardy Laws Amendment Act 1872 for a summons to be served on her husband in respect of her child to obtain maintenance for it. The magistrates dismissed the complaint holding that a married woman is not 'a single woman': the applicant appealed.

Held

She was entitled to make such an application as 'a single woman' because she was living apart from her husband under the separation order.

Pearson J:

> 'It is clear from the many cases decided under the Bastardy Laws Amendment Act 1872 that the expression "single woman" cannot be interpreted literally but has an extended meaning including some married women. In my view, the principle to be deduced from the previously decided cases is simply that a married woman who is for the time being effectively separated from her husband may be regarded as a single woman for the purposes of the Act of 1872, and the material time is the time of the application. Here we have a married woman who was living apart from her husband under a separation order. There could be no more effective separation than that. I have referred to the cases, and I have not found anything which would conflict with the apparently obvious proposition that a woman in that state can be treated as a single woman, having regard of course to the other decisions under which it becomes plain that the simple literal meaning cannot be given to that expression.'

Comment

A simple application of the mischief rule. Note the commonsense approach adopted by Pearson J in preference to a literal approach.

Letang* v *Cooper [1965] 1 QB 197; [1964] 2 All ER 929 Court of Appeal (Lord Denning MR, Danckwerts and Diplock LJJ)

- *Material aids*

Facts

The plaintiff was run over by a car negligently driven by the defendant in July 1957. The plaintiff brought an action in February 1961 which was then statute-barred for damages for personal injuries in negligence and alternatively trespass to the person. The case turned on whether a cause of action lay also in trespass and if so, whether that too was statute-barred. The question was also raised as to whether or not the court could, on a matter of construction, refer to a report of a committee leading to the passing of a statute. (The Tucker Committee Report (Cmnd 7740) expressed an intention to exclude trespass from the shorter limitation period.)

Held

The action was statute-barred. Her only action lay in negligence as the act was intentional and that was statute-barred. If an action in trespass was available, then on a true construction of s2(1) of the Law Reform (Limitation of Actions) Act 1954, trespass would be included under the words 'breach of duty', therefore such an action would also be statute-barred.

Lord Denning MR:

> 'It is legitimate to look at the report of a committee, so as to see what was the mischief at which the Act was directed. You can get the facts and surrounding circumstances from the report, so as to see the background against which the legislation was enacted. This is always a great help in interpreting it. But you cannot look at what the committee recommended, or at least, if you do look

at it, you should not be unduly influenced by it. It does not help you much, for the simple reason that Parliament may, and often does, decide to do something different to cure the mischief. You must interpret the words of Parliament as they stand, without too much regard to the recommendations of the committee: see *Assam Railways and Trading Co Ltd* v *Inland Revenue Commissioners* [1935] AC 445. In this very case, Parliament did not reduce the period to two years. It made it three years. It did not make any exception of "trespass to the person" or the rest. It used words of general import; and it is those words which we have to construe, without reference to the recommendations of the committee.'

Comment

A straightforward case applying the mischief rule as justification for referring to extraneous historical material.

Magor & St Mellons Rural District Council v *Newport Corporation* [1952] AC 189 House of Lords (Lords Simonds, Goddard, Morton, Radcliffe and Tucker)

- *Statutory construction – filling in gaps*

Facts

Due to the alteration of local government areas, the boundary of the county borough of Newport was extended under the Newport Extension Act 1934 s4 to take in parts of the two Rural Districts, Magor and St. Mellons. The Act provided for reasonable compensation to be made to the two Rural District Councils. Immediately after the Act took effect the two Rural District Councils were amalgamated under an order made by the Minister. The question was whether the new Rural District Council had a right to the compensation. The case turned on the interpretation of the order.

Held

The new Rural District Council could only make a claim as successor to the two former councils, ie if they could prove that in consequence of the alteration of the boundaries an increase of burden would be placed on the ratepayers of those councils but (Lord Radcliffe dissenting), as they were dissolved by the Order immediately after the alteration of the boundaries, no cost would have to be met by these councils after the alteration, therefore there could be no increase in burden for the ratepayers and the Council could recover nothing. The decision of the Court of Appeal was affirmed.

In the Court of Appeal Lord Denning MR, in his dissenting judgment, refused to adopt the literal approach and he looked to the intention of the Minister's Order, stating that he had no patience with an ultra-legalistic interpretation which would deprive 'the appellants of their rights altogether'. He went on to say:

> 'I would repeat what I said in *Seaford Court Estates Ltd* v *Asher*. We do not sit here to pull the language of Parliament and of Ministers to pieces and make nonsense of it. That is an easy thing to do, and it is a thing to which lawyers are often prone. We sit here to find out the intention of Parliament and of Ministers and carry it out, and we do this better by filling in the gaps and making sense of the enactment than by opening it up to destructive analysis.'

In the House of Lords the literal rule was accepted (except by Lord Radcliffe) and Lord Simons took the opportunity of criticising the observations of Lord Denning. He said that it was not the conclusion of the Master of the Rolls that he wished to criticise, but his approach to construction.

> 'It is sufficient to say that the general proposition that it is the duty of the court to find out the intention of Parliament – and not only of Parliament but of Ministers also – cannot by any means be supported. The duty of the court is to interpret the words that the

legislature has used. Those words may be ambiguous, but even if they are, the power and duty of the court to travel outside them on a voyage of discovery is strictly limited.

Ministers too must proceed to fill in the gaps. What the legislature has not written the court must write. This proposition which re-states in a new form the view expressed by the Lord Justice in the earlier case of *Seaford Court Estates Ltd* v *Asher* (to which the Lord Justice himself refers) cannot be supported. It appears to me to be a naked usurpation of the legislative function under the thin guise of interpretation, and it is guesswork with what material the legislature would, if it had discovered the gap, have filled it in. If a gap is disclosed, the remedy lies in an amending Act.'

Comment

An important case illustrating a sharp clash of judicial opinions over the extent to which a departure from a literal approach can be justified. As usual Lord Denning argues robustly for a commonsense liberal approach to do 'justice' in the case, and as usual he is rebutted by senior Law Lords for crossing the forbidden boundary separating interpretation from legislation. But in view of modern perceptions as to the legitimacy of judicial law-making, was Lord Denning simply ahead of his time?

Morris Angel & Son Ltd* v *Hollande [1993] 3 All ER 569 Court of Appeal (Dillon and Bingham LJJ)

- *Construction of regulations – Council Directive*

Facts

On an application for an interlocutory injunction to enforce a contract in restraint of trade, a question arose as to the construction of the Transfer of Undertakings (Protection of Employment) Regulations 1981 which were enacted to give effect to Council Directive (EEC) 77/187.

Held

The regulations were to be given a purposive (as opposed to a strict and literal) construction and, in the light of this approach, the injunction would be granted.

Dillon LJ:

> 'The regulations, which were laid before Parliament and have statutory force, were made to give effect to Council Directive (EEC) 77/187 on the approximation of the laws of the member states relating to the safeguarding of employees' rights in the event of transfer of undertakings, businesses or parts of businesses.
>
> There is no doubt that the protection of employees' rights was the primary objective but any contract of employment is a complex of rights and obligations on each side, and in *Lister* v *Forth Dry Dock Co Ltd* [1990] 1 AC 546 at 555 ... Lord Oliver stated that, if primary or subordinate legislation enacted to give effect to the United Kingdom's obligations under the EEC Treaty can reasonably be construed so as to conform with those obligations, a purposive construction will be applied even though perhaps it may involve some departure from the strict and literal application of the words which the legislature has elected to use (see [1990] 1 AC 546 at 559).'

Comment

An illustration of a purposive interpretation of laws emanating from a European Community source.

NWL Ltd* v *Woods [1979] 1 WLR 1294 House of Lords (Lords Diplock, Fraser and Scarman)

- *Material aids*

Facts

The owners of the Nawala, a ship registered in Norway, sold her to a Swedish company which re-registered her in Hong Kong and replaced her highly paid Norwegian crew with

a much poorer paid crew flown out from Hong Kong. The ITF, an international federation of trade unions which operated a policy of blacking ships registered under flags of convenience in order to force owners to agree to ITF terms of employment, threatened to black the ship from entering the port of Redcar if the owners refused to increase the men's wages in compliance with ITF conditions of employment. The crew were, in fact, very happy and content with their wages.

Held

Since the dispute concerned terms and conditions of employment it fell within the ambit of the Trade Union and Labour Relations Act 1974 and was a trade dispute even though it was being pursued for other motives and those motives were predominant or extraneous; accordingly, the ultimate object of ITF, to prevent shipowners from using flags of convenience, did not prevent the present dispute from being a trade dispute since it was in fact connected with terms and conditions of employment in the shipping industry.

Lord Diplock:

> 'Even if the defendants had succeeded in inducing port workers at Redcar to break their contracts of employment and black the Nawala, they would not have committed any tort in English law, because their conduct was excused by s13 of the Trade Union and Labour Relations Act 1974.
>
> I turn then to the crucial question in this appeal which I take to be this: have the defendants shown that what they did or threatened to do at Redcar was done in contemplation or furtherance of a trade dispute? That this is not a dispute in connection with terms and conditions of employment seems to me to be simply unarguable. Section 29 makes it clear that ITF qualifies as "workers" for the purpose of making it a 'dispute between employers and workers'. The fact that the Hong Kong crew were content with their existing articles and were not in dispute with the shipowners as to their own terms and conditions of employment is not, in my view, material.'

Comment

The decision in this case was reached upon a purposive construction of the relevant statute and by placing that construction in its proper context, namely a trade dispute. This enabled the court to discover the true legislative purpose.

Nokes* v *Doncaster Amalgamated Collieries [1940] AC 1014 House of Lords (Viscount Simon LC, Lords Atkin, Thankerton, Romer and Porter)

- *The golden rule*

Facts

Section 154 of the Companies Act 1929 enabled the court to order 'the transfer to the transferee company ... the whole or any part of the undertaking and of the property or liabilities of any transferor company': 'property' included 'property, rights and powers of every description' and 'liabilities' included 'duties'. The court made such an order: were contracts of service automatically transferred?

Held

They were not as, in their nature, they were incapable of being transferred.

Viscount Simon LC:

> '... the House is left with the difficult task of putting the proper construction on s154, so far as its application to current contracts of service is concerned. ... The principles of construction which apply in interpreting such a section are well-established. The difficulty is to adapt well-established principles to a particular case of difficulty. The golden rule is that the words of a statute must prima facie be given their ordinary meaning. We must not shrink from an interpretation which will reverse the previous law, for the purpose of a large part of our statute law is to make lawful that which would not be lawful without the statute, or, conversely, to prohibit results which would

> otherwise follow. Judges are not called upon to apply their opinions of sound policy so as to modify the plain meaning of statutory words, but, where, in construing general words the meaning of which is not entirely plain, there are adequate reasons for doubting whether the legislature could have been intending so wide an interpretation as would disregard fundamental principles, then we may be justified in adopting a narrower construction. At the same time, if the choice is between two interpretations the narrower of which would fail to achieve the manifest purpose of the legislation, we should avoid a construction which would reduce the legislation to futility, and should rather accept the bolder construction, based on the view that Parliament would legislate only for the purpose of bringing about an effective result.'

Comment

Viscount Simon's formulation of the golden rule of statutory construction seems to be a much more narrow one than that given in *Grey* v *Pearson* (1857) (above). Indeed, it closely resembles the literal rule!

Nothman v *Barnet London Borough Council* [1978] 1 WLR 220 Court of Appeal (Lord Denning MR, Lawton and Eveleigh LJJ)

- *Statutory construction – filling in gaps*

Facts

The contractual retirement age for teachers employed by the respondent employers was 65. The employee was dismissed at 61 and brought a complaint for unfair dismissal. The industrial tribunal held that it had no jurisdiction to hear the complaint as it was precluded by para 10(b) of Sch 1 to the Trade Union and Labour Relations Act 1974 which provides that a right to bring a complaint of unfair dismissal under para 4:

> 'does not apply to the dismissal of an employee from any employment if the employee ... (b) on or before the effective date of termination attained the age which in the undertaking in which he was employed, was the normal retiring age for an employee holding the position which he held, or, if a man, attained the age of 65, or, if a woman, attained the age of 60.'

The Employment Appeal Tribunal considered that there was a double age barrier and that although the employee could show that she had not reached the normal retiring age she could not satisfy the second qualification which provided an age limit of 60 for women. The employee appealed.

Held

The normal retiring age was when a person must or should retire and the second part of the paragraph only applied where there was no such normal retiring age. The appeal was therefore allowed.

Lord Denning MR:

> 'Faced with glaring injustice, the judges are, it is said, impotent, incapable and sterile. Not so with us in this court. The literal method is now completely out of date. It has been replaced by the approach which Lord Diplock described as the "purposive approach". He said so in *Kammins Ballrooms Co Ltd* v *Zenith Investments (Torquay) Ltd* [1971] AC 850, 899; and it was recommended by Sir David Renton and his colleagues in their valuable report on the Preparation of Legislation (1975) Cmnd 6043 pp135-148. In all cases now in the interpretation of statutes we adopt such a construction as will "promote the general legislative purposes" underlying the provision. It is no longer necessary for judges to wring the hands and say: "There is nothing we can do about it". Whenever the strict interpretation of a statute gives rise to an absurd and unjust situation, the judges can and should use their good sense to remedy it – by reading words in, if necessary so as to do what Parliament would have done, had they had the situation in mind.'

He went on to interpret the provision 'so as to

do justice' by inserting the words 'where there is no normal retiring age' before the second part.

Comment

A case remarkable for the robust language used by Lord Denning in disposing of the literal rule in favour of a purposive approach to statutory construction. At the time he was out of step with other judges, but today his views have received more sympathetic treatment, though they probably still go too far: see *Pepper* v *Hart* (1993) below.

Pepper v *Hart* [1992] 3 WLR 1032; [1993] 1 All ER 42 House of Lords (Lords Mackay of Clashfern LC, Keith of Kinkel, Bridge of Harwich, Griffiths, Ackner, Oliver of Aylmerton and Browne-Wilkinson)

- *Statutory construction – reference to Hansard*

Facts

The question having arisen whether the payment of reduced fees in respect of the sons of teaching staff at an independent school constituted a taxable benefit, for the purposes of certain provisions of the Finance Act 1976, accruing to the teachers concerned, the Appellate Committee decided to invite further argument, before a freshly constituted committee, as to whether reference could be made to the parliamentary proceedings which led to the passing of those provisions when construing them.

Held (Lord Mackay of Clashfern LC dissenting)

Such reference could be made in certain circumstances and the previous position of the House would be relaxed to that extent.

Lord Browne-Wilkinson:

> 'Under present law, there is a general rule that references to parliamentary material as an aid to statutory construction is not permissible (the exclusionary rule) (see *Davis* v *Johnson* [1978] 2 WLR 553 and *Hadmor Productions Ltd* v *Hamilton* [1982] 2 WLR 322. This rule did not always apply but was judge-made ...
>
> My Lords, I have come to the conclusion that, as a matter of law, there are sound reasons for making a limited modification to the existing rule (subject to strict safeguards) unless there are constitutional or practical reasons which outweigh them. ... I will first consider the practical difficulties.
>
> It is said that parliamentary materials are not readily available to, and understandable by, the citizen and his lawyers, who should be entitled to rely on the words of Parliament alone to discover his position. It is undoubtedly true that Hansard and particularly records of committee debates are not widely held by libraries outside London and that the lack of satisfactory indexing of committee stages makes it difficult to trace the passage of a clause after it is redrafted or renumbered. But such practical difficulties can easily be overstated ... experience in New Zealand and Australia (where the strict rule has been relaxed for some years) has not shown that the non-availability of materials has raised these practical problems.
>
> Next, it is said that lawyers and judges are not familiar with parliamentary procedures and will therefore have difficulty in giving proper weight to the parliamentary materials. Although, of course, lawyers do not have the same experience of these matters as members of the legislature, they are not wholly ignorant of them. If, as I think, significance should only be attached to the clear statements made by a minister or other promoter of the Bill, the difficulty of knowing what weight to attach to such statements is not overwhelming ...
>
> Then it is said that court time will be taken up by considering a mass of parliamentary material and long arguments about its significance, thereby increasing the expense of litigation. In my judgment, though the introduction of further admissible material will inevitably involve some increase in the use of time, this will not be

significant as long as courts insist that parliamentary material should only be introduced in the limited cases I have mentioned and where such material contains a clear indication from the minister of the mischief aimed at, or the nature of the cure intended, by the legislation. Attempts to introduce material which does not satisfy those tests should be met by orders for costs made against those who have improperly introduced the material …

There is one further practical objection which, in my view, has real substance. If the rule is relaxed legal advisers faced with an ambiguous statutory provision may feel that they have to research the materials to see whether they yield the crock of gold, ie a clear indication of Parliament's intentions. In very many cases the crock of gold will not be discovered and the expenditure on the research wasted. This is a real objection to changing the rule. However, again it is easy to overestimate the cost of such research: if a reading of Hansard shows that there is nothing of significance said by the minister in relation to the clause in question, further research will become pointless.

In sum, I do not think that the practical difficulties arising from a limited relaxation of the rule are sufficient to outweigh the basic need for the courts to give effect to the words enacted by Parliament in the sense that they were intended by Parliament to bear …

Is there, then, any constitutional objection to a relaxation of the rule? The main constitutional ground urged by the Attorney General is that the use of such material will infringe s1, art 9 of the Bill of Rights as being a questioning in any court of freedom of speech and debates in Parliament …

In my judgment, the plain meaning of art 9, viewed against the historical background in which it was enacted, was to ensure that Members of Parliament were not subjected to any penalty, civil or criminal, for what they said and were able, contrary to the previous assertions of the Stuart monarchy, to discuss what they, as opposed to the monarch, chose to have discussed. Relaxation of the rule will not involve the courts in criticising what is said in Parliament. The purpose of looking at Hansard will not be to construe the words used by the minister but to give effect to the words used so long as they are clear. Far from questioning the independence of Parliament and its debates, the courts will be giving effect to what is said and done there. …

I therefore reach the conclusion, subject to any question of parliamentary privilege, that the exclusionary rule should be relaxed so as to permit reference to parliamentary materials where: (a) legislation is ambiguous or obscure, or leads to an absurdity; (b) the material relied on consists of one or more statements by a minister or other promoter of the Bill together if necessary with such other parliamentary material as is necessary to understand such statements and their effect; (c) the statements relied on are clear. Further than this, I would not at present go …'

Lord Griffiths, agreeing with Lord Browne-Wilkinson:

'My Lords, I have long thought that the time had come to change the self-imposed judicial rule that forbade any reference to the legislative history of an enactment as an aid to its interpretation. The ever increasing volume … of legislation must inevitably result in ambiguities of statutory language which are not perceived at the time the legislation is enacted. The object of the court in interpreting legislation is to give effect so far as the language permits to the intention of the legislature. If the language proves to be ambiguous I can see no sound reason not to consult Hansard to see if there is a clear statement of the meaning that the words were intended to carry. The days have long passed when the courts adopted a strict constructionist view of interpretation which required them to adopt the literal meaning of the language. The courts now adopt a purposive approach which seeks to give effect to the true purpose of legislation and are prepared to look at much extraneous material that bears on the background against which the legislation was enacted. Why then

> cut ourselves off from the one source in which may be found an authoritative statement of the intention with which the legislation is placed before Parliament.'

Comment

The leading modern authority on statutory construction. (Note that seven Law Lords sat to hear the appeal, instead of the usual five.) All seven Law Lords agreed that the time had come to move away from the traditional literal approach toward a more purposive one, and six of them (Lord Mackay LC dissenting) held that the time had come to lift the ban on the use of Hansard as an aid to this purposive approach. Note, however, that the literal rule was not completely abandoned and that fairly strict conditions were laid down for the use of Hansard: see Lord Browne-Wilkinson's judgment for the three conditions that need to be satisfied. Despite those conditions Lord Mackay, in his dissenting judgment, expressed concern that the new approach would increase delays in litigation and add to costs. Has he been proved right?

Powell* v *Kempton Park Race Course Co Ltd [1899] AC 143 House of Lords (Earl of Halsbury LC, Lords Hobhouse, Macnaughten, Morris, Shand, Davey and James)

- *Ejusdem generis*

Facts

There was an open enclosure adjacent to a race course where members of the public and bookmakers were admitted. Some members of the public would place bets with the bookmakers who operated on an informal basis without any particular apparatus such as a booth. This use was known to the owners of the field. It was the task of the court to decide whether the enclosure was 'a place opened, kept or used' for the purposes prohibited by the Betting Act 1853. The case turned on whether the enclosure could be construed ejusdem generis with 'house office room or other place'.

Held (Lords Hobhouse and Davey dissenting)

The enclosure was not 'a place opened, kept or used' for the purposes prohibited by the Act. The enclosure was not an 'other place'. The words 'other place' had to be construed in the light of the words 'house office room' all of which were closed spaces: the enclosure was an open space. (No extract from a judgment is necessary on this point.)

Comment

A simple little case illustrating the use of the 'ejusdem generis' rule of grammatical construction.

R* v *Allen (1872) LR 1 CCR 367 Court for Crown Cases Reserved (Cockburn CJ and fourteen other judges)

- *The golden rule*

Facts

Section 57 of the Offences against the Person Act 1861 provided:

> 'Whosoever, being married, shall marry any other person during the life of the former husband or wife ...'

shall be guilty of bigamy. The word 'marry' in this context has two possible meanings. Firstly, contracting a valid marriage and secondly, going through the actual marriage service.

Held

The second interpretation would be adopted to avoid the absurd result that would occur by adopting the first (ie that no-one could ever be guilty of the offence). (No extract from a judgment is necessary on this point.)

Comment

A simple old case illustrating use of the golden rule to avoid an otherwise absurd result.

R v *Highbury Corner Magistrates' Court, ex parte Di Matteo* [1991] 1 WLR 1374 High Court (Watkins LJ and Roch J)

- *Forfeiture – car used for driving while disqualified – statutory construction*

Facts

Following conviction of, inter alia, driving while disqualified, the stipendiary magistrate ordered the forfeiting of the applicant's car under s43(1) of the Powers of Criminal Courts Act 1973.

Held

In principle, such an order could be made, but here it would be quashed as the magistrate had not considered the relevant matters set out in s43(1A) of the 1973 Act.

Watkins LJ:

> 'The argument advanced on behalf of the applicant was this: the essence of a driving offence is the actual use of a motor vehicle, whereas the forfeiture provision is in respect of property which has been used "for the purpose of committing, or facilitating the commission of any offence". That is to say the use of the property is subsidiary to the commission of an offence and not the offence itself. A strict or narrow construction of that provision of s43, it was submitted by counsel for the applicant, should be adopted by the courts because it could not have been Parliament's intention that such a general forfeiture provision should be used by the courts to confiscate motor vehicles where the essence of the offence committed was the use of the motor car.
>
> Counsel for the prosecutor argued that, as to the offence of driving whilst disqualified, the car must have been used for the purpose of committing that offence, that is to say for the very purpose of driving whilst disqualified and that, provided the other material requirements of it were satisfied, s43 applied ...
>
> In our judgment the words used in s43 should be given their natural and ordinary meaning, unless on a reading of the section there are two possible interpretations, in which case, this being a penal provision, the interpretation most favourable to a defendant should be adopted. That is to say the section should be confined to the narrower of the two possible interpretations.
>
> But we see no ambiguity in s43(1) when seeking to apply it to the facts of the present case. The applicant was convicted of an offence, namely of driving whilst disqualified. He had in his possession at the time he was apprehended the Ford Granada motor car. The remaining question for the magistrate was whether that car had been used by the applicant for the purpose of committing any offence. In this case the words "any offence" referred to the driving whilst disqualified. His conclusion that the car had been used by the applicant for the purpose of committing the offence of driving whilst disqualified, in our opinion, placed no strain on its language, but was an application of s43(1) using the ordinary and normal meaning of the words therein contained ...
>
> In the present case, in our judgment, the use of the car was an integral part of the offence. The applicant could not have committed the offence without the car ... the applicant must have intended to drive whilst disqualified when the journey in his car started.'

Comment

A case in which the court gave effect to the natural and ordinary meaning of statutory language, though there is reference in the judgment to construing a penal provision in a manner favourable to a defendant in the event of ambiguity. However, the presumption that such a provision should be construed narrowly in favour of the citizen, like other presumptions of parliamentary intention, may no longer be of utility in view of the availability

of Hansard to resolve such doubts: see *Pepper* v *Hart* (1993) (above).

R v *Judge of the City of London Court* [1892] 1 QB 273 Court of Appeal (Lord Esher MR, Lopez and Kay LJJ)

- *The literal rule*

Facts

A barge owner sued the pilot of a steamer for negligence after a collision in the River Thames in which the barge was damaged. The question before the court was whether, under the County Courts Admiralty Jurisdiction Acts, the City of London Court on its Admiralty side had jurisdiction to hear the case (in which case the court had power to award up to £300 in damages) or whether it only had jurisdiction on its common law side (in which case the maximum damages were £50).

Held

Lord Esher MR:

> 'The question we have to decide is a narrow one, viz, whether the county court has this Admiralty jurisdiction with regard to a pilot.'

Lopez LJ:

> 'I have always understood that, if the words of an Act are unambiguous and clear, you must obey those words, however absurd the result may appear; and, to my mind, the reason for this is obvious. If any other rule were followed, the result would be that the court would be legislating instead of the properly constituted authority of the country, namely, the legislature.'

Comment

A classic example of the prevalence of the literal approach in early English law.

R v *McFarlane* [1994] 2 WLR 494 Court of Appeal (Taylor of Gosforth LCJ, Popplewell and Scott Baker JJ)

- *'Clipper' a 'prostitute'? – use of mischief rule*

Facts

On the hearing of a charge of living on the earnings of prostitution, contrary to s30(1) of the Sexual Offences Act 1956, it appeared that the woman in question had been a 'clipper'. On appeal against conviction, the man contended that a clipper was not a prostitute.

Held

The appeal would be dismissed.

Taylor of Gosforth LCJ:

> 'The words "prostitute" and "prostitution" are not defined in any statute. Our attention was drawn to dictionary definitions and to three decided cases …
>
> In our judgment both the dictionary definitions and the cases show that the crucial feature in defining prostitution is the making of an offer of sexual services for reward. [Counsel for the appellant] submits that the true offence here was not one of living off immoral earnings, and that the woman in question … was not acting by way of prostitution … [Counsel] also submits that the mischief against which s30 of the Sexual Offences Act 1956 is directed is the exploitation of women. Here, the appellant was not exploiting [the woman] sexually, only dishonestly. However, if [counsel's] argument were right, the mischief aimed at in other statutes requiring proof of prostitution would not be defeated. There have been a number of statutes, from the Vagrancy Act 1824 through the Town Police Clauses Act 1847, up to and including the Street Offences Act 1959, whose object has been to prevent the nuisance of women soliciting and offering sexual favours in public places. If it were a defence to soliciting for prostitution under s1 of the 1959 Act that the accused woman was acting as a "clipper" and not as a "hooker", proof of such

offences would be extremely difficult. It would be necessary to prove not merely the offer of sexual services in a public place, but that the services were actually provided, or were at the time of the offering intended to be provided. The mischief being simply the harassment and nuisance to members of the public on the streets, the distinction between "clippers" and "hookers" is immaterial.'

Comment
A case illustrating the use of the mischief rule to resolve apparent ambiguities in statutory language.

River Wear Commissioners* v *Adamson (1877) 2 App Cas 743 House of Lords (Lord Cairns LC, Lords Gordon, Hatherley, O'Hagan and Blackburn)

- *The golden rule*

Facts
The Harbours, Docks and Piers Act 1847 stated that 'the owner of every vessel, or float of timber shall be answerable ... for any damage done by such a vessel or float of timber to the harbour, dock or pier, or the quays or works connected therewith'. The respondents were owners of a ship, the Natalian, which went aground during a violent storm near the mouth of the River Wear. The crew were rescued but the abandoned ship subsequently damaged the pier.

Held
The owners were not liable.

Lord O'Hagan:

> 'Your Lordships, exercising your appellate jurisdiction, act as a court of construction. You do not legislate, but ascertain the purpose of the Legislature; and if you can discover what that purpose was, you are bound to enforce it, although you may not approve the motives from which it springs, or the objects which it aims to accomplish.'

Lord Blackburn:

> 'In all cases the object is to see what is the intention expressed by the words used. But, from the imperfection of language, it is impossible to know what that intention is without inquiring further, and seeing what the circumstances were with reference to which words were used, and what was the object, appearing from these circumstances, which the person using them had in view.'

Comment
A case which helped to affirm and develop the golden rule of construction laid down in *Grey* v *Pearson* (1857), above.

Sweet* v *Parsley [1970] AC 132 House of Lords (Lords Reid, Morris, Pearce, Wilberforce and Diplock)

- *Presumptions*

Facts
The appellant was the sub-tenant of a farmhouse and let out rooms to tenants. She no longer lived there herself but retained a room and returned occasionally to collect rent and mail. Drugs were found on the property and she was charged with being 'concerned in the management' of premises used for drug taking subject to s5 of the Dangerous Drugs Act 1965. The prosecutor conceded that she was unaware of the existence of the drugs. She was convicted of the offence.

Held
The appeal against conviction would be allowed. Lord Diplock approved *R* v *Tolson* (1889) 23 QBD 168 in his judgment, saying that it laid down:

> '... as a general principle of construction of any enactment, which creates a criminal offence, that, even where the words used to describe the prohibited conduct would not in any other context connote the necessity for any particular mental element, they are nevertheless to be read subject to the implication that a necessary element in the offence

is the absence of a belief, held honestly and upon reasonable grounds, in the existence of the facts, which, if true, would make the act innocent.'

Comment

A case illustrating a very strong presumption, namely that a criminal offence requires proof of mens rea unless there are clear and unambiguous words creating an offence of strict liability. It is debatable whether the use of presumptions will continue if Hansard can be used to find the answer instead. Indeed, one academic has argued that the danger of using Hansard instead of a presumption is that the research may reveal an intention to do things that are not consistent with the protection of basic human rights!: see Oliver [1993] PL 5 at 12–13.

Three Rivers District Council v *Bank of England (No 2)* [1996] 2 All ER 363 Queen's Bench Division Commercial Court (Clarke J)

- *Criteria for use of Hansard as an aid to construction*

Facts

The plaintiff local authority (P) intended to sue the defendant bank (D) for the tort of misfeasance in public office. In order to support its main action P applied for leave to refer to parliamentary speeches made by ministers when moving the second readings of banking legislation. The legislation was designed to implement obligations under a European directive. P contended that the true purpose of the legislation, if construed in the context of all the relevant legislative materials, was to place certain responsibilities on D. It would be P's contention in the main action that D failed to fulfil these responsibilities. D contested the application on the ground that the criteria for the use of Hansard laid down in *Pepper* v *Hart* [1993] AC 593 (HL) were not satisfied since the construction of particular ambiguous statutory provisions would not be in issue.

Held

Leave granted. The strict conditions for the use of Hansard laid down in *Pepper* v *Hart* did not apply to cases where the purpose of the legislation in question was to implement international obligations.

In such cases a more flexible approach was desirable in order to ascertain the true purpose of legislation since it was particularly important that such legislation was construed consistently with the relevant international materials (in this case an EC directive). This flexible approach had been signalled in cases such as *Pickstone* v *Freemans plc* [1989] 1 AC 66 (HL) which were not affected by the speeches in *Pepper* v *Hart*. Commenting on the latter case, Clarke J observed:

> 'It [the House of Lords] was not considering the case where the Court might be considering the purpose or object of a statute for some reason other than the construction of a particular statutory provision. Moreover, the House was considering a purely domestic statute.
>
> In my judgment it does not necessarily follow that the principle [of *Pepper* v *Hart*] applies so narrowly to a case where the purpose of the legislation is to introduce into English law the provisions of an international convention or of a European directive, even where the question is one of construction; a fortiori to a case where the question for decision is not one of construction.'

Comment

The decision confirms the survival of the flexible purposive approach used in *Pickstone* v *Freemans plc*, above, even after the attempt to lay down strict conditions on the use of Hansard in *Pepper* v *Hart* (above).

Universal Corporation v *Five Ways Properties* [1979] 1 All ER 552 Court of Appeal (Buckley and Eveleigh LJJ)

- *Mischief rule – limitation*

Facts

The purchasers of Dorset House were unable to complete the purchase because their money was not available: the vendors rescinded the contract and purported to forfeit the deposit. The purchasers sued to recover the deposit relying, inter alia, on s49(2) of the Law of Property Act 1925 which provides that 'Where the court refuses to grant specific performance of a contract, or in any action for the return of a deposit, the court may, if it thinks fit, order the repayment of any deposit.' Walton J ordered that the claim be struck out on the ground, inter alia, that s49(2) of the 1925 Act could not be applied if the vendors would have been granted specific performance had they sought it. The purchaser appealed.

Held

The appeal would be allowed as the discretion which s49(2) of the 1925 Act conferred on the court was unqualified.

Buckley LJ:

> 'The judge, however, went on to say that ... it was obvious that there must be severe limits on the operation of the subsection. It is not, he said, designed simply to do justice between vendor and purchaser. Looking at s49(2) in its terms, having regard to the language used in it and without regard to extraneous considerations, this seems to be precisely what the section in fact is.
>
> By way of supporting, or establishing, his view, the judge asked: "... when can it be just and equitable to deprive the vendor of the whole of the moneys to which he is at law entitled?" It seems to me that this is, or may be, precisely the problem which the section presents to the court, for it confers on the judge a discretion, which is unqualified by any language of the subsection, to order or refuse repayment of the deposit, a discretion which must, of course, be exercised judicially and with regard to all relevant considerations, including the very important consideration of the terms of the contract into which the parties have chosen to enter.
>
> With respect to the judge, it does not seem to me to follow, as he thought, that a purchaser can only succeed in a claim to repayment of the deposit if the vendor's conduct has been open to criticism in some way which Walton J described as having some mark of equitable disfavour attached to it.
>
> In the course of argument, we have been referred to the principle of construction which is stated in Maxwell on Statutes where it is said that "it is a canon of interpretation that all words, if they be general and not precise, are to be restricted to the fitness of the matter, that is, to be construed as particular if the intention be particular". That, as I understand it, is a reference to the well-known doctrine of having regard to the mischief which the enactment is intended to deal with; but that doctrine, as I understand it, does not entitle the court to disregard the plain and natural meaning of wide general terms in a statute. If the language is equivocal and requires construction, then the doctrine is a proper one to refer to; but if the language is quite plain then the duty of the court is to give effect to what Parliament has said, and it seems to me that in the present case Parliament has conferred a wide and general discretion.'

Comment

The judgment of Buckley LJ emphasises that the mischief rule can be used only if the statutory language is equivocal and requires construction. The survival of the literal rule is reaffirmed. However, the modern judicial tendency is to emphasise the advantages of a purposive approach: see especially per Lord Griffiths in *Pepper* v *Hart* (1993) (above).

5 Arrest, Search, Seizure and Interrogation

Abbassy v *Commissioner of Police of the Metropolis* [1990] 1 WLR 385 Court of Appeal (Purchas, Mustill and Woolf LJJ)

- *Arrest – information to be given*

Facts

The plaintiff motorist, an Iranian, was stopped by the police and asked four times about the ownership of the vehicle: on each occasion the reply was abusive. On being told that he would be arrested unless he could satisfy the constable as to the ownership of the Mercedes, the plaintiff said that British laws meant nothing to him. The constable then told him that he was being arrested for 'unlawful possession' and he was held in custody for some two hours before being released. In an action for, inter alia, wrongful arrest and false imprisonment the judge ruled that the arrest had been unlawful as the constable's explanation of the reason for the arrest had been insufficient and the plaintiff was awarded £5,000 by way of damages. The defendants appealed.

Held

The judge had been wrong to withdraw from the jury the issue as to whether the arrest had been unlawful and the appeal would be allowed to that extent.

Purchas LJ:

> 'The powers of arrest without warrant which the (constable) purported to exercise were granted under s2(4) of the Criminal Law Act 1967, now replaced in equivalent terms by s24(6) of the Police and Criminal Evidence Act 1984. That this power should be available to constables is important for the protection of the public for obvious reasons. It is, however, of equal importance to the protection of the selfsame citizens that the statutory powers to which I have just referred should not be abused. …
>
> … I can see no mandate in the common law for a requirement that a constable exercising his powers of arrest without warrant should specify the particular crime for which the arrest is being made, provided that one or more of such alternatives present to his mind were arrestable offences. Nor does the arresting constable have to impart the information to the arrested person in the form of a technical statutory or common law definition. In my judgment, it is sufficient that commonplace words be used, the obvious meaning of which informs the person arrested of the offence or type of offences for which he is being arrested. This is quite sufficient to give him the opportunity of volunteering information which would avoid the arrest or, alternatively, although I must personally express some reservation on this aspect of the law as it appears from the authorities, permit forcible resistance against arrest. For these reasons I agree … that Leonard J was wrong to withhold from the jury the question whether a reasonable explanation was given to the … plaintiff by the (constable) and that this question, which was one essentially for the jury, should have been left to them.'

Comment

The decision may be seen as favourable to police constables in that it permits non-technical language to be used when giving reasons for an arrest. It is sufficient that the type of offence is identified.

D'Souza* v *Director of Public Prosecutions [1992] 1 WLR 1073 House of Lords (Lords Keith of Kinkel, Roskill, Jauncey of Tullichettle, Lowry and Browne-Wilkinson)

- *Power of entry – 'hot pursuit'*

Facts

A mother had been detained in hospital under the Mental Health Act 1983 and, without leave having been given under that Act, she had left the premises. Three uniformed police officers went to her home, intending to return her to the hospital. Entry having been refused, the officers broke into the premises and they were there attacked by the daughter. She was convicted of assaulting the officers in the execution of their duty and she appealed against that conviction.

Held

Her appeal would be allowed as, at the material time, the officers had not been acting in the execution of their duty.

Lord Lowry:

> 'The appellant ... had indeed assaulted the police officers and the propriety of convicting her depended on whether at the time of the assaults the police were acting in the execution of their duty. The answer to that question depended in turn on whether the police were entitled to enter by force without a warrant the premises in which the assaults occurred ...
>
> The justification for entering the house must be sought in s17 of the Police and Criminal Evidence Act 1984 ... It will be noted that, except for the power of entry to deal with or prevent a breach of the peace, sub-s (5) abolished all the common law rules relating to a constable's power of entry without a warrant. (The power to use reasonable force is found in s117(1).)
>
> The statutory provision relied on by the police in this case was, of course, s17(1)(d), and therefore, to justify entry for the purpose of recapturing the patient, she has to be a person (1) who was unlawfully at large and (2) whom the police were pursuing.
>
> The first requirement takes me to the circumstances ... in which the patient was admitted to the hospital and later left it and to the statutory background consisting of the relevant provisions of the 1983 Act ... I accept the submission of [counsel for the respondent] that the expression "unlawfully at large" does not have a technical or special meaning. A person who is detained in hospital ... is lawfully detained. If he goes absent without leave, he is then at large ... and, since he ought not to be at large and is ... liable to be taken into custody and returned to the hospital, he would inevitably appear to be *unlawfully* at large until he is taken into custody ...
>
> I turn now to the second question on the basis, which I regard as justified, that the patient was "unlawfully at large". Was she a person "whom the constables were pursuing"?
>
> That question, I admit, is a question of fact but, like all such questions, it must be answered within the relevant legal principles and paying regard to the meaning in their context of the relevant words (in this case the words "whom he is pursuing" in s17(1)(d)) ... Many of the illustrations of pursuit (which made it lawful to enter premises without a warrant in order to recapture an escaper) describe recapture by the very constable from whom the person arrested has escaped. I am not, however, saying that s17(1)(d) applies only in such circumstances. I would assume that the power of entry to recapture can apply in a case like the present, provided the constable is "pursuing" the patient. But, even so, I cannot find any evidence from which pursuit by the constables before the break-in can be inferred. The verb in the clause "whom he is pursuing" is in the present continuous tense and therefore, give or take a few seconds or minutes – this is a question of degree – the pursuit must be almost contemporaneous with the entry into the premises. There must, I consider, be an act of pursuit, that is a chase, however short in time and distance.

It is not enough for the police to form an intention to arrest, which they put into practice by resorting to the premises where they believe that the person whom they seek may be found …'

Comment

An important decision emphasising the strict conditions applying to an entry of premises without a warrant under s17 PACE 1984. One of those conditions requires proof of an act of pursuit – it is not enough for a constable to 'seek' someone by going to a dwelling in the reasonable belief that that person will be found. Such a strict construction of the statutory provision may be said to be justified to protect homes from oppressive police searches.

Jeffrey* v *Black [1978] QB 490 High Court (Widgery LCJ, Forbes and Croom-Johnson JJ)

- *Evidence admissible?*

Facts

The respondent was arrested for stealing a sandwich from a public house. After he had been charged with this offence, the police officer told him that they intended to search his premises: they did so, without his consent, and found there cannabis and cannabis resin. He was charged with unlawful possession of these drugs, but the charge was dismissed as the police officers had entered his premises unlawfully. The prosecutor appealed.

Held

The appeal would be allowed and the case sent back for rehearing before a different bench. Widgery LCJ:

'I do not accept that the common law has yet developed to the point, if it ever does, in which police officers who arrest a suspect for one offence at one point can as a result thereby authorise themselves, as it were, to go and inspect his house at another place when the contents of his house, on the face of them, bear no relation whatever to the offence with which he is charged or the evidence required in support of that offence.

However, having failed to succeed on his first point, counsel for the appellant is by no means exhausted in this matter because the next point he takes is that, even if the justices were right in holding that the entry of these two police officers was unlawful, that does not prevent any drugs or the like which they found in the house from being the subject of admissible evidence in the trial.

It is firmly established according to English law that the mere fact that evidence is obtained in an irregular fashion does not of itself prevent that evidence from being relevant and acceptable to a court. The authority for that is *Kuruma Son of Kaniu* v *R* [see below] … I have not the least doubt that we must firmly accept the proposition that an irregularity in obtaining evidence does not render the evidence inadmissible. Whether or not the evidence is admissible depends on whether or not it is relevant to the issues in respect of which it is called … But if the case is exceptional, if the case is such that not only have the police officers entered without authority, but they have been guilty of trickery or they have misled someone, or they have been oppressive or they have been unfair, or in other respects they have behaved in a manner which is morally reprehensible, then it is open to the justices to apply their discretion and decline to allow the particular evidence to be let in as part of the trial.

I cannot stress the point too strongly that this is a very exceptional situation, and the simple, unvarnished fact that evidence was obtained by police officers who had gone in without bothering to get a search warrant is not enough to justify the magistrates in exercising their discretion to keep the evidence out.'

Comment

A case illustrating the common law rule on the admissibility of illegally obtained evidence: see now s78 PACE 1984. It may be that the

common law discretion to exclude such evidence survives the statutory discretion to exclude: *R* v *Khan (Sultan)* (1996) (below).

Kuruma, Son of Kaniu* v *R [1955] 2 WLR 223 Privy Council (Goddard LCJ, Lord Oaksey and Mr L M D de Silva)

- *Evidence – method of obtaining*

Facts

The appellant had been convicted of being in unlawful possession of two rounds of ammunition: he maintained that the evidence had been illegally obtained and should not have been admitted. The law provided that police officers of or above the rank of assistant inspector could stop and search; those who had stopped and searched the appellant had been below this rank.

Held

The appeal would be dismissed as the evidence had been properly admitted.

Goddard LCJ:

> 'In their Lordships' opinion, the test to be applied in considering whether evidence is admissible is whether it is relevant to the matters in issue. If it is, it is admissible and the court is not concerned with how the evidence was obtained. While this proposition may not have been stated in so many words in any English case, there are decisions which support it and, in their Lordships' opinion, it is plainly right in principle. In *R* v *Leatham*, an information for penalties under the Corrupt Practices Prevention Act 1854, objection was taken to the production of a letter written by the defendant because its existence only became known by answers he had given to the commissioners who held the inquiry under the Act, which provided that answers before that tribunal should not be admissible in evidence against him. The Court of Queen's Bench held that, though the defendant's answers could not be used against him, yet if a clue was thereby given to other evidence, in that case the letter, which would prove the case, it was admissible. Crompton, J, said (8 Cox CC at p501):
>
> > "It matters not how you get it; did you steal it even, it would be admissible."
>
> In their Lordships' opinion, when it is a question of the admission of evidence strictly it is not whether the method by which it was obtained is tortious but excusable, but whether what has been obtained is relevant to the issue being tried. Their Lordships are not now concerned with whether an action for assault would lie against the police officers and express no opinion on that point.'

Comment

Another common law precedent on the discretion to exclude illegally obtained evidence. At common law it is very difficult to persuade the trial judge to exclude such evidence. Consider whether it is easier to do so under s78 PACE 1984, or whether the discretion is the same.

Lewis* v *Chief Constable of the South Wales Constabulary [1991] 1 All ER 206 Court of Appeal (Balcombe and Taylor LJJ)

- *Arrest – reasons given later*

Facts

The plaintiffs had been arrested on suspicion of burglary and taken to a police station. One had been told the reason for the arrest 10 minutes after it had occurred, the other some 23. They were detained for about five hours and then released. In an action for false arrest and wrongful imprisonment, they were awarded damages for unlawful detention of only 10 and 23 minutes respectively. They appealed, contending that, in view of s28(3) of the Police and Criminal Evidence Act (PACE) 1984, they were entitled to compensation for the whole period of their detention.

Held

Their appeal would be dismissed.

Balcombe LJ:

'Counsel for the plaintiffs, for whose able submissions before us I would like to pay tribute, put his case really in two ways. First, he says that, if at the moment of initial apprehension the arrest is unlawful, the act is a nullity.

I think I have already said enough to make it clear from the cases I have cited that, in my judgment, that contention is untenable. Arrest is a situation. It is a matter of fact, as was said in *Spicer* v *Holt* [1976] 3 All ER 71, [1977] AC 987. Whether a person has been arrested depends not on the legality of his arrest but on whether he has been deprived of his liberty to go where he pleases. There is no doubt that, on the facts of this case, these two ladies were deprived of their liberty at the moment that they were arrested in the car. That act clearly was not a nullity …

His more substantive argument, it seems to me, was that, whatever may have been the law before the passing of the 1984 Act, the law was changed by that Act. He accepts that if *R* v *Kulynycz* [1970] 3 All ER 881, [1971] 1 QB 367 is still good law, then inevitably his appeal must fail.

I do not accept that submission. Simply as a matter of the language used, arrest, as I have already said, is defined as a continuing act. It starts with the action of taking a person into custody and, undoubtedly, under s28(3) at that moment the person arrested should be informed of the ground of the arrest, either at that moment or as soon as is practicable after arrest and, if that is not so, that arrest, that taking into custody, is unlawful. But there is nothing in the section which provides what is the effect of the arrested person subsequently being given the reasons for the arrest. Now, clearly, a subsequent giving of the reasons cannot retrospectively make the period between the moment of arrest and the time for giving the reasons unlawful, and no one suggests that it did. The question which this court has to decide, which is precisely the same as the court had to decide in *R* v *Kulynycz* [1970] 3 All ER 881, [1971] 1 QB 367, is this. What is the effect of telling a person, who was initially arrested without being told of the reasons for his arrest, those reasons at a later time? *R* v *Kulynycz* held that thereafter his custody became lawful and, in so far as I have already said that arrest is a continuing act and is the process of being kept in custody or deprived of liberty, it seems to me there is nothing inconsistent with the wording of s28(3) to say that from that moment (when reasons are given) the arrest becomes lawful, or the continued deprivation of liberty becomes lawful, or the continued custody becomes lawful. Indeed, the contrary seems to me to be not merely a surprising, but an almost ridiculous, contention, that what the police officer should do in those circumstances is to tell the person concerned, "You are now free to go", and, the instant he says that, should place his hands immediately on that person's shoulder and say, "Now you are under arrest and you are arrested for", giving the reasons. It seems to me that Parliament cannot have intended that such a farce had to be gone through, and it is sufficient if the police officer gives the reasons and then from that moment onwards the arrest is lawful. …

So, in my judgment, the judge here was quite right in the ruling he gave that, on the jury's finding that these two ladies were deprived of their liberty, in one case for 10 minutes and in the other case for 23 minutes, before being given the reasons for their arrest, that is the period in respect of which they were entitled to sue and for which they were properly awarded damages. The appeal, therefore, in my judgment, should be dismissed.'

Comment

A useful case defining the concept of arrest and the circumstances in which what starts out as an unlawful arrest becomes a lawful arrest.

McLeod* v *Commissioner of Police of the Metropolis [1994] 4 All ER 553 Court of Appeal (Neill, Hoffmann and Waite LJJ)

• *Police powers of entry – private premises*

Facts

Arising out of a confrontation between a divorced couple at the former wife's house in relation to furniture, in which the police had intervened, a question arose in relation to police powers.

Held

On the facts, the police officers had been entitled to enter the former wife's property.

Neill LJ:

> 'I am satisfied that Parliament in s17(6) [of the Police and Criminal Evidence Act 1984] has now recognised that there is a power to enter premises to prevent a breach of the peace as a form of preventive justice. I can see no satisfactory basis for restricting that power to particular classes of premises such as those where public meetings are held. If the police reasonably believe that a breach of the peace is likely to take place on private premises, they have power to enter those premises to prevent it. The apprehension must, of course, be genuine and it must relate to the near future.
>
> What then are the facts here? ... The judge found that the police officers attended to prevent a breach of the peace and that they were reasonable in coming to the conclusion that there was a danger of such a breach. I, for my part, can see no basis for upsetting his decision on these facts. I think it right, however, to add a word of caution.
>
> It seems to me it is important that when exercising his power to prevent a breach of the peace a police officer should act with great care and discretion; this will be particularly important where the exercise of his power involves entering on private premises contrary to the wishes of the owners or occupiers. The officer must satisfy himself that there is a real and imminent risk of a breach of the peace, because, if the matter has to be tested in court thereafter there may be scrutiny not only of his belief at the time but also of the grounds for his belief.
>
> It may be necessary in some future case to consider how far in advance of a possible breach of the peace the right to enter arises. It will depend on the facts of the case, and on the nature and scale of the apprehended breach.'

Comment

A significant warning is given by Neill LJ in this case as to the need for great care and discretion when exercising the power to enter premises to prevent a breach of the peace. Clearly the judge was mindful of the risk that over-zealous police officers would be entering premises every time they heard a domestic argument and the sound of breaking crockery!

O'Hara* v *Chief Constable of the Royal Ulster Constabulary [1997] 1 All ER 129 House of Lords (Lords Goff, Mustill, Steyn, Hoffman and Hope)

• *Basis for a police officer having reasonable suspicion*

Facts

The plaintiff had been arrested during the course of an investigation into a terrorism-related murder. The arresting officer had acted under s12(1) Prevention of Terrorism (Temporary Provisions) Act 1984 (now superseded by an identically worded provision in the Prevention of Terrorism (Temporary Provisions) Act 1989), which provided, inter alia, that '... a constable may arrest without warrant a person whom he has reasonable grounds for suspecting to be a person who is or has been concerned in the commission, preparation or instigation of acts of terrorism to which this Part of this Act applies ...'. The plaintiff sought damages for unlawful arrest

and false imprisonment on the basis that the arresting officer had not had the reasonable suspicion justifying the exercise of powers under s12(1). The action was dismissed at first instance and on appeal. On appeal to the House of Lords.

Held

The appeal was dismissed. Subjectively, the arresting officer had had the necessary suspicion, hence the question was whether, objectively, he had reasonable grounds for suspecting that the plaintiff was concerned in the murder. The objective test was to be applied on the basis of whether a reasonable person would have shared the officer's opinion, given the information which was in the mind of the arresting officer. The arresting officer's suspicion did not have to be based solely on his own observations but could be based upon information received from others, even where this was given anonymously. The basis for the officer's suspicion was a briefing by a super-ior officer during which he was told that the plaintiff had been involved in the murder. The trial judge had been justified in inferring that the briefing had provided the arresting officer with sufficient information upon which to form the reasonable suspicion required by s12(1).

Lord Steyn considered the issue worthy of further examination, however, given the wide range of important police powers that used the concept of reasonable suspicion as the precondition for their being exercised.

Lord Steyn:

> 'An arrest is … not lawful if the arresting officer honestly but erroneously believes that he has reasonable grounds for arrest but there are unknown to him in fact in existence reasonable grounds for the necessary suspicion, eg because another officer has information pointing to the guilt of the suspect. It would be difficult without doing violence to the wording of the statute to read it in any other way … A strong argument can be made that in arresting a suspect without warrant a constable ought to be able to rely on information in the possession of another officer and not communicated to him … But s12(1), and similar provisions, cannot be approached in this way: they categorise as reasonable grounds for suspicion only matters present in the mind of the constable … [the rationale being that] … in framing such statutory provisions Parliament has proceeded on the long standing constitutional theory of the independence and accountability of the individual constable … This case must therefore be approached on the basis that under s12(1) the only relevant matters are those present in the mind of the arresting officer.
>
> Certain general propositions about the powers of constables under a section such as s12(1) can now be summarised. (1) In order to have a reasonable suspicion the constable need not have evidence amounting to a prima facie case. Ex hypothesi one is considering a preliminary stage of the investigation and information from an informer or a tip-off from a member of the public may be enough: *Hussien* v *Chong Fook Kam* [1970] AC 942, 949. (2) Hearsay information may therefore afford a constable a reasonable grounds to arrest. Such information may come from other officers: Hussien's case, ibid. (3) The information which causes the constable to be suspicious of the individual must be in existence to the knowledge of the police officer at the time he makes the arrest. (4) The executive "discretion" to arrest or not as Lord Diplock described it in *Holgate-Mohammed* v *Duke* [1984] AC 437, 446, vests in the constable, who is engaged on the decision to arrest or not, and not in his superior officers.
>
> Given the independent responsibility and accountability of a constable under a provision such as s12(1) of the Act of 1984 it seems to follow that the mere fact that an arresting officer has been instructed by a superior officer to effect the arrest is not capable of amounting to reasonable grounds for the necessary suspicion within the meaning of s12(1). It is accepted, and rightly accepted, that a mere request to arrest without any further information by an equal ranking officer, or a junior officer, is incapable of amounting to reasonable grounds

for the necessary suspicion. How can the badge of the superior officer, and the fact that he gave an order, make a difference? In respect of a statute vesting an independent discretion in the particular constable, and requiring him personally to have reasonable grounds for suspicion, it would be surprising if seniority made a difference. It would be contrary to the principle underlying s12(1) which makes a constable individually responsible for the arrest and accountable in law. In *R* v *Chief Constable of Devon and Cornwall, ex parte Central Electricity Generating Board* [1982] QB 458, 474 Lawton LJ touched on this point. He observed:

> "... [chief constables] cannot give an officer under command an order to do acts which can only lawfully be done if the officer himself with reasonable cause suspects that a breach of the peace has occurred or is imminently likely to occur or an arrestable offence has been committed."

Such an order to arrest cannot without some further information being given to the constable be sufficient to afford the constable reasonable grounds for the necessary suspicion. That seems to me to be the legal position in respect of a provision such as s12(1). For these reasons I regard the submission of counsel for the respondent as unsound in law. In practice it follows that a constable must be given some basis for a request to arrest somebody under a provision such as s12(1), eg a report from an informer.'

Comment

Although the case turns upon the interpretation of s12(1) of the Prevention of Terrorism (Temporary Provisions) Act 1984, it is clearly of very persuasive authority as regards the interpretation of provisions in the Police and Criminal Evidence Act 1984, and other similar enactments, where reasonable suspicion is the basis upon which the discretion vested in a police constable can be exercised.

O'Loughlin* v *Chief Constable of Essex (1997) The Times 12 December Court of Appeal (Civil Division) (Roch, Thorpe and Buxton LJJ)

- *Statutory power of entry exercised by constable – reasons to be given*

Facts

The plaintiff was arrested by police officers who visited his house in connection with a report that the plaintiff's wife had committed an act of criminal damage on a neighbour's car. The plaintiff sustained injuries whilst police officers were effecting an entry into his premises under s17(1)(b) Police and Criminal Evidence Act (PACE) 1984 ('... a constable may enter and search any premises for the purpose ... of arresting a person for an arrestable offence ...'). It was accepted that no officer had explained the reason for their wanting to enter the plaintiff's house. The plaintiff sued successfully for damages for assault, and the Chief Constable appealed.

Held (Thorpe LJ dissenting)

The appeal was dismissed.

Buxton LJ said that the obligation to inform a citizen why his liberty was being interfered with, although not absolute, was a strong one. His Lordship agreed with the view of Professor Sir John Smith that the common law duty to give reasons for an arrest – see *Christie* v *Leachinsky* [1947] AC 573 – ought to require reasons for an entry into premises unless the circumstances rendered it impracticable to do so. He continued:

> 'Freedom of the home from invasion is an interest of comparable importance to freedom from arrest and is deserving of a comparable degree of protection.'

Comment

An important decision safeguarding the consti-

tutional right of the citizen to freedom of his home from unreasonable police entry.

R v *Bryce* [1992] 4 All ER 567 Court of Appeal (Taylor of Gosforth LCJ, Macpherson and Turner JJ)

• *Confession in unrecorded interview – admissibility*

Facts

Having been arrested on suspicion of handling stolen goods, during a recorded interview, under caution, at the police station the appellant had made no comments. However, after the tape recorder had been switched off at his request, he had allegedly made a confession of which evidence was admitted at his trial.

Held

The conviction would be quashed as a fresh caution should have been given before the unrecorded interview.

Taylor of Gosforth LCJ:

> 'If this interview was correctly admitted, the effect would be to set at nought the requirements of the Police and Criminal Evidence Act 1984 and the code in regard to interviews. One of the main purposes of the code is to eliminate the possibility of an interview being concocted or of a true interview being falsely alleged to have been concocted. If it were permissible for an officer simply to assert that, after a properly conducted interview produced a nil return, the suspect confessed off the record and for that confession to be admitted, then the safeguards of the code could readily be bypassed. In our judgment there would have to be some highly exceptional circumstances, perhaps involving cogent corroboration, before such an interview could be admitted without its having such an adverse effect on the fairness of the trial that it ought to be excluded under s78 [of the 1984 Act].'

Comment

A case illustrating the importance attached by judges to the caution that should be administered prior to an interview of a suspect. Even though this requirement is a non-statutory one, breach of it may persuade the trial judges to exclude all the evidence obtained subsequent to the breach.

R v *Chief Constable of the Lancashire Constabulary, ex parte Parker* [1993] 2 WLR 428 High Court (Nolan LJ and Jowitt J)

• *Search warrant – lawfully issued and executed? – retention of unlawfully seized property*

Facts

When granting an application for search warrants under s9 of and Sch 1 to the Police and Criminal Evidence Act 1984 in respect of the two applicants' homes, the circuit judge signed a two-page document headed 'Warrant to enter and search premises' (the authorisation) and there was also a one-page document attached to it headed 'Schedule of application' setting out the articles to be sought (the schedule). In searching the applicants' premises, the police used the original authorisation and a photocopy of the schedule and supplied the applicants only with a copy of the authorisation. By way of judicial review, the applicants sought, inter alia, an order of certiorari to quash the search warrants (the warrants) and the return of the documents seized.

Held

There had been breaches of the requirements of s16(5)(b), (c) of the 1984 Act and the documents must be returned.

Nolan LJ:

> 'We turn now to the chief constable's argument that, even though the entry and search were unlawful, he is entitled to retain the documents and other materials which have been seized.
>
> The searches were purportedly made under the authority of the warrants issued

pursuant to para 12 of Sch 1. The power to seize and retain material for which a search has been authorised under para 12 is conferred by para 13. No information was extracted from a computer in the course of the search so that the police did not have recourse to s19(4) or s20(1). Nor did they need to have recourse to the powers provided upon a lawful entry by s19(1) to (3) which are, along with s19(4), additional to any other powers conferred by para 13 (see s19(5)). The only power invoked by the police was under that paragraph.

The consequence of the breaches of s16(5)(b) and (c) is that by virtue of s15(1) the entries, searches and seizures were unlawful, so depriving the respondent of any authority under para 13 to retain any of the material seized. [Counsel for the chief constable] relies, however, upon the power of retention conferred by s22(2)(a), which, he submits, is designed to authorise the retention by the police of material which has come into their hands by unlawful means ... He referred to the decision of the House of Lords in *R* v *Sang* [1979] 3 WLR 263, which established that evidence is none the less admissible if it was obtained by improper means, and he pointed out that a defendant would be protected against the unfair use of such evidence by the discretion conferred upon the trial judge under s78 of the 1984 Act.

In our judgment, this submission too much be rejected. Neither *R* v *Sang* nor s78 provides any support for the proposition that the police have a general right to retain unlawfully seized material as against its owner for use as evidence. Such a right could only be conferred by express statutory language. In our judgment s22(2)(a) cannot bear the weight which [counsel] seeks to place upon it.'

Comment

An important decision safeguarding the rights of a citizen whose property has been unlawfully searched and/or seized.

R* v *Chief Constable of the Royal Ulster Constabulary, ex parte Begley; Same, ex parte McWilliams [1997] 4 All ER 833 House of Lords (Lords Browne-Wilkinson, Berwick, Steyn, Hoffmann and Hope)

- *Whether any common law right to consult privately with a solicitor*

Facts

Both applicants were arrested in connection with terrorist offences in Northern Ireland and had their requests, to have solicitors present whilst they were being interviewed, refused. As regards the appeal brought by Begley, the Divisional Court certified the following question of law:

> 'Whether a person arrested under section 14 of the Prevention of Terrorism Act 1989 has (i) a right at common law to be accompanied and advised by his solicitor during interviews with the police or (ii) if such right did not exist at common law, can it now be said to exist in the light of the provisions of The Criminal Evidence (Northern Ireland) Order 1988 and in particular art 3 thereof.'

The appeal brought by McWilliams was wider in scope but was not considered separately.

Held

The appeals were dismissed.

Addressing the issue of whether the common law recognised a right of a detained person to have a solicitor present whilst being interrogated, Lord Browne-Wilkinson observed:

> 'Certainly, the common law recognised a general right in an accused person to communicate and consult privately with his solicitor outside the interview room. This development is reflected in the *Judges' Rules and Administrative Directions to the Police* ... this case is concerned with the ... independent question whether every accused person has an established common law right to have a solicitor present during police interviews regardless of the nature of the

> offence in respect of which he was arrested. Needless to say there is no decision or dictum in support of such a right. Indeed no such argument has ever been placed before a court. There is no academic support for the existence of such a right ... If the Judges Rules had been formulated on the supposition that a suspect already had a legal right to have his solicitor present during interview, it is inconceivable that such a right and the necessary qualifications to it would not have been spelt out in the elaborate statement of the rights of a suspect in the Judges Rules ... in *Murray* v *United Kingdom* [(1996) The Times 9 February] ... the European Court of Human Rights specifically declined to make a ruling as to whether a refusal to allow a solicitor to be present during police interviews violates art 6 [of the European Convention on Human Rights]. In these circumstances counsel for the appellants conceded that no assistance can be gained from art 6 or the jurisprudence of the European Court of Human Rights. One has therefore arrived at the position that there is no positive law to support the proposition that the common law recognised a right in a suspect to have his solicitor present during a police interview.'

Turning to the issue of whether or not the removal of the right to silence had altered the common law position as to the right to have a solicitor present during police questioning, Lord Browne-Wilkinson noted that although s58 Police and Criminal Evidence Act (PACE) 1984 had given suspects (including those arrested under s14(1) Prevention of Terrorism (Temporary Provisions) Act 1989) the legal right to consult privately with a solicitor as well as a right to have a solicitor present during interview, a different regime applied in Northern Ireland. There, a person arrested or detained under the terrorism provisions was merely entitled to consult privately with a solicitor: see s15 of the Northern Ireland (Emergency Provisions) Act 1987; s45 of the Northern Ireland (Emergency Provisions) Act 1991; s47 of the Northern Ireland (Emergency Provisions) Act 1996. The Code issued under s61 of the 1991 Act is to the same effect: Codes of Practice, para 6 and Annex B. He continued:

> 'Nowhere is there any reference to any right in a person arrested under terrorism provisions to have a solicitor present during interview. The differential treatment of persons suspected of having committed offences under the terrorism provisions in Northern Ireland is plainly part of a deliberate legislative policy ... It is of the first importance that ... Parliament re-enacted the relevant provisions [in the Northern Ireland (Emergency Provisions) Act 1996] in the same form as in the Act of 1991 on which Mr Rowe commented. The conclusion is inescapable that it is the clearly expressed will of Parliament that persons arrested under section 14(1) of the PTA should not have the right to have a solicitor present during interview. In these circumstances I would reject the invitation to develop such a right as beyond the power of the House of Lords.'

Comment

An interesting case for comparative purposes only. The common law right to consult privately with a solicitor when under arrest at a police station is largely academic in the light of the statutory right granted under s58 PACE 1984: see *R* v *Samuel* (1988) (below). However, this case, from Northern Ireland, involved different statutory provisions offering less extensive protection for suspects than s58 PACE (which gives suspects the right to have a solicitor present during interviews). The House of Lords concluded that it was deliberate legislative policy to treat Northern Ireland differently on this point.

R* v *Chief Constable of South Wales, ex parte Merrick [1994] 1 WLR 663 Queen's Bench Division (Ralph Gibson LJ and Smith J)

• *Right of a prisoner to consult privately with a solicitor*

Facts

The applicant, a remand prisoner, was being held in the cells at Cardiff magistrates' court following an unsuccessful bail application. His request to consult privately with his solicitor after the hearing was refused. The police at the court had adopted a policy of not permitting interviews between prisoners and solicitors after 10.00 am, unless there were good reasons for the interview not having taken place earlier, and it was possible to grant access given the other demands on resources. The applicant had requested an interview in the middle of the afternoon. The applicant, by way of judicial review, sought a declaration that the policy being followed at Cardiff magistrates' court was unlawful in that it resulted in a denial of his right to consult with a solicitor under s58(1) of the Police and Criminal Evidence Act (PACE) 1984.

Held

The application would be granted in part. Section 58(1) PACE 1984 did not extend to a prisoner held in custody at a court following a refusal of bail, but at common law he did have a right to consult with a legal adviser as soon as was reasonably practicable.

Ralph Gibson LJ:

> 'The right to consult a solicitor is not, so far as concerns a person in custody, a free standing right of uniform extent irrespective of the circumstances. So far as concerns questioning of a person by the police and treatment of him after arrest, and while he is in custody before charge, the primary purpose is to ensure that the questioning is fair and that his legal rights may be preserved and protected, in particular that he should understand and, if he wishes, have resort to his right to be silent: see *R* v *Walsh* (1989) 91 Cr App R 161, 163. To that end, it is necessary that the right should be secured to such a person at that stage to consult a solicitor privately at any time while the inquiry proceeds and "as soon as is practicable;" and, subject to the exceptions listed in paragraph 6.6 of PACE Code of Practice C, a person who wants legal advice may not be interviewed or continue to be interviewed until he has received it. After a person has been charged, and is in custody at a court on remand, the primary purpose of the right to consult a solicitor is to ensure that the trial, and all ancillary proceedings, such as applications for bail, are conducted fairly and effectively. To that end, it is necessary that the right should be secured to such a person at such time or times as will enable the proceedings to be fairly and effectively conducted by him or on his behalf. A significant difference between a person in detention or custody but before charge, whose conduct is under investigation by the police, on the one hand, and a person in custody after charge on remand in the cells of a magistrates' court, on the other hand, is that the court stands between the person in custody and the prosecutor, and the court, provided that complaint is made by or on behalf of the accused, is well able to ensure that any preceding failure to provide sufficient access for an accused to a solicitor is not permitted to prejudice the conduct of the proceedings on the behalf of the accused. The court can direct, or indicate its opinion – I have discussed the distinction above – that the accused is to be allowed sufficient access to his legal advisers before the hearing of the case, or of any ancillary proceeding, will proceed.'

Comment

A decision on the scope of s58 PACE 1984 (right to consult a solicitor when under arrest at a police station). The judgment of Ralph Gibson LJ also recognises a common law right to see a legal adviser 'as soon as is reasonably practicable'. The common law right may be useful, therefore, if, as in this case, it is found

that the suspect is not covered by the statutory protection.

R v *Cowan* [1995] 4 All ER 939 Court of Appeal (Criminal Division) (Taylor LCJ, Turner and Latham JJ)

• *Right of silence – effect of s35 of the Criminal Justice and Public Order Act 1994 – specimen direction to juries*

Facts

The appellant had been convicted after the trial judge had directed the jury that they could draw adverse inferences from the appellant's silence. The appellant appealed on the ground of misdirection, contending that the trial judge should have directed the jury that they could draw adverse inferences only in an exceptional case where there was no reasonable possibility of an innocent explanation for the silence. The appellant was represented by Mr Mansfield QC.

Held

The plain words of s35 of the Criminal Justice and Public Order Act 1994 did not justify confining its operation to exceptional cases. However the appeal would be allowed because, inter alia, the judge had failed to tell the jury that they could not infer guilt solely from silence. The Court of Appeal would take the opportunity to give guidance to trial judges on directing the jury under the new law.

Taylor LCJ:

> 'It should be made clear that the right of silence remains. It is not abolished by the section; on the contrary, sub-s (4) expressly preserves it. …
>
> It is further argued that the section alters the burden of proof or 'waters it down', to use Mr Mansfield's phrase. The requirement that the defendant give evidence on pain of an adverse inference being drawn is said to put a burden on him to testify if he wishes to avoid conviction.
>
> In our view that argument is misconceived. First, the prosecution have to establish a prima facie case before any question of the defendant testifying is raised. Secondly, s38(3) of the 1994 Act is in the following terms:
>
> > "A person shall not … be convicted of an offence solely on an inference drawn from such a failure or refusal as is mentioned in … section 35(3) …"
>
> Thus the court or jury is prohibited from convicting solely because of an inference drawn from the defendant's silence. Thirdly, the burden of proving guilt to the required standard remains on the prosecution throughout. The effect of s35 is that the court or jury may regard the inference from failure to testify as, in effect, a further evidential factor in support of the prosecution case. It cannot be the only factor to justify a conviction and the totality of the evidence must prove guilt beyond reasonable doubt.
>
> We therefore reject the two premises relied upon by Mr Mansfield to support his submission that s35 should only be invoked in exceptional cases. …
>
> We accept that, apart from the mandatory exceptions in s35(1), it will be open to a court to decline to draw an adverse inference from silence at trial and for a judge to direct or advise a jury against drawing such inference if the circumstances of the case justify such a course. But in our view there would need either to be some evidential basis for doing so or some exceptional factors in the case making that a fair course to take. It must be stressed that the inferences permitted by the section are only such "as appear proper". The use of that phrase was no doubt intended to leave a broad discretion to a trial judge to decide in all the circumstances whether any proper inference is capable of being drawn by the jury. If not, he should tell them so; otherwise it is for the jury to decide whether in fact an inference should properly be drawn. …
>
> … there are certain essentials which we would highlight.
>
> (1) The judge will have told the jury that the burden of proof remains upon the prosecution throughout and what the required standard is.
>
> (2) It is necessary for the judge to make

clear to the jury that the defendant is entitled to remain silent. That is his right and his choice. The right of silence remains.

(3) An inference from failure to give evidence cannot on its own prove guilt. That is expressly stated in s38(3) of the Act.

(4) Therefore, the jury must be satisfied that the prosecution have established a case to answer before drawing any inferences from silence. Of course, the judge must have thought so or the question whether the defendant was to give evidence would not have arisen. But the jury may not believe the witnesses whose evidence the judge considered sufficient to raise a prima facie case. It must therefore be made clear to them that they must find there to be a case to answer on the prosecution evidence before drawing an adverse inference form the defendant's silence.

(5) If, despite any evidence relied upon to explain his silence or in the absence of any such evidence, the jury conclude the silence can only sensibly be attributed to the defendant's having no answer or none that would stand up to cross-examination, they may draw an adverse inference....

We wish to stress, moreover, that this court will not lightly interfere with a judge's exercise of discretion to direct or advise the jury as to the drawing of inferences from silence and as to the nature, extent and degree of such inferences. He is in the best position to have the feel of the case, and so long as he gives the jury adequate directions of law as indicated above and leaves the decision to them, this court will be slow to substantiate its view for his.'

Comment

The first authoritative decision on the changes to the traditional right of silence made by the Criminal Justice and Public Order Act 1994. Taylor LCJ's judgment explores the circumstances in which juries may be directed to draw inferences from a defendant's silence. The factors set out in the judgment are clearly designed to safeguard the rights of the defendant, though Lord Taylor emphasised that in directing a jury the trial judge is probably best placed to choose adequate words of guidance to the jury.

R* v *Dunford (1990) 91 Cr App R 150 Court of Appeal (Neill LJ, Macpherson and Otton JJ)

- *Admissions – exercise of court's discretion*

Facts

Having played a 'supporting role' as a getawayman, the appellant had been convicted of, inter alia, conspiracy to rob. The Crown had maintained that the appellant had been interviewed under caution and had made admissions: the appellant had contended that the interview notes and their contents had been fabricated. The trial judge had ruled that there had been a breach of s58 of the Police and Criminal Evidence Act (PACE) 1984 (access to legal advice) but that he would not exclude the evidence in the exercise of his discretion under s78 of that Act. On his appeal, the appellant challenged this exercise of the judge's discretion.

Held

The appeal would be dismissed as, on the facts, the judge had been entitled to conclude that a solicitor's advice would not have added anything to the appellant's knowledge of his rights. Neill LJ said that it was clear that, where a challenge was made to the admissibility of evidence as to a confession or admissions on the ground that an accused man had been refused access to a solicitor, it was necessary for the court to proceed as follows:

1 To consider and determine whether a request to consult a solicitor had been made.

2 If a request had been made, to consider whether the request was refused.

3 If a request had been made and refused, to consider whether the delay in compliance with the request was permissible under s58(6) and (8). That involved determining:

a Whether the person was in police

detention for a serious arrestable offence.

b Whether the necessary authority was given by an officer of at least the rank of superintendent to keep a suspect incommunicado.

c Whether, unless subs(8)(a) applied, the officer believed that the exercise of the right to consult a solicitor would lead to one of the consequences set out in subs(8).

d Whether the officer had reasonable grounds for that belief.

4 If the judge concluded that there had been a breach of s58, it would then be necessary for him to consider whether the confession or admissions should be excluded under s78. It might also be necessary to consider whether the evidence should be excluded by any rule of common law.

It was held in *R* v *Walsh* (unreported 13 July 1989) that a breach of s58 would prima facie have an adverse effect on the fairness of the proceedings. However, the court added, rightly in their Lordships' judgment:

> 'This does not mean, of course, in every case of a significant or substantial breach of s58 or the Code of practice the evidence concerned will automatically be excluded. The task of the court is not merely to consider whether there would be an adverse effect on the fairness of the proceedings, but such an adverse effect that justice requires the evidence to be excluded ... Breaches which are in themselves significant and substantial are not rendered otherwise by the good faith of the officers concerned.'

Neill LJ continued:

> 'If a man showed, as the appellant did, that he knew that he could answer "No comment" and could refuse to sign an interview, and if a man had experience of arrest, their Lordships did not believe that a judge had to or could simply pay no attention to those facts.
>
> The very core of the trial judge's ruling depended on them since, he concluded that "in the light of the answers given in the interview it is extremely doubtful whether the solicitor's advice would have added anything to the (appellant's) knowledge of his rights. He has, I observe, previous convictions although for far less grave offences." '

Acceptance of the appellant's arguments would be wholly to deny the judge the right and the opportunity to exercise his discretion.

It had to be open to the court, even where a breach of s58 was established, to balance all the circumstances and to decide whether or not there existed such an adverse effect on the fairness of the proceedings that justice required the evidence to be excluded.

Comment

A controversial decision because it appears to dilute the safeguard provided under s58 PACE 1984 (access to legal advice). Is it enough to assert that an accused does not need this protection because he/she knows his/her legal rights already?

R v *Fulling* [1987] 2 WLR 923 Court of Appeal (Lane LCJ, Taylor and Henry JJ)

- *Criminal evidence – oppression*

Facts

A woman was arrested for allegedly obtaining property by deception. While in police custody, for two days she exercised her right to say nothing in response to persistent questioning. An officer then told her that her lover had been having an affair with another woman for the last three years and, on hearing this, the accused confessed to the charge. At her trial, she contended that the confession was inadmissible under s76(2)(a) of the Police and Criminal Evidence Act (PACE) 1984 because it had been obtained by oppression.

Held

This was not the case, even if her account of the alleged disclosure by the police officer was correct.

Lane LCJ:

'... "oppression" in s76(2)(a) should be given its ordinary dictionary meaning. The Oxford English Dictionary as its third definition of the word runs as follows: "Exercise of authority or power in a burdensome, harsh, or wrongful manner; unjust or cruel treatment of subjects, inferiors, etc; the imposition of unreasonable or unjust burdens." One of the quotations given under that paragraph runs as follows: "There is not a word in our language which expresses more detestable wickedness than oppression."

We find it hard to envisage any circumstances in which such oppression would not entail some impropriety on the part of the interrogator.'

Comment

A useful case on the definition of 'oppression' for the purpose of excluding a confession obtained by such means.

R* v *Khan (Sultan) [1996] 3 All ER 289 House of Lords (Lords Keith, Browne-Wilkinson, Slynn, Nolan and Nicholls)

• *Admissibility of evidence obtained by electronic bugging devices – illegally obtained evidence – effect of s78 Police and Criminal Evidence Act 1984 on discretion to exclude such evidence*

Facts

The police had attached an electronic listening device to the outside of a suspect's house and thereby obtained a tape recording of a conversation between the subject and a visitor which implicated the visitor in the importation of heroin. The visitor (K) was arrested, charged and convicted following a ruling from the trial judge in a voir dire that the tape recording was admissible. There is no statutory framework regulating the installation and use by the police of covert listening devices, though there are Home Office Guidelines (1984), which were apparently complied with in this case. The appeal was on the ground that the tape recording had been wrongly admitted in evidence. The Court of Appeal ([1994] 4 All ER 426) dismissed the appeal. K then appealed to he House of Lords.

Held

Appeal dismissed. The House of Lords reaffirmed the common law rule that relevant evidence obtained improperly or unfairly or even unlawfully was admissible: *R* v *Sang* [1980] AC 402 (HL). However, the House went on to hold that this common law rule was subject to the trial judge's discretion both at common law and under s78 Police and Criminal Evidence Act (PACE) 1984 to exclude relevant evidence if its admission would render the trial unfair.

On the facts the police had committed a civil trespass and criminal damage when installing the listening device. There had also been an invasion of privacy, but whether there was a right of privacy in English law was still a debatable question and the House preferred not to express a decided view on that particular issue. However, it was relevant that the invasion of privacy in this case probably breached art 8 European Convention on Human Rights (ECHR), which protects the right to respect for private and family life and home.

The House held that the trial judge had correctly taken account of all these factors and was entitled to conclude that, despite the impropriety of the way in which the evidence was obtained, the evidence was admissible. Such an approach was consistent with the approach of the European Court of Human Rights since art 6 ECHR protects the right to a fair trial and the case law under art 6 confirms that the use of material obtained in breach of art 8 does not of itself mean that the trial is unfair.

Lord Nolan:

> '... if the behaviour of the police in the particular case amounts to an apparent or probable breach of some relevant law or convention, common sense dictates that this is a consideration which may be taken into account for what it is worth. Its significance,

however, will normally be determined not so much by its apparent unlawfulness or irregularity, as upon its effect, taken as a whole, upon the fairness or unfairness of the proceedings.'

Comment

The case raised for the first time the question whether a criminal court, in considering its power under s78 PACE 1984, is required to have regard to the articles and jurisprudence of the European Convention and Court of Human Rights, which, at the date of the judgment, were not formally incorporated into domestic English law. The House of Lords answered this question in the affirmative, but this was not enough to condemn the admissibility of the evidence. No doubt all the judges were influenced by the seriousness of the charges against the accused. The Law Lords expressed surprise at the lack of statutory safeguards regulating the use of surveillance devices by the police. Such statutory regulation is now contained in ss91–108 of the Police Act 1997, but since these provisions are silent on the question of whether a breach of the Act and/or the Code of Practice issued under it should render the evidence obtained as a result of such breach inadmissible, trial judges will need to continue exercising their general discretionary exclusionary powers under s78 PACE 1984 and at common law.

R* v *Latif*; *R* v *Shahzad [1996] 1 All ER 353 House of Lords (Lords Keith, Jauncey, Mustill, Steyn and Hoffmann)

• *Admissibility of evidence obtained by undercover operations – whether discretion to exclude evidence for abuse of process and/or to exclude under s78 Police and Criminal Evidence Act 1984 for unfairness*

Facts

The two appellants had been convicted of being knowingly concerned in the importation of heroin into the United Kingdom from Pakistan. An undercover officer had assisted in the importation as part of an operation designed to lure one of the appellants (S) to England (there being no extradition treaty with Pakistan). At the trial it was argued for the defence that either the proceedings should be stayed as an abuse of process or the evidence should be excluded under s78 PACE 1984 on the ground that to admit it would prejudice the fair trial of the accused. The prosecution conceded that the behaviour of the undercover officer had been criminal, and that trickery and deception had been used to lure S to the United Kingdom. The trial judge rejected the defence submissions. At the end of the trial the accused were convicted. In conjoined appeals it was argued, inter alia, that the trial judge had wrongly exercised his discretion by allowing the trial to proceed on the evidence in question. Although the abuse of process argument and the s78 PACE 1984 admissibility argument were separate arguments it was conceded by the appellants that the two arguments stood or fell together.

Held

Appeals dismissed. The House of Lords concentrated on the abuse of process argument and held that the trial judge had correctly concluded that, in view of the serious nature of the charges against the accused, the conduct of the undercover officer had not been so unworthy or shameful as to affront the public conscience to the extent that the proceedings ought to be stayed as an abuse of process.

Lord Steyn:

'... If the court always refuses to stay such proceedings, the perception will be that the court condones criminal conduct and malpractice by law enforcement agencies. That would undermine public confidence in the criminal justice system and bring it into disrepute. On the other hand, if the court were always to stay proceedings in such cases, it would incur the reproach that it is failing to protect the public from serious crime. The

weaknesses of both extreme positions leaves only one principled solution. The court has a discretion: it has to perform a balancing exercise. If the court concludes that a fair trial is not possible, it will stay the proceedings. That is not what the present case is concerned with. It is plain that a fair trial was possible and that such a trial took place. In this case the issue is whether, despite the fact that a fair trial was possible, the judge ought to have stayed the criminal proceedings on broader considerations of the integrity of the criminal justice system. The law is settled. Weighing countervailing considerations of policy and justice, it is for the judge in the exercise of his discretion to decide whether there has been an abuse of process, which amounts to an affront to the public conscience and requires the criminal proceedings to be stayed.'

Comment

The decision has been described as a pragmatic one influenced by the very serious nature of the drug-dealing operation in question. In other jurisdictions, for example Australia, a more principled approach has been taken condemning the police and/or customs practices of controlled importations. It has been suggested that the admissibility argument under s78 PACE 1984 deserved more detailed consideration in this case by the House of Lords, and that the need to ensure a fair trial for all defendants should not be offset by concerns for the public interest in the event of the evidence being excluded: see Grevling 'Undercover Operations: Backing the Public Interest?' (1996) 112 LQR 401.

R* v *Mason [1988] 1 WLR 139 Court of Appeal (Watkins LJ, Mars-Jones and Henry JJ)

- *Criminal evidence – confession*

Facts

The appellant was arrested and questioned regarding an offence of arson – setting fire to a car. At the time of the arrest, the police had no evidence to associate the appellant with the incident, but they told him and his solicitor that his fingerprints had been found on the bottle used to perpetrate the offence. This was a deliberate falsehood, but it was sufficient to cause the appellant to confess that he had been involved. At the trial, he maintained that the confession was inadmissible, but the judge allowed the evidence to be adduced.

Held

The appeal would be allowed.

Watkins LJ:

> '... regardless of whether the admissibility of a confession falls to be considered under s76(2) [of the Police and Criminal Evidence Act 1984], a trial judge has a discretion to deal with the admissibility of a confession under s78 which, in our opinion, does no more than to restate the power which judges had at common law before the 1984 Act was passed. The power gave a trial judge a discretion whether solely in the interests of the fairness of a trial he would permit the prosecution to introduce admissible evidence sought to be relied on, especially that of a confession or an admission. That being so, we now return to the circumstances of the present case.
>
> It is obvious from the undisputed evidence that the police practised a deceit not only on the appellant, which is bad enough, but also on the solicitor whose duty it was to advise him. In effect, they hoodwinked both solicitor and client. That was a most reprehensible thing to do. It is not however because we regard as misbehaviour of a serious kind conduct of that nature that we have come to the decision soon to be made plain. This is not the place to discipline the police. That has been made clear here on a number of previous occasions. We are concerned with the application of the proper law. The law is, as I have already said, that a trial judge has a discretion to be exercised, of course on right principles, to reject admissible evidence in the interests of a defendant having a fair trial. The judge in the present case appre-

ciated that, as the quotation from his ruling shows. So the only question to be answered by this court is whether, having regard to the way the police behaved, the judge exercised that discretion correctly. In our judgment he did not. He omitted a vital factor from his consideration, namely the deceit practised on the appellant's solicitor. If he had included that in his consideration of the matter we have not the slightest doubt that he would have been driven to an opposite conclusion, namely that the confession be ruled out and the jury not permitted therefore to hear of it. If that had been done, an acquittal would have followed for there was no other evidence in the possession of the prosecution …

Before parting with this case, despite what I have said about the role of the court in relation to disciplining the police, we think we ought to say that we hope never again to hear of deceit such as this being practised on an accused person, and more particularly possibly on a solicitor whose duty it is to advise him, unfettered by false information from the police.'

Comment

An important case indicating judicial repugnance to police methods of obtaining evidence which involve duplicity – especially if the deceit is practised on the accused's legal adviser thereby affecting the advice offered to the client!

R* v *Rasool and Another [1997] 4 All ER 439 Court of Appeal (Criminal Division) (Stuart-Smith LJ, Forbes and Brian Smedley JJ)

• *Phone-tapping with consent – whether material obtained inadmissible*

Facts

C invited GB to act as a drugs courier. GB informed the police and agreed to having his telephone line tapped. On the basis of the information thus made available to the police, C was charged with conspiring to supply a Class A drug. During the trial the judge rejected a submission that, by virtue of ss1 and 9 Interception of Communications Act 1985, the evidence obtained as a result of the phone-tapping was inadmissible. C was convicted and appealed.

Held

The appeal was dismissed (Rasool's appeal being allowed on other, unconnected, grounds).

Stuart-Smith LJ (considering the effect of s9 of the Interception of Communications Act 1985):

'… So far as material, s9 provides:

"(1) In any proceedings before any court or tribunal no evidence shall be adduced and no question in cross-examination shall be asked which (in either case) tends to suggest – (a) that an offence under section 1 above has been or is to be committed by any of the persons mentioned in subsection (2) below; or (b) that a warrant has been or is to be issued to any of those persons.
(2) The persons referred to in subsection (1) above are – (a) any person holding office under the Crown …"

It is common ground that the constable who intercepted the line was within s9(2)(a). No problem arises in this case under s9(1)(b). Moreover on the face of it s9(1)(a) is not concerned with the admissibility of the contents of a telephone intercept. Furthermore since it is irrelevant to the question of admissibility of the evidence whether an offence has been committed in the obtaining of it, no proper question can in any event be asked in cross-examination to seek to establish that an offence has been committed. This was the approach of the Court of Appeal in *R* v *Effik* (1992) 95 Cr App R 427. …

… it seems to me that the general statement of the law on the construction of s9(1) to be found in the Court of Appeal's judgment in *R* v *Effik* (1992) 95 Cr App R 427, namely that it does not prevent the admission of the product of a telephone intercept to which the Act applies, is to be modified

only to the extent that it relates to a warranted intercept. Accordingly s9(1)(a) is not sufficient by itself to prevent admissibility of the substance of a consensual interception. Furthermore since on the question of admissibility, the fact that the evidence may have been obtained unlawfully is irrelevant, cross-examination to show that the intercept was not consensual cannot be entertained, quite apart from the prohibition in s9(1)(a).

In granting leave to appeal the single judge thought arguable the question whether the prohibition effected by s9(1)(a) on any enquiry as to the genuineness or existence of consent makes the admission of the evidence unfair under s78 of the Police and Criminal Evidence Act 1984. Mr Spencer did not argue this point either before the judge or this court. He confined his argument to the admissibility of the evidence, rather than on the exclusion of admissible evidence. We do not therefore need to consider this point, but we can see nothing unfair in the admission of the evidence; and this accords with the views of the Court of Appeal in *Effik*'s case the facts of which, on the assumption made by the court, involved a serious breach of the Act.

Comment

R v *Preston* [1993] 4 All ER 638 (HL) was distinguished on the ground that *Preston* concerned a telephone intercept which had been authorised by a warrant issued under s2 of the 1985 Act.

R* v *Samuel [1988] 2 WLR 920 Court of Appeal (Glidewell LJ, Hodgson and Rougier JJ)

- *Criminal evidence – access to a solicitor*

Facts

Arrested on suspicion of robbery, that day and the next the appellant was interviewed by the police on four occasions about the robbery and two burglaries, in all of which the appellant denied any involvement. During the second interview he asked for access to a solicitor, but his request was refused on the ground of likelihood of other suspects involved in the robbery being inadvertently warned. At the fourth interview the appellant confessed to the two burglaries and he was charged with those offences at 4.30 pm. At 4.45 pm a solicitor was informed of the charges, but denied access. Shortly afterwards the appellant confessed to the robbery and the solicitor was allowed to see him one hour later. At the trial, the appellant contended that evidence of the latter confession should be excluded, but it was admitted and he was convicted of robbery.

Held

The conviction would be quashed as, in the circumstances, the refusal of access to a solicitor had been unjustified and the interview in question should not have taken place. Under the Code of Practice for Detention issued under s66 of the Police and Criminal Evidence Act (PACE) 1984, access could not be denied after a person had been charged with 'a serious arrestable offence' – and one of the burglaries was such an offence.

Hodgson J:

> '... a court which has to decide whether denial of access to a solicitor was lawful has to ask itself two questions: "Did the officer believe?", a subjective test; and "Were there reasonable grounds for that belief?", an objective test.
>
> What it is the officer must satisfy the court that he believed is this: that (1) allowing consultation with a solicitor (2) will (3) lead to or hinder one or more of the things set out in paragraphs (a) to (c) of section 58(8) [of the 1984 Act]. The use of the word "will" is clearly of great importance. There were available to the draftsman many words or phrases by which he could have described differing nuances as to the officer's state of mind, for example "might", "could", "there was a risk", "there was a substantial risk" etc. The choice of "will" must have been deliberately restrictive.
>
> Of course, anyone who says that be believes that something will happen, unless he is speaking of one of the immutable laws

of nature, accepts the possibility that it will not happen, but the use of the word "will" in conjunction with belief implies in the believer a belief that it will very probably happen.

What is it that the officer has to satisfy the court he believed? The right denied is a right "to consult a solicitor privately". The person denied that right is in police detention. In practice, the only way that the person can make any of the matters set out in paragraphs (a) to (c) happen is by some communication from him to the solicitor. For the matters set out in paragraphs (a) to (c) to be made to happen the solicitor must do something. If he does something knowing that it will result in anything in paragraphs (a) to (c) happening he will, almost inevitably, commit a serious criminal offence. Therefore, inadvertent or unwitting conduct apart, the officer must believe that a solicitor will, if allowed to consult with a detained person, thereafter commit a criminal offence. Solicitors are officers of the court. We think that the number of times that a police officer could genuinely be in that state of belief will be rare. Moreover it is our view that, to sustain such a basis for refusal, the grounds put forward would have to have reference to a specific solicitor. We do not think they could ever be successfully advanced in relation to solicitors generally ... We do not know who make the decision at 4.45 pm but we find it impossible to believe that whoever did had reasonable grounds for the belief required by section 58(8).'

Comment

An important decision emphasising that the right of access to legal advice granted by s58 PACE 1984 is of fundamental constitutional importance and should be denied only in very exceptional circumstances. In the normal situation breach of s58 will result in the exclusion from trial of all evidence obtained subsequent to such breach. Contrast, however, *R* v *Dunford* (1990) (above).

R* v *Sang [1980] AC 402 House of Lords (Viscount Dilhorne, Lords Diplock, Salmon, Fraser of Tullybelton and Scarman)

• *Discretion to refuse evidence – agents provocateurs*

Facts

The appellant pleaded not guilty to a charge that he conspired with others to utter forged United States banknotes. Requesting a trial within a trial, his counsel said that he hoped to establish that the appellant had been induced to commit the offence by an informer acting on the instructions of the police and that but for such persuasion the appellant would not have committed the offence. Counsel then hoped that the judge would rule, in the exercise of his discretion, that no evidence of the offence so incited should be admitted and that he would direct the entry of a not guilty verdict. The judge ruled that he had no discretion to exclude the evidence.

Held

Although a judge always had a discretion to refuse to admit evidence if he thought its prejudicial effect outweighed its probative value, here the evidence should not have been excluded, whether or not it had been obtained as a result of the activities of an agent provocateur.

Lord Diplock:

'The decisions in *R* v *McEvilly*, *R* v *Lee* and *R* v *Mealey*, *R* v *Sheridan* that there is no defence of "entrapment" known to English law are clearly right. Many crimes are committed by one person at the instigation of others. From earliest times at common law those who counsel and procure the commission of the offence by the person by whom the actus reus itself is done have been guilty themselves of an offence, and since the abolition by the Criminal Law Act 1967 of the distinction between felonies and misdemeanours can be tried, indicted and punished as principal offenders. The fact that the counsellor and procurer is a policeman or a police informer, although it may be of rele-

vance in mitigation of penalty for the offence, cannot affect the guilt of the principal offender; both the physical element (actus reus) and the mental element (mens rea) of the offence with which he is charged are present in his case.

My Lords, this being the substantive law on the matter, the suggestion that it can be evaded by the procedural device of preventing the prosecution from adducing evidence of the commission of the offence, does not bear examination. …

…What it really involves is a claim to a judicial discretion to acquit an accused of any offences in connection with which the conduct of the police incurs the disapproval of the judge. The conduct of the police where it has involved the use of an agent provocateur may well be a matter to be taken into consideration in mitigation of sentence; but under the English system of criminal justice it does not give rise to any discretion on the part of the judge himself to acquit the accused or to direct the jury to do so, notwithstanding that he is guilty of the offence. …

I understand your Lordships to be agreed that whatever be the ambit of the judicial discretion to exclude admissible evidence it does not extend to excluding evidence of a crime because the crime was instigated by an agent provocateur. …

I turn now to the wider question that has been certified. It does not purport to be concerned with self-incriminatory admissions made by the accused himself after commission of the crime, though in dealing with the question I will find it necessary to say something about these. What the question is concerned with is the discretion of the trial judge to exclude all other kinds of evidence that are of more than minimal probative value … I would hold that there has now developed a general rule of practice whereby in a trial by jury the judge has a discretion to exclude evidence which, though technically admissible, would probably have a prejudicial influence on the minds of the jury, which would be out of proportion to its true evidential value.'

Comment

An important common law decision on the general power of trial judges to exclude relevant evidence obtained by illegal or unfair police methods. Note that Lord Diplock's judgment lays emphasis on the issue of relevancy and the public interest in convicting guilty persons; he takes the view that the rules of evidence are not designed to 'punish' the police for misconduct by excluding relevant material obtained by such misconduct. Contrast the exercise of the statutory discretion under s78 PACE 1984 in cases such as *R* v *Mason* (1988) (above). See also *R* v *Khan (Sultan)* (1996) (above) on the continuing relevance of the common law discretion.

R* v *Self [1992] 1 WLR 657 Court of Appeal (Watkins LJ, Swinton Thomas and Garland JJ)

- *Scope of citizen's power of arrest*

Facts

The appellant, who was believed to have stolen a bar of chocolate, was arrested by a store detective and another member of the public. During the course of the arrest the appellant assaulted those trying to apprehend him.

The appellant was ultimately acquitted of theft, but convicted of assault with intent to resist or prevent lawful apprehension, contrary to s38 of the Offences Against the Person Act 1861. The appellant now contended that as he had been acquitted on the theft charge, neither the store detective nor any other member of the public could have been empowered to arrest him under s24(5) of the Police and Criminal Evidence Act (PACE) 1984, since this required proof that an arrestable offence had been committed. It followed, therefore, that the detention had not been lawful, and thus he should not have been convicted under s38.

Held

The appeal would be allowed.

Garland J:

'… in the judgment of this court, the words of s24 do not admit of argument. Subsection (5) makes it abundantly clear that the powers of arrest without a warrant where an arrestable offence has been committed require as a condition precedent an offence committed. If subsequently there is an acquittal of the alleged offence no offence has been committed. The power to arrest is confined to the person guilty of the offence or anyone who the person making the arrest has reasonable grounds for suspecting to be guilty of it. But of course if he is not guilty there can be no valid suspicion … to which reference has been made.

If it is necessary to go further, one contrasts the words of subs(5) with subs(6), the very much wider powers given to a constable who has reasonable grounds for suspecting that an arrestable offence has been committed. However, it is said on behalf of the Crown that the court should not be assiduous to restrict the citizen's powers of arrest and that, by going back to subs(4) and looking at the words there, "anyone who is in the act of committing an arrestable offence", perhaps those words can be used to cover the sort of situation that arose in this case where somebody is apparently making good his escape. Having committed the offence of theft, can it be said, asks Mr Sleeman, that the thief is not in substance still committing the offence while running away?

He asks, rhetorically, should the court have to inquire into the exact moment when the ingredients of theft come together – dishonesty, appropriation, intention permanently to deprive – when to analyse the offence carefully may produce absurd results so that in one set of circumstances the offence may be complete and the situation fall within subs(5) and in another be still being committed and fall within subs(4).

The view of this court is that little profit can be had from taking examples and trying to reduce them to absurdity. The words of the statute are clear and applying those words to this case there was no arrestable offence committed. It necessarily follows that the two offences under s38 of the Offences Against the Person Act 1861 could not be committed because there was no power to apprehend or detain the appellant.'

Comment

A case illustrating the more limited scope of a citizen's arrest compared with police powers of arrest. It appears that the statutory provisions in s24 PACE 1984 merely confirm the common law position on this point: see *Walters* v *W H Smith and Son Ltd* (1914) (below).

Walters v *W H Smith and Son Ltd* [1914] 1 KB 595 High Court (Isaacs CJ)

- *Scope of citizen's power of arrest*

Facts

The plaintiff was employed by the defendants at a bookstall in King's Cross Station; he also owned a newsagent's shop (which was a breach of his contract of employment). Over a period of several months the bookstall suffered a series of thefts of money and books and, consequently, the defendants set a trap for the thief by secretly marking some of the stock, including a book entitled *Traffic*. When they later sent an agent round to the newsagent's shop to buy a copy of the book it was found to bear the secret mark. On being interviewed by the defendants the plaintiff admitted taking the book but said that he had intended to pay for it. The plaintiff was arrested and he was subsequently prosecuted for theft. On being found not guilty the plaintiff sued the defendants for false imprisonment.

Held

He had been falsely imprisoned since the plaintiffs were wrong in believing that he had committed a crime.

Isaacs CJ:

'When a person, instead of having recourse to legal proceedings by applying for a judi-

cial warrant for arrest or laying an information or issuing other process well known to the law, gives another into custody, he takes a risk upon himself by which he must abide, and if in the result it turns out that the person arrested was innocent, and that therefore the arrest was wrongful, he cannot plead any lawful excuse unless he can bring himself within the proposition of law which I have enunciated in this judgment.

In this case, although the defendants thought, and indeed it appeared that they were justified in thinking, that the plaintiff was the person who had committed the theft, it turned out in fact that they were wrong. The felony for which they had the plaintiff into custody had not in fact been committed, and, therefore, the very basis upon which they must rest any defence of lawful excuse for the wrongful arrest of another fails them in this case. Although I am quite satisfied not only that they acted with perfect bona fides in the matter but were genuinely convinced after reasonable inquiry that they had in fact discovered the perpetrator of the crime, it now turns out that they were mistaken, and it cannot be established that the crime had been committed for which they gave the plaintiff into custody; they have failed to justify in law the arrest, and there must, therefore, be judgment for the plaintiff.'

Comment

An old common law decision on the scope of citizen's arrest: see now s24 PACE 1984 and *R* v *Self* (1992) (above).

6 Criminal Procedure

Elguzouli-Daf v *Commissioner of Police of the Metropolis* [1995] 1 All ER 833 Court of Appeal (Civil Division) (Steyn, Rose and Morritt LJJ)

• *Whether Crown Prosecution Service is under a duty of care to those it prosecutes*

Facts

The plaintiff had been charged with sexual offences but subsequently the Crown Prosecution Service informed him that the prosecution would be discontinued. The plaintiff had spent 22 days in custody and sued the Crown Prosecution Service, claiming that it had been negligent in not discontinuing the prosecution at an earlier date. His action was struck out on the ground that there was no sustainable cause of action because the Crown Prosecution Service did not owe a duty of care to those whom it prosecuted. The plaintiff appealed.

Held

The appeal would be dismissed. There were compelling policy considerations which precluded the recognition of a duty of care in these circumstances. There might be rare cases where a private law duty of care would arise if it was shown that the Crown Prosecution Service had by its conduct assumed a responsibility to a particular defendant.

Morritt LJ:

> 'The CPS was created by the Prosecution of Offences Act 1985. It is not a body corporate but a collection of individuals with statutory functions to perform. At the head is the Director of Public Prosecutions. Below but answerable to the Director are the Chief Crown Prosecutors. The third category is the staff appointed by the Director (s1(1), (6)). The Director is appointed by and under the superintendence of the Attorney-General (ss2(1) and 3(1)). The duties of the Director are set out in s3(2) and include the duty:
>
> > "... (b) to institute and have the conduct of criminal proceedings in any case where it appears to him that – (i) the importance or difficulty of the case makes it appropriate that proceedings should be instituted by him; or (ii) it is otherwise appropriate for proceedings to be instituted by him ..."
>
> By s1(6) every Crown Prosecutor has all the powers of the Director as to the institution and conduct of proceedings but must exercise those powers under the direction of the Director.
>
> By s10(1) the Director is required to –
>
> > "issue a Code for Crown Prosecutors giving guidance on general principles to be applied by them – (a) in determining, in any case – (i) whether proceedings for an offence should be instituted or, where proceedings have been instituted, whether they should be discontinued; or (ii) what charges should be preferred; and (b) in considering, in any case, representation to be made by them to any magistrates' court about the mode of trial suitable for that case."
>
> The code includes a paragraph, para 4, dealing with the sufficiency of evidence to start or maintain a prosecution (see *Archbold's Pleading, Evidence and Practice in Criminal Cases* (46th edn, 1994) vol 2, p1765, App D). It points out the importance of admissible, substantial and reliable evidence that a criminal offence has been committed by an identifiable person and the possible defences which might

affect the likelihood or otherwise of a conviction.

Thus, although the CPS is the authorised department for the purposes of bringing proceedings against the Crown under s17(3) of the Crown Proceedings Act 1947, the relevant statutory duties are cast on the Director and, through the Director, the Crown prosecutors and the staff of the service. In this case neither plaintiff alleges that there is a breach of any such statutory duty actionable by him, whether because of direct and substantial damage sustained by him or otherwise. In these circumstances "It would be strange that a common law duty of care should be superimposed on such a statutory framework" (see *Yuen Kun-yeu* v *A-G of Hong Kong* [1987] 2 All ER 705 at 713, [1988] AC 175 at 195 per Lord Keith of Kinkel).

I do not think that the imposition of either of the duties contended for is required by the relationship between the CPS and the plaintiffs or that it would be fair, just and reasonable for the law to do so. There are a number of reasons why I reach that conclusion. None of them may be sufficient in itself but the overall combination is in my judgment compelling.

First, there is the analogy with civil litigation. One party to a civil action does not owe a duty of care to the other, nor does his solicitor (see *Business Computers International Ltd* v *Registrar of Companies* [1987] 3 All ER 465, [1988] Ch 229 and *Al-Kandari* v *J R Brown & Co (a firm)* [1988] 1 All ER 833, [1988] QB 665). The reason is obvious: the duty to the other side might conflict with the duty to his own client. The analogy is not precise because criminal proceedings and the role of the prosecutor are different from civil proceedings and the role of a plaintiff in them. But the respects in which the roles differ appear to me to suggest that the prosecutor is an a fortiori case. Some of his duties, and in particular where they differ from those of a plaintiff, are equated with those of a minister of justice. In that respect a liability in negligence would be even more inapposite than in the case of the opposing party or his solicitor in civil litigation.

Second, not only would it be surprising to find a common law duty in the circumstances that the CPS is a recent creature of statute but under no statutory duty to individuals, but it would suggest that in this field at least the independent torts of malicious prosecution and misfeasance in a public office are unnecessary. In the case of the former, a plaintiff has to establish the absence of reasonable and probable cause and malice. In the case of the latter, knowledge of the want of power is an essential element. If the plaintiffs are right, want of reasonable care will suffice. To conclude that the duties for which the plaintiffs contend do exist would be to disregard the danger to which Lord Templeman referred in *Downsview Nominees Ltd* v *First City Corp Ltd* [1993] 3 All ER 626 at 638, [1993] AC 295 at 316, namely –

> "of extending the ambit of negligence so as to supplant or supplement other torts, contractual obligations, statutory duties or equitable rules in relation to every kind of damage including economic loss ..."

I do not understand that warning to have lost its relevance by virtue of the decision of the House of Lords in *Spring* v *Guardian Assurance plc* [1994] 3 All ER 129, [1994] 3 WLR 354.

Third ... policy considerations similar to those which weighed with Lord Keith of Kinkel in the context of the police in *Hill* v *Chief Constable of West Yorkshire* [1988] 2 All ER 238 at 243, [1989] AC 53 at 63 would be as applicable in this field to exclude a general duty of care. ...

I do not wish to be thought to be casting doubt on the decision of Tudor Evans J in *Welsh* v *Chief Constable of the Merseyside Police* [1993] 1 All ER 692 in so far as that decision was grounded on the assumed fact that there had been a voluntary assumption of responsibility. As such, liability would rest on the well-established principles of *Hedley Byrne & Co Ltd* v *Heller & Partners Ltd* [1963] 2 All ER 575, [1964] AC 465.'

Comment

A decision which establishes that as a general rule the Crown Prosecution Service is under no private law duty of care to those it prosecutes. Consider whether this immunity is justified, particularly in view of current public concerns about the efficiency and quality of CPS work.

R v *Central Criminal Court, ex parte Guney* [1996] 2 All ER 705 House of Lords (Lords Goff, Jauncey, Slynn, Steyn and Hoffmann)

• *Provision of surety as a condition of bail – whether surety's liability continuing after the arraignment of the accused – accused fleeing jurisdiction after arraignment*

Facts

The respondent had acted as a surety in the sum of one million pounds for Mr Asil Nadir, who had been charged with serious fraud offences. Mr Nadir had been granted bail and turned up at the Central Criminal Court for arraignment. No formal surrender to custody took place, though he went through the process of arraignment.

Counsel and the trial judge took the view that the arraignment was not a formal surrender to custody. Subsequently counsel for prosecution and defence privately agreed that bail arrangements could continue. Mr Nadir later absconded and the respondent was ordered to forfeit his surety. He successfully appealed against forfeiture to the Court of Appeal. The Serious Fraud Office appealed to the House of Lords against that decision.

Held

Appeal dismissed. Forfeiture of surety could not be required where arraignment had taken place because arraignment amounted to a surrender to the custody of the court and from that moment the further detention of an accused person lay solely within the discretion and power of the trial judge. This principle applied to all criminal cases, including serious fraud cases.

Lord Steyn:

> 'The duty of a defendant who has been granted bail by the magistrates' court is to surrender to the custody of the court at the required time and place. Depending on arrangements at various trial centres, a person desiring to surrender to bail may be required to report to a particular office or a particular official. ...
>
> Through the years the arrangements have been simplified. Nowadays a defendant is usually simply required to go to a particular courtroom where he may surrender to a dock officer, if there is one, or to a court official, such as the usher. It also has to be borne in mind that in a small but significant number of cases a defendant will be required to surrender to custody in a courtroom not equipped for the hearing of criminal cases, ie without cells or a dock.
>
> The present appeal raises the question of what happens when the defendant, although present in court, is not officially asked to surrender but is formally arraigned. Does he remain on bail after arraignment until the judge orders otherwise? If the answer is in the affirmative, and there is an adjournment, short or long, the defendant is presumably free to leave unless the judge directs otherwise. That in my judgment is a position which is calculated to create uncertainty, confusion and practical difficulties. There will always be cases where the system for surrender before arraignment breaks down. The situation demands a clear cut rule. It is imperative that there should be an objectively ascertainable formal act which causes a defendant's bail to lapse at the beginning of a trial. In my judgment that formal act can only be the arraignment of a defendant. The arraignment of a defendant involves: (1) calling the defendant to the bar by name: (2) reading the indictment to him; and (3) asking whether he is guilty or not . ...
>
> When a defendant who has not previously surrendered to custody is so arraigned he thereby surrenders to the custody of the

court. From that moment the defendant's further detention lies solely within the discretion and power of the judge. Unless the judge grants bail the defendant will remain in custody pending and during his trial. This is a readily comprehensible system which causes no problems for the administration of justice.'

Comment

A commonsense victory for providers of sureties.

R v Crown Court at Maidstone, ex parte Lever [1995] 2 All ER 35 Court of Appeal (Civil Division) (Butler-Sloss and Hoffmann LJJ and Sir Tasker Watkins)

- *Bail – whether to order forfeiture of sureties upon absconding of the accused*

Facts

The appellant had stood surety of £40,000 for the accused who was charged with drugs offences. When the appellant discovered that the accused may have absconded he informed the police. In fact the local police station had been aware of the accused's failure to report to it one evening as required by the conditions of bail, and had failed to inform anyone of that failure. The accused was not found and did not appear at his trial. The judge ordered forfeiture of £35,000, despite the lack of culpability of the appellant and the negligence of the local police. The appellant had applied for judicial review. The Divisional Court dismissed the application and he appealed to the Court of Appeal.

Held

The appeal would be dismissed. The trial judge's decision could not be treated as irrational or unfair. The basis of forfeiture was not the culpability of the surety but the non-attendance of the accused. However, the culpability of the surety and the negligence of the accused were relevant factors in deciding whether it would be just to remit some or all of the recognisances. The trial judge had taken account of those factors in remitting about 15 per cent of the recognisance and there was no ground on which the court could interfere with the judge's exercise of discretion.

Butler-Sloss LJ:

> 'The power of a judge to estreat some or the whole of a recognisance upon the application of a surety is to be found in r21 of the Crown Court Rules 1982, SI 1982/1109. The general principle is that the purpose of a recognisance is to bring the defendant to court for trial. The basis of entreatment is not as a matter of punishment of the surety, but because he has failed to fulfil the obligation which he undertook. The starting point on the failure to bring a defendant to court is the forfeiture of the full recognisance. The right to estreat is triggered by the non-attendance of the defendant at court. It is for the surety to establish to the satisfaction of the trial court that there are grounds upon which the court may remit from forfeiture part or, wholly exceptionally, the whole recognisance. The presence or absence of culpability is a factor but the absence of culpability, as found in this case by the judge, is not in itself a reason to reduce or set aside the obligation entered into by the surety to pay in the event of a failure to bring the defendant to court. The court may, in the exercise of a wide discretion, decide it would be fair and just to estreat some or all of the recognisance.
>
> Unless the exercise of the judge's discretion is outside that which a reasonable judge on the facts would have done, or was an irrational or perverse decision, judicial review will not lie. ...'

Comment

A case which illustrates the scope of the trial judge's discretion to order forfeiture of all or part of the recognisance in cases where the defendant fails to appear at trial.

R* v *Crown Court at Reading, ex parte Bello [1992] 3 All ER 353 Court of Appeal (Civil Division) (Purchas, Parker and Stuart-Smith LJJ)

- *Surety – forfeiture of recognisance*

Facts

The applicant had stood as surety for the accused and he had been ordered to forfeit £5,000, half of his recognisance. He had contended that this order should be set aside because (a) he was not notified that the accused was required to attend Reading Crown Court on 3 February 1986, (b) the accused was already then in police custody in The Netherlands, and (c) he (the applicant) was blameless.

Held

The appeal would not be allowed as it had not been shown that the accused was ever required to attend Reading Crown Court whether for trial, sentence or anything else, either on 3 February 1986 or on any other date.

Parker LJ:

> '… the failure of the accused to surrender when required triggers the power to forfeit but the court, before deciding what should be done, must inquire into the question of fault. If it is satisfied that the surety was blameless throughout it would then be proper to remit the whole of the amount of the recognisance and in exceptional circumstances this would in my judgment be the only proper course. Suppose for example the accused and the surety were on the way to court when both of them were seriously injured in a motor accident and taken to hospital. On no basis could it be said that the justice of the case required any part of the recognisance to be forfeit. …
>
> I turn to the contention that ignorance of the date when a defendant is required to appear at court is by itself a ground for non-forfeiture. There is in my judgment force in this contention. The surety undertakes to ensure the appearance of the defendant at court when required. It is an undertaking to the court of which failure to observe may result in the forfeiture of very large sums of money. It therefore appears that justice should require that the surety is notified by the court of the date upon which the defendant is required to appear. Suppose, for example, that on the occasion when bail is granted it is estimated that the trial is unlikely to take place for at least six months After three months, however, the court is notified that the defendant intends to plead and the case is listed for seven days hence. The surety is not notified because he is on a walking holiday in the Himalayas. Using Lord Denning MR's own words in *Ex p Green* [1975] 2 All ER 1073 at 1077, [1976] QB 11 at 19 the court should do 'what the justice of the case requires'. For my part I cannot see that in such a situation the justice of the case can possibly require forfeiture. In my judgment, however, it is impossible to say that ignorance of the date *must* be an answer to proceedings for forfeiture. Each case will depend on the facts. It may be, for example, that the surety is warned that the case is liable to be listed at some time in a particular week and that he should watch the list because it may come into the list suddenly. It may be that the court for administrative reasons cannot do better than this. If in such a case the surety does not watch the list ignorance would be unlikely, as it seems to me, to be an answer.
>
> In my judgment, however, the court should always notify sureties when a date is fixed and, if no date is fixed, notify them between what dates the case is likely to be listed. Such warning should be given as far in advance as possible.'

Comment

A case which shows that the trial judge must inquire into the question of fault before deciding whether to order forfeiture of all or part of the recognisance following a failure by the defendant to surrender to custody.

R* v *Horseferry Road Magistrates' Court, ex parte K [1996] 3 All ER 719 Queen's Bench Division (Kennedy LJ and Forbes J)

• *Magistrates re-opening mode of trial proceedings after entry of not guilty plea at summary trial but before commencement of evidence – whether jurisdiction to do so*

Facts

The applicant had been charged with affray and common assault. The charges had been treated as suitable for summary trial, where the applicant entered a plea of not guilty. Before any evidence had been given the stipendiary magistrate realised from a review of the psychiatric reports that there was a possible defence of insanity. The magistrate then reopened the mode of trial procedure and concluded that the applicant should be committed for trial at the Crown Court on the ground that a hospital order under s41 of the Mental Health Act 1983 might be required if the defence were successful. Under s25(2) of the Magistrates' Courts Act (MCA) 1980 magistrates have jurisdiction to reopen mode of trial proceedings if they have begun to try the information summarily. The applicant contended that a summary trial had not commenced in his case and that therefore the magistrate could not rely on s25(2). He sought judicial review.

Held

Application dismissed. It was possible for a summary trial to begin after the entry of a not guilty plea but before evidence had been called, for example where the magistrates heard submission on points of law. In the present case the magistrate had jurisdiction under s25(2) to reopen the mode of trial procedure and it had been appropriate to do so because the possible defence of insanity was relevant to the available powers of the court to deal with the accused – a factor specified in s19(3) MCA 1980.

Forbes J:

'... where there is a plea of guilty in the magistrates' court to an information which charges an offence triable either way, the court has not at any stage "begun to try the information summarily" for the purposes of s25(2) of the 1980 Act, because there is nothing to try in the narrow sense. The reason that this is so is, as it seems to us, obvious. The process of determining the guilt or innocence of the defendant in such circumstances is rendered unnecessary by the defendant's own admission of guilt.

In our opinion, the same reasoning cannot be applied to a plea of not guilty. It must be remembered that it is the plea of not guilty which puts the defendant's guilt in issue and creates the need for a "trial" in the narrow sense. In that respect, we take the view that a plea of not guilty can be said to initiate the process of determining guilt, ie it is an essential and necessary introduction to the trial. Whether the plea of not guilty does or does not form part of the actual process of determining guilt or innocence will depend on the particular facts of the case. If, as a fact, all that happens following a plea of not guilty is that the court puts the matter over to another day for trial, then the process of determining guilt or innocence, although initiated, has still not begun. ...

... there are a number of possible circumstances in which, after a plea of not guilty and before the commencement of the evidence, it can become apparent that the court has embarked upon the process of determining the guilt or innocence of the accused and thus has "begun" the trial in question. We do not consider that it is either necessary or desirable to try and enumerate all the possible circumstances in which this could occur. However, we are satisfied that one such possible circumstance can arise where, as in the instant case, the defence makes and the magistrate considers submissions in support of an application for a preliminary ruling of law which has a direct and immediate bearing on the conduct and content of the process of determining the guilt or innocence of the accused.'

Comment

The decision clarifies the law concerning the time when a summary trial begins and the consequent powers of the magistrates to reconsider the mode of trial question if an either-way offence is being tried summarily.

R v *Metropolitan Police Commissioner, ex parte Blackburn* [1968] 2 WLR 893 Court of Appeal (Lord Denning MR, Salmon and Edmund-Davies LJJ)

- *Decision to prosecute*

Facts

As the result of a policy decision, the Commissioner of Police of the Metropolis failed to prosecute gaming clubs in London under the Betting, Gaming and Lotteries Act 1963. The applicant, a private citizen, complained that illegal gaming was being carried on and applied for an order of mandamus directing the Commissioner to reverse the policy decision. The application was refused and the applicant appealed to the Court of Appeal. The respondent argued that he did not owe a duty to the public to enforce the law and had an absolute discretion not to prosecute.

Held

The respondent owed a duty to the public to enforce the law which he could be compelled to perform. While he had a discretion not to prosecute, his discretion to make policy decisions was not absolute.

Lord Denning MR:

> 'Although the chief officers of police are answerable to the law, there are many fields in which they have a discretion with which the law will not interfere. For instance, it is for the Commissioner of Police of the Metropolis, or the chief constable, as the case may be, to decide in any particular case whether inquiries should be pursued, or whether an arrest should be made, or a prosecution brought. It must be for him to decide on the disposition of his force and the concentration of his resources on any particular crime or area. No court can or should give him direction on such a matter. He can also make policy decisions and give effect to them, as, for instance, was often done when prosecutions were not brought for attempted suicide. But there are some policy decisions with which, I think, the courts in a case can, if necessary, interfere. Suppose a chief constable were to issue a directive to his men that no person should be prosecuted for stealing any goods less than £100 in value. I should have thought that the court could contest it. He would be failing in his duty to enforce the law.'

Comment

An important decision on the scope of the discretion to prosecute. Although the discretion is a wide one, Lord Denning's judgment makes it clear that there is a duty to enforce the law so that the discretion can only be exercised in regard to the particular facts of a case and not in regard to the wider issue of whether it is desirable to enforce the particular law in question.

R v *Pitman* [1991] 1 All ER 468 Court of Appeal (Lane LCJ, Alliott and Auld JJ)

- *Private discussion between judge and counsel – plea bargaining*

Facts

In the course of a trial for allegedly causing death by reckless driving, the judge asked counsel to see him in his private room. He said that he believed there was no defence to the charge and that the accused should plead guilty: if he did so, when it came to sentencing, he would receive substantial credit. Although the accused's counsel had previously advised him to plead not guilty, in the light of the discussion with the judge he changed his plea and on conviction he was

sentenced to nine months' imprisonment and disqualified for four years.

Held

There had been a material irregularity and the conviction would therefore be quashed.

Lane LCJ:

'... There is it seems a steady flow of appeals to this court arising from visits by counsel to the judge in his private room. No amount of criticism and no amount of warnings and no amount of exhortation seems to be able to prevent this happening. In this case it was an invitation from the judge which caused counsel to visit him in his room.

The dangers of such visits scarcely need emphasising. They were set out in *R* v *Harper-Taylor and Bakker* (1988) 138 NLJ 80 at 80–81, decided in this court on 10 February 1988, in which Mustill LJ delivered this passage which is worthy of note:

"A first principle of criminal law is that justice is done in public, for all to see and hear. By this standard, a meeting in the judge's room is anomalous: the essence, and indeed the purpose, being that neither the defendant nor the jury nor the public are there to hear what is going on. Undeniably, there are circumstances where the public must be excluded. Equally, the jury cannot always be kept in court throughout. The withdrawal of the proceedings into private, without even the defendant being there, is another matter. It is true, as this court stated in *R* v *Turner (Frank)* [1970] 2 All ER 281 at 285, [1970] 2 QB 321 at 326, that there must be freedom of access between counsel and the judge when there are matters calling for communications or discussions of such a nature that counsel cannot in the interests of his client mention them in open court. Criminal trials are so various that a list of situations where an approach to the judge is permissible would only mislead; but it must be clear that communications should never take place unless there is no alternative. Apart from the question of principle, seeing the judge in private creates risks of more than one kind, as the present case has shown. The need to solve an immediate practical problem may combine with the more relaxed atmosphere of the private room to blur the formal outlines of the trial. Again, if the object of withdrawing the case from open court is to maintain a degree of confidence, as it plainly must be, there is room for misunderstanding about how far the confidence is to extend; and in particular, there is a risk that counsel and solicitors for the other parties may hear something said to the judge which they would rather not hear, putting them into a state of conflict between their duties to their clients, and their obligation to maintain the confidentiality of the private room. The absence of the defendant is also a potential source of trouble. He has to learn what the judge has said at second hand and may afterwards complain (rightly or no) that he was not given an accurate account. Equally, he cannot hear what his counsel has said to the judge, and hence cannot intervene to correct a mis-statement or an excess of authority: a factor which may not only be a source of unfairness to the defendant, but which may also deprive the prosecution of the opportunity to contend that admissions made in open court in the presence of the client and not repudiated by him may be taken to have been made with his authority: *R* v *Turner (Bryan)* (1975) 61 Cr App R 67."

We have thought it necessary to cite that portion from that judgment in full in order to draw to the attention of courts up and down the country a point which we hope may at last go home, because this case is a prime example of the sort of difficulties which arise when those injunctions are disregarded.'

Comment

One of the leading authorities on the legality of the practice of plea bargaining. Lord Lane's judgment gives stern warnings about the dangers of the practice and, in particular, the

undesirability of secret discussions and sentence canvassing.

R v *Tower Bridge Metropolitan Stipendiary Magistrate, ex parte Chaudhry* [1993] 3 WLR 1154 High Court (Kennedy LJ and Bell J)

• *Private prosecution – magistrate's refusal to issue summons*

Facts

The applicant's motor cyclist son having died as a result of injuries received in a collision with a van and the Crown Prosecution Service having laid informations against the van driver alleging three relatively minor road traffic offences, the applicant had laid an information alleging that the death had been caused by reckless driving. The magistrate refused to issue such a summons and the applicant applied for judicial review of this decision.

Held

The application would be dismissed.

Kennedy LJ:

> 'Underlying all of [counsel's] submissions is of course the individual's right to prosecute, and before us no one has questioned it. …
>
> … I see no conflict between the existence of that right and of the discretion of a magistrate to decide whether or not to issue a summons. After all … an individual prosecutor does not have the unfettered right to pursue his prosecution to trial. By virtue of s6(2) of the 1985 Act the Director of Public Prosecutions may, at any stage, take over in order to abort (see *Raymond* v *Attorney General* [1982] QB 839), and he may even bring the magistrates' court proceedings to an end by notice pursuant to s23 of the 1985 Act. So, as it seems to me, in any given case, a private prosecutor will have two hurdles to surmount. He will have to persuade a magistrate to issue a summons, and thereafter, if he wishes to retain control of the case, he may have a persuade the Director of Public Prosecutions not to take it over. But in reality, the criteria applied by the magistrate and the Director will be different. The magistrate should have regard to all of the relevant circumstances of which he is aware … such as whether the incident giving rise to the information which he is considering has already been investigated by a responsible prosecuting authority which is pursuing what it considers to be the appropriate charges against the same proposed defendant. If so, as [counsel for the van driver] pointed out, the magistrate may have in mind the provisions of the *Guide for Crown Prosecutors* issued under s10 of the Prosecution of Offences Act 1985, which requires the Crown Prosecution Service generally to charge the most serious offence revealed by the evidence but to have regard to the public interest, the interests of the victim, and the prospects on the available evidence of securing a conviction (which may not be very high where recklessness is alleged). If a summons for a more serious charge is issued on the application of a private prosecutor, the discretion of the Crown prosecutor is overridden in a way which may well appear to the defendant and to those who represent him to be oppressive, and so, whilst I would not go so far as to suggest that a magistrate should never at the behest of a private prosecutor issue a summons against a defendant who, in respect of the same matter, already has to answer one or more informations laid by the Crown, it seems to me that unless there are special circumstances, such as apparent bad faith on the part of the public prosecutor, the magistrate should be very slow to take that step. He will be all the more hesitant because he knows that the Director can, and in reality may well, take over the proceedings of the private prosecutor. That too is a relevant factor even if, as [counsel for the applicant] contends, the magistrate in the present case was to some extent guessing when he said that it seemed to him that the Crown Prosecution Service *would* take over Mrs Chaudhry's prosecution.
>
> If a magistrate does decide to issue a summons, the Director in deciding whether

or not to exercise her powers under s6(2) of the 1985 Act will no doubt look at the evidence in a way that the magistrate was not expecting to do when he decided to issue the summons, so the functions are different, but I do not accept that the discretion of the magistrate is anything like so confined as [counsel for the applicant] would have us accept. In my judgment the magistrate in the present case ... was right to have regard to the action already taken by the Crown Prosecution Service and to the Director's powers under s6(2) of the 1985 Act, and accordingly this court cannot and should not interfere with his conclusion, arrived at in the exercise of his discretion, that in the interests of justice a summons should not be issued.'

Comment

Whilst any citizen has a general right to bring a private prosecution, this decision makes it clear that the right is subject to conditions, in particular the need to persuade a magistrate to issue a summons.

R* v *Turner [1970] 2 WLR 1093 Court of Appeal (Parker LCJ, Widgery LJ and Bean J)

- *Plea bargaining*

Facts

The defendant pleaded not guilty at his trial to a charge of theft. After having spoken to the judge, his counsel advised him in strong terms to change his plea to guilty in order to reduce the likelihood of a custodial sentence. Believing that counsel was relaying a statement made by the judge (although this had never in fact been implied), the defendant changed his plea and was found guilty. He appealed against conviction on the ground that he did not have a free choice in retracting the plea of not guilty and pleading guilty.

Held

Allowing the appeal, counsel could properly advise the defendant in strong terms to change his plea provided that it was made clear to him that the ultimate choice was freely his; but that, if the advice was conveyed as that of someone who has seen the judge, a defendant should be disabused of any impression that the judge's views were being repeated. As the defendant may have felt that the views expressed were those of the judge he could not be said to have had a free choice in changing his plea, and that, accordingly, the plea of guilty should be treated as a nullity and a venire de novo ordered.

Parker LCJ:

> 'The judge should, subject to the one exception referred to hereafter, never indicate the sentence which he is minded to impose. A statement that on a plea of guilty he would impose one sentence but that on a conviction following a plea of not guilty he would impose a severer sentence is one which should never be made. This could be taken to be undue pressure on the accused, thus depriving him of that complete freedom of choice which is essential. Such cases, however, are in the experience of the court happily rare. What on occasions does appear to happen however is that a judge will tell counsel that, having read the depositions and the antecedents, he can safely say that on a plea of guilty he will, for instance, make a probation order, something which may be helpful to counsel in advising the accused. The judge in such a case is no doubt careful not to mention what he would do if the accused were convicted following a plea of not guilty. Even so, the accused may well get the impression that the judge is intimating that in that event a severer sentence, maybe a custodial sentence, would result, so that again he may feel under pressure. This accordingly must also not be done.
>
> The only exception to this rule is that it should be permissible for a judge to say, if it be the case, that whatever happens, whether the accused pleads guilty or not guilty, the sentence will or will not take a particular form eg a probation order or a fine, or a custodial sentence.'

Comment

This case probably remains the leading common law authority on the scope of plea bargaining. The safeguards suggested by Lord Parker were later confirmed in a *Practice Direction* [1976] Crim LR 561.

R v *Wood Green Crown Court, ex parte Howe* [1992] 1 WLR 702 High Court (Watkins LJ and Anthony Evans J)

• *Bail – forfeiture and withdrawal of recognisance*

Facts

On 14 November 1988 the applicant (for judicial review) stood surety for her brother in the sum of £35,000, knowing that (then) she would be unable to pay that amount if he failed to appear. The trial was rescheduled for 3 April 1989 and the brother kept in touch with the applicant until 7 March 1989. On the following day the applicant reported the brother's disappearance to the police and recorded a wish to withdraw her surety. The Crown Court judge refused to allow withdrawal of the recognisance and, the brother having failed to appear on 3 April, on 17 April he ordered forfeiture of its full amount.

Held

The application would be granted and the case remitted for rehearing.

Watkins LJ:

> 'It is accepted by the applicant that the burden of showing that the order for forfeiture should not be made rests upon her. This is in accordance with the authorities already referred to.
>
> The undertaking to pay the amount of the recognisance if the defendant fails to appear gives rise to a serious obligation which is owed by the surety to the court. It is therefore an equally serious matter for the surety to mislead the court as to his or her means when the undertaking is given. There is no authority directly in point on the question whether, when the surety has undertaken to pay a sum which he cannot afford, the court can properly and should order forfeiture of the full amount, or otherwise order payment of such a large sum that the surety must necessarily default and therefore will become liable to serve a term of imprisonment for non-payment. ...
>
> ... The learned judge referred to "two disquieting features" which are often present in cases of this sort. Persons, especially close relatives, are often put under enormous pressure by defendants and by circumstances to stand surety in sums which they cannot afford to pay. This happened here ...
>
> The second disquieting feature, as we understand the judge's remarks, was that as soon as her brother disappeared the applicant "went round to a police station and made a statement", which was easy to do but which did not show "quite the diligence that is required". In other words, the undertaking that a defendant will appear in court is not discharged merely by taking even the utmost care to ensure that he does ...
>
> The finding that the degree of culpability was very high is one that cannot be faulted in the present case. Whether it was so high as to result in the full amount being forfeited is more debatable ... It seems clear to us that in the circumstances of this case she was entitled to a large measure of credit.
>
> Where the ruling must also be criticised, in our view, lies in the fact that no separate consideration was given to the applicant's inability to pay the full amount which was forfeited. The authorities require that consideration be given to the surety's "means" ... There may be cases where the culpability is so great that payment may be ordered of an amount which makes a prison sentence likely, but nothing which we have seen makes the present case one of that sort.
>
> We hold for these reasons that the judge's ruling must be set aside, and we shall remit the application for rehearing in the light of the judgment and of such further evidence and submissions as may be placed before the court ...'

Comment

An important decision on the rights of sureties, particularly in regard to the right to withdraw (available only if the defendant appears at court) and in regard to ability to pay (the court is bound to consider this before ordering payment of a particular sum as surety).

Williams v *Bedwellty Justices* [1996] 3 All ER 737 House of Lords (Lords Keith, Goff, Jauncey, Browne-Wilkinson and Cooke)

• *Admission of inadmissible evidence during committal proceedings – whether judicial review available to quash committal for error of law*

Facts

The applicant had been charged with conspiracy. The only evidence put forward at the committal proceedings was in the form of incriminating statements from the other alleged conspirators. After committal the Crown served witness statements from those other alleged conspirators. The applicant applied for judicial review of the committal on the ground that the statements given at the committal were inadmissible on the ground of hearsay and that there was no other evidence to support the committal. The application failed at first instance. The applicant then appealed direct to the House of Lords by way of the 'leap frog' appeal procedure.

Held

Appeal allowed and certiorari granted to quash the committal. The committal had been flawed by the reception of inadmissible hearsay evidence and this flaw could not be cured by the later service of witness statements. Examining justices were required by s6(1) of the Magistrates' Courts Act 1980 to consider the admissibility of the Crown's evidence.

However, a judicial review should be granted only where there had been a really substantial error on the committal proceedings leading to manifest injustice for the accused. In the present case such an error had occurred and the committal must be quashed because no alternative remedy would give the appellant the opportunity to cross-examine the makers of the witness statements before trial.

Lord Cooke:

> '... it would be both illogical and unsatisfactory to hold that the law of judicial review should distinguish in principle between a committal based solely on inadmissible evidence and a committal based solely on evidence not reasonably capable of supporting it. In each case there is in truth no evidence to support the committal and the committal is therefore open to quashing on judicial review. None the less there is a practical distinction. If justices have been of the opinion on admissible evidence that there is sufficient to put the accused on trial, I suggest that normally on a judicial review application a court will rightly be slow to interfere at that stage. The question will more appropriately be dealt with on a no case submission at the close of the prosecution evidence, when the worth of that evidence can be better assessed by a judge who has not heard it, or even on a pre-trial application grounded on abuse of process. In practice, successful judicial review proceedings are likely to be rare in both classes of case, and especially rare in the second class.'

Comment

The decision clarifies the scope of judicial review over committals.

7 The Jury System

Attorney-General v *Associated Newspapers Ltd* [1994] 2 WLR 277 House of Lords (Lords Keith of Kinkel, Bridge of Harwich, Goff of Chieveley, Lowry and Lloyd of Berwick)

• *Contempt of court – secrets of jury room*

Facts

The *Mail on Sunday* published particulars of a jury's deliberations in a fraud trial at the Central Criminal Court. The information was obtained from two members of the jury by an independent researcher. The newspaper, its editor and the journalist concerned were found to be in breach of s8 of the Contempt of Court Act 1981.

Held

Their appeals would be dismissed.

Lord Lowry:

> '[Counsel] for the appellants, accepted … that, if the word "disclose" in s8 was to be given the unrestricted meaning contended for by the Attorney General, a contempt was proved. But he submitted that the scope of s8(1) could be either widely or narrowly interpreted and that in context the word "disclose" applied only to a revelation by a juror to another person and not to a further revelation by that person or by another person in his turn. While conceding, frankly but also unavoidably, that what the appellants did amounted to disclosure in the ordinary sense of that word, he contrasted publication with disclosure and contended that the word "disclose" must here be given a restricted meaning.
>
> The cardinal rule, as stated in the textbooks on interpretation, for example in *Maxwell on the Interpretation of Statutes* (12th edn, 1969) pp28–29, is that words in a statute prima facie bear their plain and ordinary meaning. If that rule is applied without modification, then the appellants disclosed the relevant particulars. There is no conflict or contrast between publication and disclosure. The latter activity has many manifestations and publication is one of them. To disclose is to expose to view, make known or reveal and in its ordinary meaning the word aptly describes *both* the revelation by jurors of their deliberations *and* further disclosure by publication in a newspaper of the same deliberations, provided always – and this will raise a question of fact – that the publication amounts to disclosure and is not a mere republication of already known facts.
>
> I have looked in vain, first in s8 and then in the other provisions of the 1981 Act, for a clue which might justify the imposing of a restriction on the natural meaning and effect of the word "disclose". Indeed, as I have observed, the concluding words of s8(2) seem to me to point away from the restriction contended for. Still following ordinary English usage, I can find no principle which lays down that something which has been disclosed by A to B cannot be further disclosed by B to C and by C, in his turn, to the public at large …
>
> One could instance the case of a jury-keeper who is told about or overhears the jury's deliberations. Can he not be guilty of disclosure if he reveals what he has heard to a newspaper? And are the newspaper's reporter and publisher immune if the deliberations are published? I scarcely think so. So far as the test of absurdity helps to decide the issue, my verdict is overwhelmingly on the side of the Attorney General.'

Comment

An important decision showing the scope of s8 of the Contempt of Court Act 1981 in protecting the secrecy of the jury room. Disclosure of jury deliberations, even if obtained indirectly, will be a contempt. There is no defence based on the 'public's right to know'; freedom of the press takes second place to the need to preserve the independence of the jury system. However, s8 does not protect the secrecy of jury deliberations that occur outside the jury room: *R* v *Young* [1995] 2 WLR 430 (CA).

H v *Ministry of Defence* [1991] 2 WLR 1192 Court of Appeal (Lord Donaldson of Lymington MR, Woolf and Mann LJJ)

- *Personal injury action – jury trial*

Facts

The defendants admitted liability for negligence which led to the amputation of a major part of a soldier's penis. Damages remained to be determined and the soldier applied for trial by jury. The judge granted his application in view of the exceptional circumstances and the defendants appealed against this decision.

Held

The appeal would be allowed.

Lord Donaldson of Lymington MR:

> 'We have reluctantly, but firmly, come to the conclusion that the judge's discretionary order was wrong and we think that the basis of the error was either a failure to appreciate the significance of the shift in emphasis created by the enactment of s69 of the Supreme Court Act 1981 in place of s6 of the Administration of Justice (Miscellaneous Provisions) Act 1933 or his acceptance of the submission that the retention of a judicial discretion necessarily involved the proposition that there must be some claims for compensatory damages in personal injury cases which were appropriate to be tried by jury or both. It follows that we are entitled, and indeed bound, to exercise a fresh discretion.
>
> There was some discussion in argument as to the propriety of an appellate court declaring a policy or guidelines for the exercise of a judicial discretion, but it was rightly accepted that this could and should be done, provided that it was made clear that every case had to be considered on its own merits and that, if the rationale of the policy was not wholly applicable, even if the case fell within the terms of that policy, a judge was always free to depart from it. This too we unreservedly accept.
>
> The policy should be that stated in *Ward* v *James* [1966] 1 QB 273, namely that trial by jury is normally inappropriate for any personal injury action in so far as the jury is required to assess compensatory damages, because the assessment of such damages must be based upon or have regard to conventional scales of damages. The very fact that no jury trial of a claim for damages for personal injuries appears to have taken place for over 25 years affirms how exceptional the circumstances would have to be before it was appropriate to order such a trial and the enactment of s69 of the 1981 Act strengthens the presumption against making such an order.
>
> Although [counsel for the defendants] in the court below was unable to suggest a case where trial by jury of a personal injuries claim would be appropriate and this undoubtedly contributed to the judge's decision, we think that there might well be such a case, albeit not one in which only compensatory damages are being sought. If, for example, personal injuries resulted from conduct on the part of those who were deliberately abusing their authority, there might well be a claim for exemplary damages and this could place the case in an exceptional category which, since it is not expressly contemplated by s69, would fall within the general judicial discretion with its bias against a trial by jury, but yet is not dissimilar to a claim for malicious prosecution or false imprisonment in respect of which there is a legislative intention that there shall be a

jury trial, unless there are contra-indications. That is not this case.

We will allow the appeal and order trial by a judge alone.'

Comment

The decision confirms the policy laid down in *Ward* v *James* (1966) (below) that trial by jury is normally inappropriate for any personal injury action in so far as the jury is required to assess compensatory damages. In rare cases where a civil jury is permitted the judge is entitled to give the jury clear and precise guidance on how to assess appropriate compensation: see *Thompson* v *Commissioner of Police of the Metropolis* (1997) (below).

John* v *MGN Ltd [1996] 2 All ER 35 Court of Appeal (Civil Division) (Sir Thomas Bingham MR, Neill and Hirst LJJ)

• *Guidance to civil juries on assessing compensation in defamation cases*

Facts

The musician Elton John had successfully sued the defendant newspaper group for defamation. The jury had awarded damages of a total sum of £350,000, comprising £75,000 compensatory damages and £275,000 exemplary damages. The defendants appealed against the award to the Court of Appeal.

Held

The jury's award would be set aside and a figure of £75,000 would be substituted, comprising £25,000 compensatory damages and £50,000 exemplary damages. Changes of practice would be introduced to provide guidance for defamation juries in performing their role of assessing damages.

Sir Thomas Bingham MR:

'... There could never be any precise, arithmetical formula to govern the assessment of general damages in defamation, but if such cases were routinely tried by judges sitting alone there would no doubt emerge a more or less coherent framework of awards which would, while recognising the particular features of particular cases, ensure that broadly comparable cases led to broadly comparable awards. This is what has happened in the field of personal injuries since these ceased to be the subject of trial by jury and became, in practice, the exclusive preserve of judges. There may be even greater factual diversity in defamation than in personal injury cases, but this is something of which the framework would take account.

The survival of jury trial in defamation actions has inhibited a similar development in this field. Respect for the constitutional role of the jury in such actions, and judicial reluctance to intrude into an area of decision-making reserved to the jury, have traditionally led judges presiding over defamation trials with juries to confine their jury directions to a statement of general principles, eschewing any specific guidance on the appropriate level of general damages in the particular case ...

... Whatever the theoretical attractions of this approach, its practical disadvantages have become ever more manifest. A series of jury awards in sums wildly disproportionate to any damage conceivably suffered by the plaintiff has given rise to serious and justified criticism of the procedures leading to such awards. This has not been the fault of the juries. Judges, as they were bound to do, confined themselves to broad directions of general principle, coupled with injunctions to the jury to be reasonable. But they gave no guidance on what might be thought reasonable or unreasonable, and it is not altogether surprising that juries lacked an instinctive sense of where to pitch their awards. They were in the position of sheep loosed on an unfenced common, with no shepherd ... Any legal process should yield a successful plaintiff appropriate compensation, that is, compensation which is neither too much nor too little. But there is continuing evidence of libel awards in sums which appear so large as to bear no relation to the ordinary values of life. This is most obviously unjust to defendants. But it serves no

public purpose to encourage plaintiffs to regard a successful libel action, risky though the process undoubtedly is, as a road to untaxed riches. Nor is it healthy if any legal process fails to command the respect of lawyer and layman alike, as is regrettably true of the assessment of damages by libel juries. We are persuaded by the arguments we have heard that the subject should be reconsidered. This is not a field in which we are bound by previous authority … We can for our part see no reason why the parties' respective counsel in a libel action should not indicate to the jury the level of award which they respectively contend to be appropriate, nor why the judge in directing the jury should not give a similar indication. The plaintiff will not wish the jury to think that his main object is to make money rather than clear his name. The defendant will not wish to add insult to injury by underrating the seriousness of the libel. So we think the figures suggested by responsible counsel are likely to reflect the upper and lower bounds of a realistic bracket. The jury must, of course, make up their own mind and must be directed to do so. They will not be bound by the submission of counsel or the indication of the judge. If the jury make an award outside the upper or lower bounds of any bracket indicated and such award is the subject of appeal, real weight must be given to the possibility that their judgment is to be preferred to that of the judge.

The modest but important changes of practice described above would not in our view undermine the enduring constitutional position of the libel jury. Historically, the significance of the libel jury has lain not in their role of assessing damages, but in their role of deciding whether the publication complained of is a libel or no. The changes which we favour will, in our opinion, buttress the constitutional role of the libel jury by rendering their proceedings more rational and so more acceptable to public opinion.'

Comment

This is a landmark decision which further restricts the scope of the jury's discretion in awarding compensation in defamation cases. Note that the Defamation Act 1996 has abolished trial by jury for defamation claims of £10,000 or less.

R* v *Comerford [1998] 1 All ER 823 Court of Appeal (Criminal Division) (Bingham LCJ, Potts and Butterfield JJ)

- *Empanelling the jury – challenge*

Facts

On the morning following the commencement of the defendant's trial the Crown made an application to the trial judge in chambers seeking the discharge of the jury. The application was made in the presence only of prosecuting counsel and two senior Customs and Excise officials (the defendant had been charged with attempting to possess cocaine with intent to supply). One of the officials gave sworn evidence to the judge, who then discussed matters with counsel. Being satisfied that there had been interference with the jury the trial judge, upon redemption of the trial, discharged that jury, but did so without prior notification to the defence and without stating his reasons for the discharge.

The Crown then applied, in the presence of the defence, for police protection for the fresh jury, but giving no reasons and calling no evidence in support of the application. Defence counsel opposed the application but the judge directed that protection should be given at the highest level. He further ruled that the jurors should be empanelled by numbers rather than their names, which would normally be announced in open court. No challenges were made as the jury was empanelled in this manner. The defendant was convicted and appealed on the basis of an irregular empanellment.

Held

Appeal dismissed.

Bingham LCJ:

'It is a truism that the jury is the lynch-pin of trial on indictment. The proper functioning of the jury is crucial to the fair and effective conduct of the trial. To that end statute regulates the composition of juries, the selection of jurors and the challenging of jurors. To that end also, almost infinite care is taken in directing the jury on the proper approach to their task, on the relevant law and on the facts. But all these rules and procedures are rendered of little effect if the integrity of an individual juror, and thus of the jury as a whole, is compromised. Such a compromise occurs when any juror, whether because of intimidation, bribery of any other reason, dishonours or becomes liable to dishonour his or her oath as a juror by allowing anything to undermine or qualify the juror's duty to give a true verdict according to the evidence. …

The question we must answer is whether we consider this conviction unsafe because the trial judge made an order for the protection of the jury without requiring the Crown to give reasons to the defence and without requiring it to call evidence in the presence of the appellant or his counsel. The defence have now been informed, which they were not informed at the trial, that there was apparently compelling evidence before the trial judge that an attempt had been made or would be made to nobble the first jury, and that a person had been observed during the swearing of the first jury, in the public gallery, making a written note of the jurors' names. There were further disclosures, made to the judge on oath, and known to us, which remain secret and unknown to the defence. Both prosecuting counsel and the judge felt constrained at the trial to withhold these disclosures from the defence, and the Crown remain concerned that no disclosure should be made, even now, beyond those which have been made.

It is plainly highly desirable that all possible information should be disclosed to the defence, and that all exchanges with the judge should so far as possible take place openly in the presence of the defendant or his representatives. Any ex parte communication between the Crown and the trial judge gives rise to a feeling of unease. Such communications should be kept to a minimum. On the facts of this case, however, we are satisfied that the trial judge was presented with apparently reliable sworn evidence.which obliged him to discharge the first jury, and fully justified his discretionary decision to order a high level of protection for the fresh jury when empanelled. Even if the defence had been told a little more than they were, the judge would have been bound to make these orders, and the defence must surely have inferred that the first jury were thought likely to have been nobbled, even if they knew nothing of the grounds for such belief. While we can understand the concern of the appellant and his advisers, there is nothing in the procedure adopted in relation to jury protection which causes us to consider this conviction unsafe.'

Lord Bingham went on to consider whether the omission to name the jurors in open court rendered the trial a nullity, leaving the court no choice but to quash the conviction. He concluded that such an omission would not render the trial a nullity, unless it violated the legal right of the appellant or made the proceedings unfair to him. Lord Bingham was satisfied that no such violation or unfairness occurred.

Comment

The withholding of the jurors' names as they were being sworn in represented a departure from the usual practice but did not affect rights of challenge because the defence is entitled by s5(2) of the Juries Act 1974 to reasonable facilities for inspecting the panel from which the jurors who tried him were or would be drawn. Names of jurors could therefore be ascertained by the defence in this manner for the purpose of deciding whether to make any challenge. The departure from the usual practice of reading out the names of the jurors in open court therefore did not infringe the rights of the defence and was a necessary device to thwart the intentions of those seeking to

nobble a jury. The risk that jurors in such a procedure might draw adverse inferences against the defence was offset by the courts' practice in such cases to warn the jury not to hold it against the defendant that protective measures had been taken. (The trial judge had given such a warning to the jury in the present case.)

R* v *Ford [1989] 3 WLR 762 Court of Appeal (Lane LCJ, Rose J and Sir Bernard Caulfield)

- *Entitled to a multiracial jury?*

Facts

A black man was convicted of driving a conveyance taken without authority and reckless driving. At his trial, the Crown Court judge had declined to accede to an application for a multiracial jury: he appealed against conviction, inter alia, on that ground.

Held

The trial judge had been right to refuse this application, although the man's appeal would be allowed on other grounds.

Lane LCJ:

> 'The most common cases in which this question has arisen have involved questions of ethnic groups where it has been suggested that the jury should consist partly or wholly of members of that same ethnic group. Those applications provide particular difficulty for the judge and the present case is a very good example. They arise without warning and are usually argued without any reference to authority, as indeed was very largely the case in the present instance …
>
> It has never been suggested that the judge has a discretion to discharge a whole panel or part panel on grounds that would not found a valid challenge. Similarly, in the absence of evidence of specific bias, ethnic origins could not found a valid ground for challenge to an individual juror. The alleged discretion of the judge to intervene in the selection of the jury does not therefore fall within any acknowledged category of judicial power or discretion …
>
> Responsibility for the summoning of jurors to attend for service in the Crown Court and the High Court is by statute clearly laid on the Lord Chancellor. That is clear from s2 of the Juries Act 1974 and from s5 … It is not the function of the judge to alter the composition of the panel or to give any directions about the district from which it is to be drawn. The summoning of panels is not a judicial function, but it is specifically conferred by statute on an administrative officer …
>
> It should also be remembered that the mere fact that a juryman is, for instance, of a particular race or holds a particular religious belief cannot be made the basis for a challenge for cause on the grounds of bias or on any other grounds. If therefore a judge were to exercise his discretion to remove a juror on either of these grounds, he would be assuming bias where none was proved. Such a course is not only unjustified in law, but also indeed might be thought to be seriously derogatory of the particular juryman himself. Further, any attempt to influence the composition of the jury on these grounds would conflict with the requirement that the jury to try an issue before a court shall be selected by ballot in open court from the panel as summoned (see the Juries Act 1974 s11) …
>
> The conclusion is that, however well intentioned the judge's motive might be, the judge has no power to influence the composition of the jury, and that it is wrong for him to attempt to do so. If it should ever become desirable that the principle of random selection should be altered, that will have to be done by way of statute and cannot be done by any judicial decision.
>
> We wish to make two final further points. It appears to have been suggested in some of the cases that there is a "principle" that a jury should be racially balanced … No authority is cited by those who have argued for the existence of the principle. In our judgment such a principle cannot be correct, for it would depend on an underlying premise that jurors of a particular racial

origin or holding particular religious beliefs are incapable of giving an impartial verdict in accordance with the evidence.

Secondly, the principles we have already set out apply not only where it is argued that a jury of a particular composition ought to be empanelled because of the nature of the particular case or particular defendants, but also where complaint is made that the panel was not truly "random", for instance that the population of a particular area contained 20 per cent of persons of West Indian origin but that only a much lower percentage of such persons was to be found on the panel. For the judge to entertain any such application would equally involve his seeking to investigate the composition of the panel in a manner which, for reason already indicated, lies outside his jurisdiction, and lies within the jurisdiction of the Lord Chancellor.'

Comment

An important decision which reaffirms the principle that random selection is the basis for producing a fair and impartial jury. However, this view was not shared by members of the Royal Commission on Criminal Justice (1993) Cmnd 2263, who recommended that trial judges ought to have discretion to ensure that a jury panel is composed of at least three members of the same ethnic minority background as the defendant in order to ensure public confidence in the impartial administration of justice.

This suggestion has not been implemented by statute.

R* v *Gough [1993] 2 WLR 883 House of Lords (Lords Goff of Chieveley, Ackner, Mustill, Slynn of Hadley and Woolf)

- *Apparent bias – test*

Facts

The appellant and his brother had been charged with robbery, but the brother had been discharged at the committal stage and the appellant indicted for allegedly conspiring with his brother to commit robbery. At the trial, one of the jurors was the brother's next door neighbour, but she had not connected him with the proceedings until he shouted out in court after the appellant's conviction. The Court of Appeal dismissed the appellant's appeal against conviction, believing that there had been no danger that the appellant might not have had a fair trial.

Held

The Court of Appeal had applied the correct test and, on the facts, the appeal would be dismissed.

Lord Goff of Chieveley:

> 'I wish to express my understanding of the law as follows. I think it possible, and desirable, that the same test should be applicable in all cases of apparent bias, whether concerned with justices or members of other inferior tribunals, or with jurors, or with arbitrators. Likewise, I consider that, in cases concerned with jurors, the same test should be applied by a judge to whose attention the possibility of bias on the part of a juror has been drawn in the course of a trial, and by the Court of Appeal when it considers such a question on appeal. Furthermore, I think it unnecessary, in formulating the appropriate test, to require that the court should look at the matter through the eyes of a reasonable man, because the court in cases such as these personifies the reasonable man; and in any event the court has first to ascertain the relevant circumstances from the available evidence, knowledge of which would not necessarily be available to an observer in court at the relevant time. Finally, for the avoidance of doubt, I prefer to state the test in terms of real danger rather than real likelihood, to ensure that the court is thinking in terms of possibility rather than probability of bias. Accordingly, having ascertained the relevant circumstances, the court should ask itself whether, having regard to those circumstances, there was a real danger of bias on the part of the relevant member of the tribunal in question, in the

sense that he might unfairly regard (or have unfairly regarded) with favour, or disfavour, the case of a party to the issue under consideration by him; though, in a case concerned with bias on the part of a magistrates' clerk, the court should go on to consider whether the clerk has been invited to give the magistrates advice and, if so, whether it should infer that there was a real danger of the clerk's bias having infected the views of the magistrates adversely to the applicant.'

Comment

The leading authority on the test used for establishing apparent bias. Prior to the decision there had been two tests arising from conflicting lines of authority – the 'reasonable suspicion' of bias test and the 'real likelihood' of bias test. The House of Lords in this case suggested that the 'real likelihood' test was to be preferred but should be reformulated as the 'real danger of bias' test. This test appears to place a heavier burden on the person complaining of bias than the 'reasonable suspicion' test and hence the decision might be regarded as undermining previous safeguards designed to protect the citizen from apparently unfair procedures.

R* v *Mason [1981] QB 881 Court of Appeal (Lawton LJ, Davies and Balcombe JJ)

- *Jury vetting*

Facts

Mason was convicted at Northampton Crown Court on counts of burglary and handling stolen goods. He made application for leave to appeal against his conviction. His main ground of appeal was that before his trial the police in Northamptonshire had vetted the names of those summoned to attend the Crown Court to form a jury panel against criminal records kept locally. They had supplied prosecuting counsel with particulars of the convictions of those on the panel which he had used for the purpose of asking some members of the panel, having convictions but not disqualified by those convictions from serving, whose names were called to serve on the jury to stand by for the Crown. It was alleged that this was in breach of the guidelines issues by the Attorney-General.

Held

The application would be dismissed. Some scrutiny of jury panels was necessary if disqualified persons were to be excluded from sitting on juries.

Lawton LJ:

'... The facts which have been revealed show that some scrutiny of jury panels is necessary if disqualified persons are to be excluded from juries. The police are the only authority able to do this. Since it is a criminal offence for the person to serve on a jury knowing that he is disqualified, for the police to scrutinise the list of potential jurors to see if any are disqualified is to do no more than to perform their usual function of preventing the commission of offences. In the course of looking at criminal records convictions are likely to be revealed which do not amount to disqualifications. We can see no reason why information about such convictions should not be passed on to prosecuting counsel. He may consider that a juror with a conviction for burglary would be unsuitable to sit on a jury trying a burglar; and if he does so he can exercise the Crown's rights. Many persons, but not burglars, would probably think that he should.

The practice of supplying prosecuting counsel with information about potential jurors' convictions has been followed during the whole of our professional lives, and almost certainly for generations before us. It is not unlawful, and has not until recently been thought to be unsatisfactory. We have not been concerned in any way with, and make no comment on, the giving to prosecution counsel of information other than that relating to convictions, or with the desirability of making other inquiries about

members of a jury panel. In so far as the obiter dicta of this court in *R* v *Crown Court at Sheffield, ex parte Brownlow* [1980] 2 All ER 444 at 453, [1980] 2 WLR 892 at 900 differ from what we have decided in this case we justify our presumption by the knowledge that we have been able to examine the issues raised in greater depth than our brethren were able to do.'

Comment

This case decided that jury-vetting practices were lawful and sometimes necessary in the public interest. Lawton LJ's judgment points out that earlier judicial views suggesting that jury-vetting might be unconstitutional – see *R* v *Sheffield Crown Court, ex parte Brownlow* (1980) (below) – had been expressed without the aid of detailed research and proper reflection.

R* v *Obellim [1997] 1 Cr App R 355 Court of Appeal (Criminal Division) (Stuart-Smith LJ, Buckley J and Judge Hyam)

• *Effects of notes from the jury – whether judge can order security check on jury during course of trial*

Facts

During a criminal trial the judge received a note from the jury which led him to suspect that one of the jurors had a lot of knowledge about police powers and might be disqualified because of previous convictions. The judge ordered a security check on the jury. The defence counsel was unaware of the incident until the jury returned their verdicts of guilty when they handed the judge another note complaining about the security check. The judge apologised to the jury for ordering the check. The appeals were based on the ground of material irregularity under the Criminal Appeal Act 1968.

Held

Appeals allowed and convictions quashed.

Stuart-Smith LJ said that jury notes were from the whole jury and that it was not appropriate for a trial judge to make inquiries as to which juror had been mainly responsible for writing the note. It was also questionable whether the judge in this case should have ordered a security check and in any event he should not have done so without letting defence counsel know about it. Consequently there had been a material irregularity because there was a real danger that the defence case had been prejudiced for the following reasons:

1. the juror subjected to the investigation might have been reluctant to ask further questions or express his opinion further;
2. other jurors might have treated any views expressed by that juror with suspicion once they knew that he was being investigated;
3. the other jurors might have been afraid to ask questions of the trial judge once it was known that a security investigation might result from such active participation in the trial;
4. the homogeneous nature of the jury was adversely affected by one juror being singled out in that way, and
5. the jury might have assumed that defence counsel had condoned the security check.

Comment

A sensible decision protecting the jury from improper pressure from the trial judge.

R* v *Oliver (1995) The Times 6 December Court of Appeal (Criminal Division) (Roch LJ, Douglas Brown and Blofeld JJ)

• *Guidance on directions to be given to juries who are to allowed to separate before reaching their verdicts: effects of s43 of the Criminal Justice and Public Order Act 1994*

Facts
Blofeld J said that the grounds of appeal were in no way concerned with the facts of the case but were entirely concentrated on matters connected with the jury, which in this case had been allowed to separate after being sent out to consider its verdict.

Held
Appeal against conviction dismissed. Blofeld J said that nothing had happened to give rise to a successful ground of appeal, but that since the power to allow a jury to separate during consideration of its verdict was a new one, the following guideance should be given on how to direct a jury prior to such a separation:

1 That the jury must decide the case on the evidence and the arguments that they had seen and heard in court and not on anything they might have seen or heard or that they might see or hear outside the court.
2 That the evidence had been completed and that it would be wrong for any juror to seek for or to receive further evidence or information of any sort about the case.
3 That the jury must not talk to anyone about the case save to the other members of the jury and then only when they are deliberating in the jury room.

   They must not allow anyone to talk to them about that case unless that person was a juror and he or she was in the jury room deliberating about the case.
4 That when they left court they should try to set the case they were trying on one side until they returned to court and retired to their jury room to continue the process of deliberating about their verdict or verdicts.

Blofeld J also said that it was not necessary for the judge to use any precise form of words provided the matters set out above were properly covered in whatever words he chose to use, and that it would be desirable for that direction to be given in full on the first dispersal by the jury and for a brief reminder to be given at each subsequent dispersal.

There might be particular circumstances in a particular case when it would be appropriate for a judge to give further directions.

Roch LJ and Douglas Brown J agreed.

Comment
A useful case setting out the conditions on which a jury may be permitted to separate after retiring to consider its verdict. The power to permit a jury to separate in this situation was granted by s43 of the Criminal Justice and Public Order Act 1994 and this case was the first one to interpret the implications of the new power.

R* v *Sheffield Crown Court, ex parte Brownlow [1980] 1 WLR 892 Court of Appeal (Lord Denning MR, Shaw and Brandon LJJ)

- *Jury vetting*

Facts
Two police officers had been committed for trial by jury on assault charges. The defence solicitors made application to the county prosecuting solicitors asking for an investigation into the records of all those persons in the panel from whom the jury could be drawn. The defence wished to know if any prospective jury members had previous convictions. The prosecuting solicitors refused. The defence therefore made application to the trial judge who made an order that the chief constable should carry out such an investigation.

The Chief Constable applied for certiorari for the judge's order to be quashed but the Divisional Court held that it had no jurisdiction to review the trial judge's order. The Chief Constable then appealed to the Court of Appeal. Section 10(5) of the Courts Act 1971 made an important exception to the general rule that the High Court can review the decisions of Crown Court judges, by exempting 'matters relating to trial on indictment.'

Held (the Master of the Rolls dissenting)
The order of the trial judge was a 'matter relat-

ing to trial on indictment' and therefore could not be reviewed by the High Court, therefore the court had no jurisdiction. The appeal would be dismissed.

Important obiter comments were made by the Court of Appeal concerning jury vetting.

Lord Denning MR:

> 'To my mind it is unconstitutional for the police authorities to engage in "jury vetting". So long as a person is eligible for jury service, and is not disqualified, I cannot think it right that, behind his back, the police should go through his record so as to enable him to be asked to "stand by for the Crown", or to be challenged by the defence. If this sort of thing is to be allowed, what comes of a man's right of privacy? He is bound to serve on a jury when summoned. Is he thereby liable to have his past record raked up against him – and presented on a plate to prosecuting and defending lawyers – who may use it to keep him out of the jury – and, who knows, it may become known to his neighbours and those about him?'

Comment

Shaw LJ shared the opinion of the Master of the Rolls that jury vetting was unconstitutional and thought the use of a special knowledge given by facilities for access to criminal records enabling the prosecution to ask for a 'standby' in respect of anyone on a jury panel who appeared unsuitable to act as a juror would be an abuse as contrary to the tenor and principle of jury service.

> 'Juries must not be exposed to prodding and probing if they were to discharge their duties fearlessly and impartially.'

He added that it was conceivable that in 'very special cases' it may be in the public interest to allow jury vetting but it should then require express permission from the Attorney-General.

Brandon LJ expressed 'serious doubts' about whether there should be any jury vetting, and opined that if it were to be permitted by the prosecution in certain cases it should be permitted in the same circumstances by the defence.

However it appears that all three judges in the Court of Appeal were wrong in these views, which were apparently expressed without the aid of detailed research and studied reflection: see the comments of Lawton LJ in *R* v *Mason* [1981] QB 881 (above).

R* v *Thompson [1962] 1 All ER 65 Court of Appeal (Parker LCJ, Slade and Widgery LJJ)

- *The secrecy of the jury room*

Facts

The appellant was convicted of offences by a jury quite late in the day and the sentence was to be pronounced the following day. Before this a member of the public was informed by a juror that all of the jurors were in favour of acquitting the appellant until the foreman produced to them a list of his previous convictions. They then agreed to convict him. The application before the Court of Appeal was limited to a ruling as to whether there was jurisdiction to enquire into what had occurred in the jury room.

Held

There was no jurisdiction and the appeal would therefore be dismissed. The court emphasised the need to preserve secrecy in the jury room. Parker LCJ quoted the view of Atkin LJ in *Ellis* v *Deheer* [1922] All ER Rep at 454:

> 'The court does not entertain or admit evidence by a juryman of what took place in the jury room either by way of explaining the grounds on which the jury arrived at their conclusion or by way of a statement as to what he believes its effect to be. The reason why that evidence is not admitted is both in order to secure the finality of decisions of fact arrived at by a jury, and also, which is a matter of of great importance, for the protection of jurymen themselves to

prevent their being exposed to pressure that might otherwise be put on them with a view to explaining the reasons which activated them individually in arriving at their verdict. To my mind, it is a principle which is of the very highest importance in the interests of justice to maintain, and an infringement of the rule appears to me to be a very serious interference with the administration of justice.'

Comment

The case remains the leading common authority on the secrecy of the jury room. Note that the case can be distinguished if the jury's deliberations occur outside the jury room: *R* v *Young* [1995] 2 WLR 430 (CA).

Racz v *Home Office* [1994] 2 WLR 23 House of Lords (Lords Templeman, Goff of Chieveley, Jauncey of Tullichettle, Browne-Wilkinson and Mustill)

- *Trial by jury – court's discretion*

Facts

The plaintiff remand prisoner claimed damages for misfeasance in public office in respect of the period for which he had been held – allegedly without justification – in a strip cell. Was he entitled to trial by jury?

Held

On the facts, the Court of Appeal had properly exercised its jurisdiction to refuse a jury trial and his appeal against that decision would therefore be dismissed.

Lord Jauncey of Tullichettle:

'[Counsel for the plaintiff], while accepting that s69(3) [of the Supreme Court Act 1981] created a presumption against jury trial, argued that issues, including the question of exemplary damages which were likely to arise when this case went to trial, were so closely related to those which would arise in a case of false imprisonment, where a right to jury trial existed, that the above presumption should be rebutted and discretion exercised in favour of allowing a jury trial. He went on to submit that the Court of Appeal had failed in exercising their discretion adequately to take into account: (1) the above-mentioned close relationship, (2) that this was a case of the individual against the state and (3) that exemplary damages were sought which were more appropriately assessed by a jury.

My Lords, if there were any discernible connection between all four types of tort enumerated in s69(1) there might be some force in the above argument as to close relationship. However, that is not the case. I can see no logical connection between, say, libel and false imprisonment, nor common factor in slander and malicious prosecution. Each tort is capable of being committed by a private individual or by an official of the state, and all in very different circumstances. One is left with a strong impression that Parliament has retained these four torts for historical rather than for any logical reason, from which it follows that the similarity to any of these of some other tort is not a factor which must be taken into account by the court in determining, in the exercise of its discretion, whether it is appropriate to rebut the presumption against jury trial created by s69(3) …

I do not think that there is any justification for criticising the manner in which the Court of Appeal as a whole exercised its jurisdiction … Had it been necessary for this House to exercise its discretion afresh as to the mode of trial, I should have had no hesitation in coming to the conclusion which was reached by the Court of Appeal. I would only add that the apparent uncertainty as to the precise ambit of the tort of misfeasance in public office, with the consequent likelihood of prolonged legal argument in the absence of the jury, would have been a further factor militating against trial by jury.'

Comment

A decision illustrating the general reluctance

of judges to order trial by a civil jury. The power to order such a trial is usually reserved for the four torts listed in s69(1) of the Supreme Court Act 1981 (fraud, defamation, malicious prosecution and false imprisonment), and this decision shows that the similarity of some other tort to any of the listed torts is not a factor to be taken into account when exercising the discretion to order a civil jury.

Rantzen v *Mirror Group Newspapers* [1993] 3 WLR 953 Court of Appeal (Neill, Staughton and Roch LJJ)

• *Defamation – damages – reduction on appeal*

Facts

In an action for libel, the jury awarded the plaintiff television presenter £250,000 by way of damages. The defendant newspaper appealed, inter alia, pursuant to s8 of the Courts and Legal Services Act 1990 and RSC O.59 r11(4), contending that the damages were excessive.

Held

The appeal would be allowed and an award of £110,000 substituted for the jury's award.

Neill LJ:

> 'How then should the Court of Appeal interpret its power to order a new trial on the ground that the damages awarded by the jury were excessive? How is the word "excessive" in s8(1) of the 1990 Act to be interpreted?
>
> After careful consideration we have come to the conclusion that we must interpret our power so as to give proper weight to the guidance given by the House of Lords and by the court in Strasbourg. In particular we should take account of the following passage in Lord Goff's speech in *A-G* v *Guardian Newspapers Ltd (No 2)* [1990] 1 AC 109 at 283–284:
>
> > "The exercise of the right to freedom of expression under art 10 [of the Convention for the Protection of Human Rights and Fundamental Freedoms] may be subject to restrictions (as are prescribed by law and are necessary in a democratic society) in relation to certain prescribed matters which include 'the interests of national security' and 'preventing the disclosure of information received in confidence'. It is established in the jurisprudence of the European Court of Human Rights that the word 'necessary' in this context implies the existence of a pressing social need, and that interference with freedom of expression should be no more than is proportionate to the legitimate aim pursued. I have no reason to believe that English law, as applied in the courts, leads to any different conclusion."
>
> If one applies these words it seems to us that the grant of an almost limitless discretion to a jury fails to provide a satisfactory measurement for deciding what is "necessary in a democratic society" or "justified by a pressing social need". We consider therefore that the common law if properly understood requires the courts to subject large awards of damages to a more searching scrutiny than has been customary in the past. It follows that what has been regarded as the barrier against intervention should be lowered. The question becomes: could a reasonable jury have thought that this award was necessary to compensate the plaintiff and to re-establish his reputation? …
>
> We return to the facts of the present case. A very substantial award was clearly justified … The jury were entitled to conclude that the publication of the article and its aftermath were a terrible ordeal for Miss Rantzen. But, as has been pointed out, Miss Rantzen still has an extremely successful career as a television presenter. She is a distinguished and highly respected figure in the world of broadcasting … We have therefore been driven to the conclusion that the court has power to, and should, intervene. Judged by any objective standards of reasonable compensation or necessity or proportional-

ity the award of £250,000 was excessive. We therefore propose to exercise our powers under s8(2) of the 1990 Act and O.59 r11(4) and substitute the sum of £110,000.'

Comment

One of the first cases to be use the power granted to the Court of Appeal (Civil Division) to quash an 'excessive' award of compensation and to substitute a new award. The power is contained in s8 of the Courts and Legal Services Act 1990 and may be used to order a new trial if the Court of Appeal prefers to do so. The decision is an illustration of what the appeal judges regarded as an 'excessive' award, though it should be noted that they also have power to increase an award regarded as 'inadequate' (or to order a new trial).

Sim v *Stretch* [1936] 2 All ER 1237 House of Lords (Lords Atkin, Russell and Macmillan)

- *The jury as 'right-thinking members of society'*

Facts

The plaintiff's housemaid went to work for the defendant. The defendant sent a telegram to the plaintiff containing the following message: 'Edith has resumed her service with us today. Please send her possessions and the money you borrowed, also her wages to Old Barton – Sim'. The plaintiff claimed damages for libel, alleging that these words were defamatory, implying that the plaintiff was in financial difficulties, had been forced to borrow money from his housemaid, had been unable to pay her wages and was uncreditworthy.

Held

There had been no libel since the words were not reasonably capable of a defamatory meaning.

Lord Atkin:

> 'The question, then, is whether the words in their ordinary signification are capable of being defamatory. Judges and textbook writers alike have found difficulty in defining with precision the word "defamatory". The conventional phrase exposing the plaintiff to hatred, ridicule and contempt is probably too narrow. The question is complicated by having to consider the person or class of persons whose reaction to the publication is the test of the wrongful character of the words used. I do not intend to ask your Lordships to lay down a formal definition, but after collating the opinions of many authorities I propose in the present case the test: would the words tend to lower the plaintiff in the estimation of right-thinking members of society generally? Assuming such to be the test of whether words are defamatory or not there is no dispute as to the relative functions of judge and jury, of law and fact. It is well settled that the judge must decide whether the words are capable of a defamatory meaning. That is a question of law: is there evidence of a tort? If they are capable, then the jury is to decide whether they are in fact defamatory.'

Comment

The decision is based on the assumption that members of a jury will be 'right-thinking members of society'. That view, taken by Law Lords in 1936 at a time when property qualifications determined the right to serve on a jury, might not be shared by senior judges today. Note Lord Denning's views as to the need for interviews and character references in order to check on the 'responsibility' of potential jurors: *What Next in the Law?* (1982) pp70–78.

Thompson* v *Commissioner of Police of the Metropolis [1997] 2 All ER 762 Court of Appeal (Civil Division) (Lord Woolf MR, Auld LJ and Sir Brian Neill)

• *Civil actions against police for false imprisonment, assault and malicious prosecution – directions to be given to the jury as to how to assess compensatory and exemplary damages*

Facts

In successful civil actions against the police for unlawful conduct juries awarded sums representing compensatory and exemplary damages. The Commissioner appealed against the awards.

Held

When assessing damages awarded to members of the public for unlawful conduct against them by the police, juries should in future be given guidance by the trial judge as to the amount of compensatory damages regarded as appropriate in personal injury cases for particular injuries, and the figure which the trial judge considered it would be appropriate to award in the circumstances of the case. When assessing exemplary damages, juries should be told that such damages ought not to be less than £5,000 and might be as much as £25,000, with an absolute maximum of £50,000 in cases where officers of at least the rank of superintendent had been directly involved in the misconduct.

Lord Woolf MR:

> 'The appeals were test cases brought because of the size of some awards being made by juries in cases against the police. The court has provided guidance as to directions which in future should be given by judges to juries which should produce greater consistency and certainty as to awards and, in particular, avoid the award of excessive sums to plaintiffs as exemplary damages which are awarded as a civil punishment.'

Comment

The decision may be seen as a logical extension of the principle permitting judicial guidance to juries in personal injury cases, since actions against the police for misconduct usually contain a personal injury element. However, the real problem facing the Court of Appeal was the need to curb huge awards of exemplary damages, and the new guidance on this matter may be seen as an application of the policy followed in the defamation case of *John* v *MGN Ltd* (1996) (above). In that case trial judges were permitted for the first time to give detailed guidance to civil juries in assessing compensation for defamation. It was hoped that such guidance would end the tendency towards excessive awards. A similar hope was expressed in the present case in regard to the new guidance on exemplary damages.

Ward* v *James [1966] 1 QB 273 Court of Appeal (Lord Denning MR, Sellers, Pearson, Davies and Diplock LJJ)

• *Civil juries – personal injury cases – value of jury system*

Facts

In May 1962, the plaintiff was being driven in a car by the defendant in Germany. There was an accident in which the plaintiff was very seriously injured, becoming a permanent quadriplegic. In December 1962, he brought an action against the defendant for damages for negligence; the question in the action was substantially what damages the plaintiff should be awarded.

On the plaintiff's application, trial by jury was ordered by the master on 23 July 1963, an appeal to the judge being dismissed on 30 July 1963. The defendant appealed against the dismissal to the Court of Appeal.

Held

Appeal dismissed. Although trial by jury was ordered in this case, the Court of Appeal went on to make observations strongly discouraging the use of civil juries.

Lord Denning MR:

> 'Let it not be supposed that this court is in any way opposed to trial by jury. It has been the bulwark of our liberties too long for any of us to seek to alter it. Whenever a man is on trial for serious crime, or when in a civil case a man's honour or integrity is at stake, or when one or other party must be deliberately lying, then trial by jury has no equal. But in personal injury cases trial by jury has given place of late to trial by judge alone, the reason being simply this, that in these cases trial by judge alone is more acceptable to the great majority of people.
>
> Rarely in these cases does a party ask for a jury. When a solicitor gives advice it runs in this way: If I were you I should not ask for a jury. I should have a judge alone. You know where you stand with a judge and if he goes wrong you can always go to a Court of Appeal. But as for a jury you never know what they will do and if they go wrong there is no putting them right. The Court of Appeal hardly ever interferes with the verdict of the jury. So the client decides on judge alone. That is why trials have declined. It is because they are not asked for.'

Comment

Lord Denning's judgment caused some controversy since it appeared that judicial policy was undermining the traditional safeguard of jury trial. However, the policy has been consistently applied ever since so that civil juries are extremely rare today: see *H* v *Ministry of Defence* (1991) (above).

8 Civil Procedure

Afzal and Others* v *Ford Motor Co Ltd and Other Appeals [1994] 4 All ER 720 Court of Appeal (Civil Division) (Neill, Beldam and Steyn LJJ)

• *Automatic references to small claims arbitration*

Facts

(*Note*: At the time of this case the small claims jurisdiction was limited to £1,000. From 8 January 1996 it has been limited to £3,000.)

The plaintiff employees had brought a number of actions against their various employers, claiming personal injury in the workplace. In most cases the claims did not exceed £1,000 and these were automatically referred for arbitration by the district judge. In sixteen of the claims the plaintiff employees sought for the reference to arbitration to be rescinded, arguing that the issues of employers' liability for personal injury were too complex for this method of resolution and that, since there was a limit on the costs recoverable in arbitrated claims, their trade union would be deterred from assisting them, thereby putting them at a serious disadvantage in negotiating compensation settlements out of court. The judge granted the applications and the defendant employer appealed.

In three other claims the plaintiff employees had sought to avoid the automatic reference to arbitration by overstating their claim (at £3,000), even though there was no reasonable prospect of recovering such a sum. In these cases, heard in court in the usual way, the trial judge held that they should have been dealt with by arbitration and awarded only those costs appropriate to an arbitration. The employees appealed against this award for costs.

Held

1 The motor company's appeals would be allowed and the cases would be remitted for individual consideration by the district judge under the arbitration procedure; and
2 the intentional overstatement of the amount involved in a claim in order to avoid automatic arbitration was a clear misuse of process, and although it was possible to penalise parties in terms of costs after an ordinary trial the preferable course was to remit individual cases to the district judge for consideration. To that extent the employees' appeals against the awards of costs would be allowed and the cases would be remitted for individual consideration by the district judge as to whether to order the arbitration procedure

Beldam LJ:

> 'We have no doubt that the judge was wrong to approach small employers' liability claims as a class of case which it was unreasonable to allow to proceed at arbitration. When he said that he did not think that in any of the cases "the facts are now so simple or straightforward that they should be dealt with by way of arbitration", he may have been misled by the elaboration introduced by the traditional pleadings which had been filed on both sides. If he had concentrated on an underlying assertion to be found in virtually every case that the employer had exposed the employee to a risk of injury of which he knew or ought to have known, the cases might well have appeared less complex.
>
> Court-based small claims arbitration is intended to be a greatly simplified proce-

dure for determining claims. The district judge remains an adjudicator and the process adversarial but, as the code makes clear, the aim of the procedure is to get away from the rigid rituals which characterise ordinary litigation and which have dictated the arguments of the parties in the appeals. The following points seem to us significant in interpreting the rules.

(1) The district judge cannot rescind an automatic reference to arbitration under Ord 19, r3(1) merely because a question of law is involved or the facts are complex. ...

(2) The law applicable in employers' liability claims is often straightforward. ...

(3) The hardship of an employee representing himself against his legally represented employer is a hardship likely to be faced in all cases where the means of the parties are unequal. ...

(4) ... cases which need a degree of expert understanding will be subject to compulsory arbitration. ...

For these reasons, we consider the judgment of Judge Paynter Reece rescinding arbitration in the 16 cases cannot be supported ...

... In our judgement they should be remitted for individual consideration by the district judge.'

On the appeal by the employees against the award of costs and on the issue of misuse of process, Beldam LJ said:

'Mr Burke QC for the employees stoutly resisted the suggestion that it was a misuse of the procedure in the County Court Rules to place a value, for example £3,000 on the sum claimed as damages to avoid the consequences of automatic reference to arbitration. He submitted that in so doing a plaintiff's advisers were seeking to obtain no more than a legitimate juridical advantage. He likened it to forum shopping for the purpose of obtaining a higher award of damages as, for example, was done in *MacShannon* v *Rockware Glass Ltd* [1978] 1 All ER 625, [1978] AC 795. We would reject such an analogy. The intentional overstatement of the amount involved in a claim to avoid a procedure which has been laid down by Parliament and incorporated in rules of the court is in our judgment a clear misuse of process. ...

... we would adopt the following as the most satisfactory formula: "Could the plaintiff reasonably expect to be awarded more than £1,000?" If the plaintiff could not reasonably expect to be awarded more than £1,000, it is a misuse of process to claim damages limited to £3,000. ...

As the rules relating to payment into court do not apply where the amount involved is under £1,000, we see no reason why a defendant faced with an inflated claim should not state in his defence that the claim cannot reasonably exceed £1,000 and should be automatically referred to arbitration. Further, where liability is admitted, the injuries are simple and the medical report is agreed, there is no reason why the defendant should not state his estimate of the amount involved. In small claims arbitration the parties are expected to state their cases informally. One way or another we think that parties seeking to take advantage of the benefits of small claims arbitration could easily overcome the difficulties which appeared of such concern in argument. The question for the district judge would be no more difficult than those he would have to consider if of his own motion or on the application of a party he had to consider whether to order trial in court. An interpretation of the rules cannot be justified which would require every case to proceed to trial and to the award of the judge to decide whether there had been a misuse of the process of the court. ...

... In a case where there is misuse of process the court must be able to ensure that cases which should be automatically referred to arbitration do not go to trial. It seems to us that it is contrary to the intent and purpose of Ord 19 that the district judge should be powerless to prevent a misuse of process.'

Neill and Steyn LJJ agreed.

Comment

An interesting case on the small claims juris-

diction, showing that judges are vigilant to ensure that the jurisdiction is not by-passed by unscrupulous parties who intentionally overstate a claim in order to avoid the automatic reference to arbitration.

American Cynamid Co v *Ethicon Ltd* [1975] AC 396 House of Lords (Viscount Dilhorne, Lords Diplock, Cross, Salmon and Edmund-Davies)

- *Interlocutory injunctions*

Facts

The plaintiff owned a patent relating to design and manufacture of surgical stitches. The defendants were about to market a product which, it was claimed, infringed that patent. The plaintiffs applied for an interlocutory injunction to restrain the launch pending trial of the action.

Held

The injunction should be granted. Leaving aside the complicated scientific evidence which supported and denied the claim, the balance of convenience favoured restraint upon a venture which had not yet been put into effect.

Lord Diplock:

> 'My Lords, when an application for an interlocutory injunction to restrain a defendant from doing acts alleged to be in violation of the plaintiff's legal right is made on contested facts, the decision whether or not to grant an interlocutory injunction has to be taken at a time when ex hypothesi the existence of the right or the violation of it, or both, is uncertain and will remain uncertain until final judgment is given in the action … The object of the interlocutory injunction is to protect the plaintiff against injury by violation of his right for which he could not adequately be compensated in damages recoverable in the action if the uncertainty were resolved in his favour at trial; but the plaintiff's need for such protection must be weighed against the corresponding need of the defendant to be protected against injury resulting from his having been prevented from exercising his own legal rights for which he could not be adequately compensated under the plaintiff's undertaking in damages if the uncertainty were resolved in the defendant's favour at trial. The court must weight one need against another and determine where "balance of convenience" lies …
>
> In those cases where the legal rights of the parties depend on facts that are in dispute between them, the evidence available to the court at the hearing of the application for an interlocutory injunction is incomplete. It is given on affidavit and has not been tested by oral cross-examination …
>
> The court … must be satisfied that the claim is not frivolous or vexatious; in other words, that there is a serious question to be tried. It is no part of the court's function at this stage of the litigation to try to resolve conflicts of evidence on affidavit as to facts on which the claims of either party may ultimately depend nor to decide difficult questions of law which call for detailed argument and mature considerations. These are matters to be dealt with at the trial … So unless the material available to the court at the hearing of the application for an interlocutory injunction fails to disclose that the plaintiff has any real prospect of succeeding in his claim for a permanent injunction at trial, the court should go on to consider whether the balance of convenience lies in favour of granting or refusing the interlocutory relief that is sought.
>
> As to that, the governing principle is that the court should first consider whether if the plaintiff were to succeed at the trial in establishing his right to a permanent injunction he would be adequately compensated by an award of damages for the loss which he would have sustained as a result of the defendant's continuing to do what was sought to be enjoined between the time of the application and the time of the trial. If damages in the measure recoverable at common law would be adequate remedy and the defendant would be in a financial posi-

tion to pay them, no interlocutory injunction should normally be granted, however strong the plaintiff's claim appears to be at that stage. If, on the other hand, damages would not provide an adequate remedy for the plaintiff in the event of his succeeding at the trial, the court should then consider whether, on the contrary hypothesis that the defendant were to succeed at the trial in establishing his right to do that which was sought to be enjoined, he would be adequately compensated under the plaintiff's undertaking as to damages for the loss he would have sustained by being prevented from doing so between the time of the application and the time of the trial. If damages in the measure recoverable under such an undertaking would be an adequate remedy and the plaintiff would be in a financial position to pay them, there would be no reason on this ground to refuse an interlocutory injunction.

It is where there is doubt as to the adequacy of the respective remedies in damages available to either party or to both, that the question of balance of convenience arises. It would be unwise to attempt even to list all the various matters which may need to be taken into consideration in deciding where the balance lies, let alone suggest the relative weight to be attached to them. These will vary from case to case.'

Comment

The leading authority on the granting of interlocutory injunctions. Lord Diplock's judgment sets out the factors comprising the 'balance of convenience' test used to decide whether such an injunction should be issued in a particular case.

Birkett* v *James [1977] 3 WLR 39 House of Lords (Lords Diplock, Simon, Salmon, Edmund-Davies and Russell)

- *Dismissal for want of prosecution*

Facts

In 1972 the plaintiff issued a writ against the defendant for £1 million which he alleged had been repayable in 1970. The defendant denied that he owed the plaintiff any money. The plaintiff took no further action until 1975 (eight months before the limitation period expired) when he gave notice that he intended to proceed. Two months later the defendant applied for an order to dismiss the action for want of prosecution.

Held

The application would not be successful. The power of the court to dismiss an action for want of prosecution should be exercised only where the plaintiff's default had been intentional and contumelious, or where there had been inordinate and inexcusable delay on his or his lawyers' part, giving rise to substantial risk that a fair trial would not be possible or would seriously prejudice the defendant.

Lord Edmund-Davies:

> 'In my judgment, the proper attitude to adopt in relation to a plaintiff's dilatoriness both before and after action brought was accurately dealt with in the following words by Sachs LJ in *Davies* v *Radio Rentals Ltd*, a case where the plaintiff sustained personal injuries in March 1967 and made no complaint or claim before issuing his writ in January 1970:
>
> > "... it can well be said that as regards the past three years ... the Statute of Limitations had not applied and that those three years cannot be taken into account per se against the plaintiff as unnecessary delay ... But ... it has been said time and again in these courts that where a plaintiff leaves to the very last minute the issue of a writ, and particularly when there has been no letter before action either, it is the duty of the plaintiff and his solicitor to use all diligence so as not to allow any unnecessary delay to eventuate which might make for difficulties at the trial owing to witnesses having a lessened memory – and thus to there being an additional

serious impediment to the ascertainment of the truth." '

Comment

The leading authority on the power to dismiss for want of prosecution. The case established that the power can be exercised where delay is intentional and 'contumelious' (ie a stubborn refusal to proceed), or where delay is inordinate, inexcusable and prejudicial to the defence.

Hastie and Jenkerson v *McMahon* [1991] 1 All ER 255 Court of Appeal (Lloyd, Glidewell and Woolf LJJ)

- *Service by fax*

Facts

An order had required that 'The plaintiffs serve on the defendant by 4.30 pm on 19 December 1988 a list of documents …': they had caused a clearly legible list of documents to be transmitted by fax to the defendant's solicitors by 4.10 pm on 19 December 1988. The issue was whether service by fax could be good service.

Held

The plaintiffs had complied with the order: service by fax could be good service, subject to any requirement of the order requiring service of a particular document and any requirement of the Rules of the Supreme Court.

Woolf LJ:

'… Special considerations apply to writs and other documents used for initiating legal proceedings and nothing in this judgment is intended to apply to such documents. However, that class of document apart, are there any legal reasons why advantage should not be taken of the progress in technology which fax represents to enable documents to be served by fax, assuming that this is not contrary to any of the Rules of the Supreme Court?

The purpose of serving a document is to ensure that its contents are available to the recipient and whether the document is served in the conventional way or by fax the result is exactly the same. Counsel on behalf of the defendant submits that what is transmitted by fax is not the document but an electronic message. However, this submission fails to distinguish between the methods of transmission and the result of the transmission by fax. What is produced by the transmission of the message by fax admittedly using the recipient's machine and paper is the document which the other party intended should be served. Counsel for the defendant submits that the service of a document in connection with legal proceedings requires a formal step and the mere production of the document by the recipient's own machine lacks the necessary degree of formality for service of a document in legal proceedings. There can be situations where a certain degree of ceremony is required for service as Mackinnon LJ points out in *Re Sharpley & Manby's Arbitration* [1942] 1 All ER 66 at 68, [1942] 1 KB 217 at 220, as for example under the Sheriff's Court (Scotland) Act 1907, which provides that notices 'may be given', inter alia, 'by a messenger at arms'. However, in the ordinary case, in order to comply with an order as was made by Master Hodgson in this case, I can see no reason why there should be any need for ceremony. What is required is that a legible copy of the document should be in the possession of the party to be served. This transmission by fax achieves. I therefore conclude that service by fax can be good service subject to any requirement of the order requiring service of a particular document, and any requirement of the Rules of the Supreme Court. …

The problem from the point of view of parties using fax as a means of service other than by agreement is that it may be difficult for a party to prove that a legible copy of the document has in fact been printed at the recipient's premises. As to this … clearly unless and until there is a special provision contained in the Rules of the Supreme Court expressly authorising service by fax a party

to legal proceedings will be taking a considerable risk in relying on service by fax unless there is consent to this form of service.'

Comment

A sensible decision recognising the practicability of using fax as a method of service (other than for service of the writ).

Joyce v *Liverpool City Council*

[1995] 3 All ER 110 Court of Appeal (Civil Division) (Sir Thomas Bingham MR, Hirst and Aldous LJJ)

• *Automatic references to small claims arbitration: claims for specific performance and injunctions against landlords in respect of breach of repairing covenants*

Facts

The plaintiff had brought an action against the defendant local authority for damages and an order for specific performance in relation to the authority's statutory housing repair obligations. The action was heard in ordinary county court proceedings. The plaintiff succeeded but was awarded only fixed costs on the ground that the action should have been heard in arbitration under the small claims jurisdiction. The plaintiff appealed against the costs order to the Court of Appeal.

Held

Appeal would be dismissed. The district judge had power to award remedies of specific performance and/or injunction in housing disputes heard under the small claims procedure and therefore references to arbitration were appropriate. The order for costs reflected that position.

Sir Thomas Bingham MR:

> '... A circuit judge, acting within his jurisdiction and subject to express exceptions not here relevant, may exercise all the powers of a High Court judge. These include the power to grant both interlocutory and final injunctions (other than Anton Piller orders and Mareva injunctions) whether or not any claim is made to money or any other relief within the jurisdiction of the county court ... He may do so at any stage of the proceedings ... The district judge, acting within his jurisdiction under the 1984 Act or any other Act or the rules, has all the powers of a judge ... His power to grant injunctions before or after the hearing in proceeding which he has jurisdiction to determine under Ord 21, r5 "or otherwise" is confirmed by Ord 13, r6(2). The expression "or otherwise" must cover proceedings automatically referred for arbitration by the district judge, since these undoubtedly are proceedings which the district judge has power to hear and determine and these are also proceedings which the district judge is authorised to hear and determine under the 1984 Act and the rules. Save that there is, under the general law, no power to make a declaration or, probably, order specific performance as an interlocutory remedy, what is true of an injunction is true of these other remedies. It makes no difference that the small claims procedure conducted by the district judge is, in our view ineptly, described as arbitration: he remains a salaried judicial officer throughout; his powers and procedures are governed by the 1984 Act and the rules; his award takes effect as a judgment (s64(3) of the 1984 Act); the hearing is in practice conducted at and in the name of the county court.
>
> We are in complete and respectful agreement with the decisions of the judges below on this jurisdictional question ...'

Comment

A decision which illustrates the usefulness of the small claims procedure. However, whilst the district judge has the power to award the remedies of specific performance and/or injunction it should be noted that difficulties of enforcement of such awards have been encountered by those using the small claims court.

Restick v *Crickmore* [1994] 1 WLR 420 Court of Appeal (Butler-Sloss, Stuart-Smith LJJ and Sir Tasker Watkins)

• *Proceedings wrongly commenced in High Court*

Facts

Five personal injury claims were wrongly commenced in the High Court and, in each case, the judge struck them out under s40 of the County Courts Act 1984. The plaintiffs appealed.

Held

The appeals would be allowed.

Stuart-Smith LJ:

'Once the conditions set out in the opening words of s40(1) are fulfilled, the court is required to do one of two things, to transfer the proceedings to the county court or strike it out. It plainly has a choice between the two courses of action. For my part, I cannot see that the use of the word "shall", positioned where it is, requires the court to adopt one course rather than the other, simply because the necessary precondition for exercising choice (b) is also fulfilled. What the court cannot do is retain the action in the High Court. In this respect the discretion is different from that in sub-s (2), where the court has a discretion whether to retain or transfer the action. In my judgment, the meaning of the section is plain and not ambiguous. The court is required to make a choice between the two alternatives, but it can only strike out if the additional condition is satisfied, namely that the person bringing the proceedings knew, or ought to have known, of the requirement. But otherwise the choice or discretion is unfettered ...

The construction I prefer accords with the well-established policy of the courts, which is this: provided proceedings are started within the time permitted by the statute of limitations, are not frivolous, vexatious or an abuse of the process of the court and disclose a cause of action, they will not as a rule be struck out because of some mistake in procedure on the part of the plaintiff or his advisers. Save where there has been a contumelious disobedience of the court's order, the draconian sanction of striking out an otherwise properly constituted action, simply to punish the party who has failed to comply with the rules of court, is not part of the court's function. No injustice is involved to the defendant in transferring an action which has been started in the wrong court to the correct court.

The ordinary sanction for failure to comply with the requirements will be in costs. Moreover, the Supreme Court Act 1981, s51, as amended by the 1990 Act, deals with costs in the High Court and county courts. Subsections (6) and (7) provide for wasted costs awards to be given against legal advisers in respect of costs incurred as a result of their improper, unreasonable or negligent acts or omissions ...

It may be asked in what circumstances should the court exercise the power to strike out? I would be reluctant to attempt to lay down any guidelines which might be thought to fetter the undoubted discretion of the judge. Where the action should plainly have been started in the county court, and the failure to do so was not due to a bona fide mistake, but can be seen as an attempt to harass a defendant, deliberately run up unnecessary costs, be taken in defiance of a warning of the defendants as to the proper venue or where a party, or more likely his solicitor, persistently starts actions in the wrong court, it may well be desirable for the court to apply the more draconian order of striking out. These are merely examples and are not intended to be an exhaustive list. It may also be in a particularly blatant case where the value of the plaintiff's claim is so obviously of a very low order the action should be struck out if there are no extenuating circumstances.

Since none of the judges in these cases considered that they had any discretion to transfer, it is necessary for this court to exercise the discretion. In all the cases I am sat-

isfied that the two conditions in s40(1) are satisfied.'

Comment

The case confirms the general policy of courts of not striking out proceedings commenced in the wrong court because of some mistake in procedure on the part of the plaintiff or his/her advisers. The ordinary sanction for such a mistake is a reduction in costs.

Ridehalgh v *Horsefield* [1994] 3 WLR 462 Court of Appeal (Sir Thomas Bingham MR, Rose and Waite LJJ)

- *Wasted costs order – where appropriate*

Facts

At the conclusion of four actions the judge in each case made an order under s51(6) of the Supreme Court Act 1981 (as substituted by s4 of the Courts and Legal Services Act 1990) against the other side's solicitor requiring him personally to pay the costs thrown away in the proceedings as a result of 'improper, unreasonable or negligent' conduct on his part. The solicitors appealed in each case. In a fifth action the judge had made a wasted costs order against the unsuccessful party's counsel on the ground that the counsel had unreasonably accepted a brief at short notice and, in effect, had pursued a hopeless case. Counsel appealed on the basis that s62 of the 1990 Act preserved the immunity from suit enjoyed by an advocate in relation to the conduct of litigation. In a sixth action solicitors who had represented parties in the county court were invited by the Court of Appeal to show cause why wasted costs orders should not be made against them in respect of their conduct of litigation based on misunderstanding of the law.

Held

All the appeals were allowed and the solicitors' application to show cause in the sixth action would also be allowed.

Sir Thomas Bingham MR:

' *"Improper, unreasonable or negligent"*
A number of different submissions were made on the correct construction of these crucial words in the new s51(7) of the Supreme Court Act 1981. In our view the meaning of these expressions is not open to serious doubt.

"Improper" means what it has been understood to mean in this context for at least half a century. The adjective covers, but is not confined to, conduct which would ordinarily be held to justify disbarment, striking off, suspension from practice or other serious professional penalty. It covers any significant breach of a substantial duty imposed by a relevant code of professional conduct. But it is not in our judgment limited to that. Conduct which would be regarded as improper according to the consensus of professional (including judicial) opinion can be fairly stigmatised as such whether or not it violates the letter of a professional code.

"Unreasonable" also means what it has been understood to mean in this context for at least half a century. The expression aptly describes conduct which is vexatious, designed to harass the other side rather than advance the resolution of the case, and it makes no difference that the conduct is the product of excessive zeal and not improper motive. But conduct cannot be described as unreasonable simply because it leads in the event to an unsuccessful result or because other more cautious legal representatives would have acted differently. The acid test is whether the conduct permits of a reasonable explanation. If so, the course adopted may be regarded as optimistic and as reflecting on a practitioner's judgment, but it is not unreasonable.

The term "negligent" was the most controversial of the three. It was argued that ... conduct cannot be regarded as negligent unless it involves an actionable breach of the legal representative's duty to his own client, to whom alone a duty is owed. We reject this approach ... Since the applicant's right to a wasted costs order against a legal representative depends on showing that the

latter is in breach of his duty to the court it makes no sense to superimpose a requirement under this head (but not in the case of impropriety or unreasonableness) that he is also in breach of his duty to his client ...we are clear that "negligent" should be understood in an untechnical way to denote failure to act with the competence reasonably to be expected of ordinary members of the profession.

In adopting an untechnical approach to the meaning of negligence in this context, we would however wish firmly to discountenance any suggestion that an applicant for a wasted costs order under this head need prove anything less than he would have to prove in an action for negligence ...

Pursuing a hopeless case
A legal representative is not to be held to have acted improperly, unreasonably or negligently simply because he acts for a party who pursues a claim or a defence which is plainly doomed to fail ...

As is well known, barristers in independent practice are not permitted to pick and choose their clients ... As is also well known, solicitors are not subject to an equivalent cab-rank rule, but many solicitors would and do respect the public policy underlying it by affording representation to the unpopular and the unmeritorious. Legal representatives will, of course, whether barristers or solicitors, advise clients of the perceived weakness of their case and of the risk of failure. But clients are free of reject advice and insist that cases be litigated ...

It is, however, one thing for a legal representative to present, on instructions, a case which he regards as bound to fail; it is quite another to lend his assistance to proceedings which are an abuse of the process of the court. Whether instructed or not, a legal representative is not entitled to use litigious procedures for purposes for which they were not intended, as by issuing or pursuing proceedings for reasons unconnected with success in the litigation or pursuing a case known to be dishonest, nor is he entitled to evade rules intended to safeguard the interests of justice, as by knowingly failing to make full disclosure on ex parte application or knowingly conniving at incomplete disclosure of documents. It is not entirely easy to distinguish by definition between the hopeless case and the case which amounts to an abuse of the process, but in practice it is not hard to say which is which and if there is doubt the legal representative is entitled to the benefit of it ...

Immunity ...
Although we are satisfied that the intention of this legislation is to encroach on the traditional immunity of the advocate by subjecting him to the wasted costs jurisdiction if he causes a waste of costs by improper, unreasonable or negligent conduct, it does not follow that we regard the public interest considerations on which the immunity is founded as being irrelevant or lacking weight in this context. Far from it. Any judge who is invited to make or contemplates making an order arising out of an advocate's conduct of court proceedings must make full allowance for the fact that an advocate in court, like a commander in battle, often has to make decisions quickly and under pressure, in the fog of war and ignorant of developments on the other side of the hill. Mistakes will inevitably be made, things done which the outcome shows to have been unwise. But advocacy is more an art than a science. It cannot be conducted according to formulae. Individuals differ in their style and approach. It is only when, with all allowances made, an advocate's conduct of court proceedings is quite plainly unjustifiable that it can be appropriate to make a wasted costs order against him.'

Comment

A useful decision on the scope of the power to make wasted costs orders. Is Sir Thomas Bingham MR's judgment over-protective of advocates? For the scope of advocates' immunity generally: see *Rondel* v *Worsley* (1969) in Chapter 10.

Roebuck* v *Mungovin [1994] 2 WLR 290 House of Lords (Lords Goff of Chieveley, Jauncey of Tullichettle, Lowry, Browne-Wilkinson and Slynn of Hadley)

• *Dismissal for want of prosecution – prejudice to defendant*

Facts

Having been injured in a road accident in August 1984, in April 1986 the plaintiff issued a writ and in July the defendant served a defence admitting liability but putting damages in issue. On the same day the defendant asked for further and better particulars: no reply was received. Correspondence passed between solicitors between April 1990 and 14 May 1991 when the plaintiff's solicitors said that a schedule of special damages (first promised on 18 October 1990) would be finalised at the end of the month. No such schedule having been received, the defendant's solicitors applied to strike out the action for want of prosecution.

Held

The action would be struck out.

Lord Browne-Wilkinson:

> '... Where a plaintiff has been guilty of inordinate and inexcusable delay which has prejudiced the defendant, subsequent conduct by the defendant which induces the plaintiff to incur further expense in pursuing the action does not, in law, constitute an absolute bar preventing the defendant from obtaining a striking out order. Such conduct of the defendant is, of course, a relevant factor to be taken into account by the judge in exercising his discretion whether or not to strike out the claim, the weight to be attached to such conduct depending upon all the circumstances of the particular case. At one extreme, there will be cases like the present where the defendant's actions are minor (as compared with the inordinate delay by the plaintiff) and cannot have lulled the plaintiff into any major additional expenditure; in such a case a judge exercising his discretion will be likely to attach only slight weight to the defendant's actions. At the other extreme one can conceive of a case where, the plaintiff having been guilty of inordinate delay, the defendant has for years thereafter continued with the action thereby leading the plaintiff to incur substantial legal costs; in such a case the judge may attach considerable weight to the defendant's activities. But it is for the judge in each case in exercising his discretion to decide what weight to attach in all the circumstances of the case to the defendant's actions and I trust that in the future there will be few occasions on which the Court of Appeal will be invited to review his decision on the point.'

Comment

A decision which sets out the factors that may be relevant to the judge's balancing exercise when deciding upon an application for dismissal for want of prosecution.

Shtun* v *Zalejska [1996] 3 All ER 411 Court of Appeal (Civil Division) (Neill, Peter Gibson and Hobhouse LJJ)

• *Jurisdiction to dismiss for want of prosecution*

Facts

In October 1984 P commenced proceedings against D claiming a beneficial interest in property registered in D's name. In April 1985 D served a defence and counterclaim, claiming that P had given her the property at the time of the purchase in 1978. Pleadings closed in July 1985. P issued a summons for directions in December 1986 and D served further and better particulars in January 1988. P set down the action in April 1988 but was taken out of the list pending discovery. It was not until May 1993 that P served a notice of intention to proceed and in September 1993 D applied for dismissal for want of prosecution

on the ground of prejudice resulting from P's delay. The only evidence of prejudice was the affidavit evidence of D's solicitors to the effect that the property ownership issue would depend on the recollections of the parties to the oral agreement made at the time of the purchase in 1978.

Held

Action dismissed for want of prosecution.

Where the prejudice relied on took the form of impairment of witnesses' recollections, it was not essential in every case that there should be evidence of particular respects in which potential witnesses' memories had faded; the court was entitled to draw appropriate inferences from the facts of each case. On the particular facts P's improper delay had clearly increased D's disadvantage by a significant margin causing more than minimal prejudice: *Birkett* v *James* [1977] 2 All ER 801; [1978] AC 297 applied.

Peter Gibson LJ:

> 'As the law now stands, the following propositions seem to me to be uncontroversial, ...
>
> (1) In a case where there has been no contumelious conduct by the plaintiff, the court, if it is to strike out an action for want of prosecution, must be satisfied (a) that there has been inordinate and inexcusable delay on the part of the plaintiff or his lawyers and (b) that such delay will give rise to a substantial risk that it is not possible to have a fair trial of issues in the action or is such as is likely to cause or to have caused serious prejudice to the defendants, either as between themselves and the plaintiff, or between each other, or between them and a third party (see *Birkett* v *James* [1977] 2 All ER 801 at 805, [1978] AC 297 at 319 per Lord Diplock).
>
> (2) The delay that must be shown to have caused such risk or such likelihood of prejudice is the delay after the issue of proceedings (see [1977] 2 All ER 801 at 808, [1978] AC 297 at 322).
>
> (3) But where the plaintiff delays in issuing proceedings and by such delay causes prejudice, the additional prejudice which must be shown to justify dismissal of the action need not be great, provided that it is more than minimal (see [1977] 2 All ER 801 at 809, [1978] AC 297 at 323).
>
> (4) Further, once the plaintiff is guilty of further delay, the prejudice caused by the totality of the period of his delay can be looked at ...
>
> (5) The prejudice may take a variety of forms, but one recognised form is the impairment of the memory of witnesses (see *Birkett* v *James* [1977] 2 All ER 801 at 808, [1978] AC 297 at 321) ...
>
> (6) Save in exceptional cases, an action will not be struck out for want of prosecution before the expiry of the relevant limitation period (see *Birkett* v *James* [1977] 2 All ER 801 at 808, [1978] AC 297 at 321).'

Comment

The extract from the judgment quoted above contains a useful summary of the circumstances in which an action may be dismissed for want of prosecution.

Tolstoy-Miloslavsky (Count)* v *Lord Aldington [1996] 2 All ER 556 Court of Appeal (Civil Division) (Rose, Roch and Ward LJJ)

- *Wasted costs orders*

Facts

P's solicitor, acting without fee, issued a writ against D seeking to set aside an award of libel damages obtained by D against P on the ground that the judgment had been obtained by fraud. D successfully applied to strike out the statement of claim as an abuse of process. D also applied for an order that P's solicitors pay his costs.

Held

A wasted costs order could be made under s51(6) and (7) Supreme Court Act 1981 because on the particular facts P's solicitors had acted improperly and unreasonably in

bringing the fresh proceedings, which were regarded as a collateral attack on the jury's verdict in the libel action, following an unsuccessful attempt to appeal that verdict. The fresh proceedings had been instituted to harass D and in bringing them P's solicitors had made a serious error of judgment: *Ridehalgh* v *Horsefield* [1994] 3 All ER 848 applied.

The Court of Appeal went on to observe that the jurisdiction to make a wasted costs order must be exercised with care and only in a clear case:

Rose LJ:

> '... acting without fee, and doing so in a hopeless case, or even in a case struck out for abuse of process ... is not conduct which itself would justify the making of a wasted costs order.'

Comment

The decision is a salutary warning to solicitors tempted to help clients whose primary motivation is to harass others rather to vindicate genuine claims.

9 Civil and Criminal Appeals

Evans v *Bartlam* [1937] AC 473 House of Lords (Lords Atkin, Thankerton, Russell, Wright and Roche)

- *Orders of masters and registrars*

Facts

The appellant owed money to a bookmaker and agreed that, if he was given time to pay, and if he was not declared a defaulter at Tattersalls, he would repay the debt within a reasonable time. The bookmaker later sued him for failure to keep his promise and was granted judgment, the appellant failing to appear at the hearing. On being asked to grant more time to pay the judgment debt, the bookmaker again agreed, but subsequently the appellant made an application to have the judgment set aside, and for leave to defend the action. The application was dismissed by the master; on appeal the judge in chambers granted the application and gave leave to defend on terms. The bookmaker then appealed to the Court of Appeal which directed that the order of the master be restored. The appellant then appealed to the House of Lords.

Held

There was no reason to interfere with the discretion of the judge in chambers who thought it proper to set aside the judgment and, unless it was clear that the judge's discretion had been wrongly exercised, his order should be affirmed.

Lord Atkin:

> 'While the appellate court, in the exercise of its appellate power, is no doubt entirely justified in saying that normally it will not interfere with the exercise of the judge's discretion except on grounds of law, yet, if it sees that, on other grounds, the decision will result in injustice being done, it has both the power and the duty to remedy it.'

Comment

The leading authority on the scope of a civil trial judge's discretion. Whilst this is a wide discretion with which appeal judges are reluctant to interfere, it is open to review on grounds of error of law or causing injustice.

Griffiths v *Jenkins* [1992] 2 WLR 28 House of Lords (Lords Bridge of Harwich, Griffiths, Ackner, Lowry and Browne-Wilkinson)

- *High Court – power to order re-hearing*

Facts

The respondents were alleged to have fished in a private stream and stolen three trout: the justices dismissed the charges. The prosecutor appealed to the Divisional Court by way of case stated and, but for the fact that two of the justices had retired, the court would have remitted the case to the justices with a direction to continue the hearing. The Divisional Court ruled that it had no power to remit the case to a freshly constituted bench and the prosecutor appealed against this decision.

Held

Although the Divisional Court could have remitted the case to a different bench of justices, in the circumstances it would now be inappropriate to do so. Accordingly, the appeal would be dismissed.

Lord Bridge of Harwich:

> 'My conclusion is that there is always power in the court on hearing an appeal by case stated under s6 of the Summary Jurisdiction Act 1857 to order a rehearing before either the same or a different bench when that appears to be an appropriate course and the court, in its discretion, decides to take it. It is axiomatic, of course, that a rehearing will only be ordered in circumstances where a fair trial is still possible. But where errors of law by justices have led to an acquittal which is successfully challenged and where the circumstances of the case are such that a rehearing is the only way in which the matter can be put right, I apprehend that the court will normally, though not necessarily, exercise its discretion in favour of that course. I recognise that very different considerations may apply to the exercise of discretion to order a rehearing following a successful appeal against conviction by the defendant in circumstances where the error in the proceedings which vitiated the conviction has left the issue of the defendant's guilt or innocence unresolved. In some such cases to order a rehearing may appear inappropriate or oppressive. But this must depend on how the proceedings have been conducted, the nature of the error vitiating the conviction, the gravity of the offence and any other relevant considerations. It would be most unwise to attempt to lay down guidelines for the exercise of such a discretion and I have no intention of doing so ...
>
> Unfortunately any rehearing of the present case, if the House were to order one, would take place more than three years after the date when the offences were alleged to have been committed. As I have said, they were of a relatively trivial character; the evidence for the prosecution suggested an illegal catch by the respondents of three trout. Moreover, the errors of law which vitiated the acquittals were not prompted by submissions advanced on behalf of the defence, but arose from points which the justices took of their own motion. In these circumstances I would not think it appropriate now to order a rehearing. The effect of this ... is that the order of the Divisional Court will stand and the appeal, therefore, will technically fall to be dismissed. But in substance, of course, the appellant has succeeded on the important issue of law in the appeal ...'

Comment

A useful illustration of the circumstances in which an order for a rehearing may or may not be appropriate.

Hadmor Productions Ltd* v *Hamilton [1983] 1 AC 191 House of Lords (Lords Diplock, Fraser of Tullybelton, Scarman, Bridge of Harwich and Brandon of Oakbrook)

• *Functions of appeal court in civil appeal when reviewing exercise of trial judge's discretion*

(The facts and decision are not important in this context. It is the statement on reviewing a trial judge's discretion which is of significance here.)

Lord Diplock:

> '... I think appropriate to remind your Lordships of the limited function of an appellate court in an appeal of this kind. An interlocutory injunction is a discretionary relief and the discretion whether or not to grant it is vested in the High Court judge by whom the application for it is heard. On an appeal from the judge's grant or refusal of an interlocutory injunction the function of an appellate court, whether it be the Court of Appeal or your Lordships' House, is not to exercise an independent discretion of its own. It must defer to the judge's exercise of his discretion and must not interfere with it merely on the ground that the members of the appellate court would have exercised the discretion differently. The function of the appellate court is initially one of review only. It may set aside the judge's exercise of his discretion on the ground that it was

based on a misunderstanding of the law or of the evidence before him or on an inference that particular facts existed or did not exist, which, although it was one that might legitimately have been drawn on the evidence that was before the judge, can be demonstrated to be wrong by further evidence that has become available by the time of the appeal, or on the ground that there has been a change of circumstances after the judge made his order that would have justified his acceding to an application to vary it. Since reasons given by judges for granting or refusing interlocutory injunctions may sometimes be sketchy, there may also be occasional cases where even though no erroneous assumption of law or fact can be identified the judge's decision to grant or refuse the injunction is so aberrant that it must be set aside on the ground that no reasonable judge regardful of his duty to act judicially could have reached it. It is only if and after the appellate court has reached the conclusion that the judge's exercise of his discretion must be set aside for one or other of these reasons that it becomes entitled to exercise an original discretion of its own.'

Comment

The decision follows the general policy established by *Evans* v *Bartlam* (1937) (above). The decision shows that the reluctance to interfere with a trial judge's discretion will tend to be greater in the area of awards of interlocutory injunctions where a delicate balancing exercise is undertaken to determine where the balance of convenience lies.

R* v *Berry [1991] 1 WLR 125 Court of Appeal (Watkins LJ, Anthony Lincoln and Tucker JJ)

• *House of Lords' decision – further appeal on other grounds?*

Facts

Berry applied to relist his appeal against his Crown Court conviction of making explosives for which he was sentenced to eight years' imprisonment. An earlier appeal against his conviction had been allowed by the Court of Appeal ([1984] 1 WLR 824) but, on appeal by the Crown on a point of law certified as of general public importance, the House of Lords ([1984] WLR 1274) directed that his conviction be restored. The grounds of the application were that the Court of Appeal should consider grounds of his original appeal which had been argued before, but not decided upon by, the Court of Appeal and which had not been decided by the House of Lords when disposing of the Crown's appeal on the certified question.

Held

The application would be refused.

Watkins LJ:

'In contemplating our decision on the merits of this application we have regarded as essential the need to preserve the concept that in appeals from the Crown Court there must be finality either in the Court of Appeal, Criminal Division or in the House of Lords. Let it be supposed there had been no appeal to the House of Lords in this case following in the Court of Appeal a decision upon the only decided point and that had gone against the appellant leaving arguable grounds unresolved. In that event, in our view, a case for relisting might possibly have been established. Here the position is that the omission by this court to deal with the other arguable grounds, as they are probably rightly claimed to be, could have been cured in the House of Lords, which on the authority of *A-G for Northern Ireland* v *Gallagher* [1961] 1 WLR 619 has the power, in order to avoid injustice, to go beyond the certified point and deal with other grounds deemed to be properly advanced. Lord Denning in *Gallagher* said ([1961] WLR 619 at 642):

"If it were necessary to consider any other point in order to dispose of the appeal I will certainly be prepared to do so; for I take the view that, once leave to appeal is given to your Lordships' House, all points are open as well as the point stated."

Thus, once an appeal reaches the House of Lords we take the view that a party to the appeal has a final opportunity within the appellate system laid down in the Criminal Appeal Act 1968 to bring such points as he wishes to make to the notice of the House. It is, of course, a matter for the discretion of the House of Lords how far, if at all, it will allow points other than that certified to be developed doubtless bearing in mind the structure of the whole of s2 of the 1968 Act which sets out the several separate bases upon which an appeal must be allowed. We should interpolate here that we do not accept the submission that the existence of those several bases gives rise to the notion that an appellant thereby has the right to more than one appeal. He has but one appeal, which may involve a number of points touching upon one or more of those bases.

The House of Lords regards itself we believe and, in our view, we say, with respect, rightly as giving a final judgment in the appeal before it. Having done so it makes its order. In the present case the order was in effect that the conviction of the applicant be restored. It was restored accordingly. It would be extraordinary and, in our opinion, unthinkable if the Court of Appeal (Criminal Division) were to be in a position thereafter to pronounce upon other grounds of appeal and thereby destroy the order of the House of Lords by again quashing the conviction.

Our conclusion is that we are powerless to do what the applicant asks for.'

Comment

A sensible decision designed to prevent constant relisting applications by disappointed appellants. Contrast *R* v *Mandair* (1994) (below).

R v *Chelmsford Crown Court, ex parte Chief Constable of Essex* [1994] 1 WLR 359 High Court (Glidewell LJ and Cresswell J)

- *Crown Court – judicial review*

Facts

During a Crown Court trial, the judge ruled that certain police evidence was inadmissible but should nevertheless be disclosed to the defence. After the trial, judicial review was sought of the order to disclose.

Held

The application would be dismissed.

Glidewell LJ:

'Does this court have jurisdiction to grant the relief sought? I use the word "jurisdiction" here in its proper or narrow sense, that is to say does this court have the power, as a matter of law, to grant the relief sought?

The answer to the question depends largely upon the provisions of the Supreme Court Act 1981 …

[Counsel for the Chief Constable] argues that if s29(3) prevents this court from making orders of mandamus, prohibition or certiorari in relation to matters relating to trial on indictment, nevertheless it does not remove or limit this court's powers under s31 to grant a declaration in relation to trial on indictment in the Crown Court where it would be appropriate to do so.

If that were not so, he argues, as indeed as I have said … there may well be no means of challenging such a decision. A defendant, if convicted, can appeal to the Court of Appeal, Criminal Division but the prosecution, or as here, the police, have no redress where the court in the course of a trial makes a wrong decision in law.

In reply, [counsel for the Attorney General] advances a fundamental argument which again has not been the subject of any decided authority … The argument is this: the power of this court to supervise by way of judicial review is exercisable over inferior courts and tribunals but not over superior courts. The Crown Court is a superior court of record and therefore, as a general proposition, this court has no supervisory power in relation to the Crown Court exercising its jurisdiction. This proposition is derived from s1 of the Supreme Court Act 1981 …

It follows, submits [counsel], that broadly speaking the Crown Court is in exactly the same position as the High Court, being a superior court. Its decisions are not open to challenge in the High Court. However, when the Crown Court was created by the Courts Act 1971 and took over the jurisdiction formally exercised by courts of oyer and terminer and general gaol delivery sitting at assizes and quarter sessions, it was recognised by the parliament that in some respects it was desirable to subject some of its decisions to the supervisory jurisdiction of this court.

Sections 28 and 29(3) of the Supreme Court Act 1981 therefore expressly granted to this court powers which it would not otherwise have to supervise the decisions of the Crown Court in relation to matters there defined ... It is wrong, submits [counsel], to regard s29(3) as imposing a limitation. On the contrary, what ss28 and 29(3) did was to grant to this court jurisdiction and powers which this court otherwise would not have had ...

I am persuaded that [counsel for the Attorney General's] argument is correct. It provides a logical analysis of the structure of the Supreme Court Act 1981, particularly of those parts of that Act which relate to the Crown Court. It reflects the proper position of the Crown Court in the hierarchy of the courts established under the 1981 Act and earlier under the 1971 Act. It reflects the fact that, generally speaking, challenges to decisions of the Crown Court, save those which derive from original decisions of the magistrates' court, will normally find their way not to this court but to the Court of Appeal, Criminal Division.

Therefore, in my view, this court does not have jurisdiction to grant the declaration sought.'

Comment

The decision illustrates the rule that judicial review is not available over any matter decided upon during a trial on indictment. Any challenge must be made through the statutory appeal route, not the judicial review procedure.

R* v *Gilfoyle [1996] 3 All ER 883 Court of Appeal (Criminal Division) (Beldam LJ, Scott Baker and Hidden JJ)

- *Power of Court of Appeal to receive fresh evidence under s23 Criminal Appeal Act 1968*

Facts

The appellant had been convicted of his wife's murder and had applied to the court to receive fresh evidence in the form of witness statements which had been ruled inadmissible at his trial. The appellant contended that these statements, if believed, would increase a lurking doubt about the safety of his conviction.

Held

Appeal dismissed. The fresh evidence would not have been likely to have affected the jury's verdict and was not of such weight that the verdict should be regarded as unsafe and unsatisfactory. The following observations were made about the scope of the powers of the Court of Appeal under s23 of the 1968 Act.

Beldam LJ:

'In our judgment, the court has not only the power to receive admissible evidence which would afford a ground for allowing the appeal but has a wider discretion, if it thinks it necessary or expedient in the interests of justice, to order any witness to attend for examination and to be examined before the court, whether or not he testified at the trial. We are satisfied that the interests of justice are not simply confined to receiving evidence which would result in an appeal being allowed, particularly when the court is being asked to review as unsafe and unsatisfactory the verdict of a jury after an impeccable summing up on the ground that it has a lurking doubt. In *Stirland* v *DPP* [1944] 2 All ER 13 at 17, [1944] AC 315 at 324 Viscount Simon LC said

"... a miscarriage of justice may arise from the acquittal of the guilty no less than from the conviction of the innocent".

In reviewing the jury's decision a court, required to consider what is necessary or expedient in the interests of justice must, it seems to us, be able to review the evidence given at the trial as well as admissible evidence which could have been given. Take the case of an appeal based on an error of law leading to the wrongful admission of evidence. Could the court receive admissible evidence which has since come to light which would, beyond doubt, have proved the same point? Or as here, where the court is being asked to consider "fresh" evidence which it is said reinforces a lurking doubt, can the court receive admissible evidence which tends to dispel such doubt?

In our view s23 of the 1968 Act confers upon a court a discretion confined only by the requirement that the court must be satisfied that it is necessary or expedient in the interests of justice to require the evidence to be given.'

Comment

The decision on the scope of s23 probably survives the amendments made by the Criminal Appeal Act 1995, but since some authorities have argued that the amendments have restricted the nature of the discretion to receive fresh evidence this point remains to be settled.

R* v *Graham (HK) and Others [1997] 1 Cr App R 302 Court of Appeal (Criminal Division) (Bingham LCJ, Blofeld and Cresswell JJ)

• *Unsafe convictions – alternative verdicts – retrials – effects of Criminal Appeal Act 1995*

Facts

Appeals were lodged by seven convicted persons. They contended that their convictions for mortgage fraud were unsafe following the reinterpretation of the criminal law relating to dishonesty in *R* v *Preddy* [1996] 3 All ER 481 (HL).

Held

Appeals allowed. All the convictions were quashed for being unsafe, but in four of the appeals convictions of alternative offences could be and were substituted using the power under s3 Criminal Appeal Act 1968.

Bingham LCJ:

(1) on unsafe verdicts and the effect of s2(1) Criminal Appeal Act 1995:

'If the court was satisfied, despite any misdirection of law or any irregularity in the conduct of the trial or any fresh evidence, that the conviction was safe the court would dismiss the appeal.

But if, for whatever reason, the court concluded that the appellant was wrongly convicted of the offence charged, or was left in doubt whether the appellant was rightly convicted of that offence or not, then it must of necessity consider the conviction unsafe.

The court was then subject to a binding duty to allow the appeal. It could make no difference that the appellant might, if duly indicted, have been rightly convicted of some other offence. Where the condition in s2(1)(a) as it now stood was satisfied, the court had no discretion to exercise ...

... A conviction would not be regarded as unsafe because it was possible to point to some drafting or clerical error, or omission, or discrepancy, or departure from good or prescribed practice ...

But if it was clear as a matter of law that the particulars of offence specified in the indictment could not, even if established, support a conviction of the offence of which the defendant was accused, a conviction of such offence had, in their Lordships' opinion, to be considered unsafe. If a defendant could not in law be guilty of the offence charged on the facts relied on no conviction of that offence could be other than unsafe ...'

(2) on substituting alternative verdicts under s3 of the 1968 Act:

> '... The prosecution would have to establish two requirements:
>
> 1. That the jury could, on the indictment, have found the appellant guilty of some other offence, offence B, and
>
> 2. that the jury must have been satisfied of facts which proved the appellant to be guilty of offence B.
>
> As to the first, it would be sufficient if, looking at the indictment, not the evidence, the allegation in the particular count in the indictment expressly or impliedly included an allegation of offence B.
>
> A count charging offence A impliedly contained an allegation of offence B if the allegation in the particular count would ordinarily involve an allegation of offence B and on the facts of the particular case did so.
>
> As to the second, their Lordships' court had only the verdict of the jury on which to go. The fact that the jury did not have a proper direction as to offence B was a highly relevant consideration, as was the question whether there were reasonable grounds for concluding that the conduct of the defence would have been materially affected if the appellant had been charged with offence B ...'

Lord Bingham pointed out that s3 of the 1968 Act has usually been used in relation to public order offences or offences of violence, as in those cases there was a clear hierarchy of offences at common law or under statute. In the present appeals the Court of Appeal was asked to use the power in regard to offences of dishonesty and this was difficult because of the complex statutory framework governing many and various offences of dishonesty. Lord Bingham expressed the hope that appropriate legislation would be enacted with all deliberate speed so as to remove the anomaly exposed by *R* v *Preddy* (above) and to establish a clear hierarchy of statutory offences involving dishonesty.

(3) on ordering retrials under s7(2) of the 1968 Act, as amended by s43 Criminal Justice Act 1988:

> '... The conditions which permitted the court to order a retrial were twofold: the court had to allow the appeal and consider that the interests of justice required a retrial.
>
> The first condition was either satisfied or it was not. The second required an exercise of judgment and would involve consideration of the public interest and the legitimate interests of the defendant.
>
> The public interest was generally served by the prosecution of those reasonably suspected on available evidence of serious crime, if such prosecution could be conducted without unfairness to or oppression of the defendant.
>
> The legitimate interests of the defendant would often call for consideration of the time which had passed since the alleged offence, and any penalty the defendant might already have paid before the quashing of the conviction.'

Comment

The decision is a useful analysis of the changes made by the Criminal Appeal Act 1995, as well as an application of surviving provisions of the Criminal Appeal Act 1968.

R* v *Harrow Crown Court, ex parte Dave [1994] 1 WLR 98 High Court (Kennedy LJ and Pill J)

- *Conviction by justices – reasons for dismissing appeal*

Facts

Having been convicted by justices of assault occasioning actual bodily harm, a woman appealed to the Crown Court. Dismissing the appeal, the Crown Court judge said simply: 'Over the course of three days we have had ample opportunity to hear and to assess the witnesses. It is our unanimous conclusion that this appeal must be dismissed.' The woman sought judicial review on the ground, inter alia, that the Crown Court should have given reasons for dismissing her appeal.

Held

The application would be allowed.

Pill J:

> 'The Crown Court is a judicial body making decisions which affect the rights of individuals. As an appellate tribunal it is presided over by a judge. It has to decide questions of fact and law, and it operates within the statutory framework of the 1981 Act, so the courts will readily imply such additional procedural safeguards as will ensure the attainment of fairness ...
>
> So, in our judgment, the weight of authority is now in favour of the conclusion that when the Crown Court sits in an appellate capacity it must give reasons for its decision. The custom has become, or ought to have become, universal ... The Crown Court judge giving the decision of the court upon an appeal must say enough to demonstrate that the court has identified the main contentious issues in the case and how it has resolved each of them ... The appellant was entitled to know the basis upon which the prosecution case had been accepted by the court. In the present case, that involved knowing the process by which the apparently powerful points in favour of the defence had been rejected. A refusal to give reasons may amount to the denial of natural justice ...
>
> We would quash the decision ... and remit the case to the Crown Court for the rehearing. We were told by counsel that, in that event, the prosecution will not offer evidence at the Crown Court with the result that the appeal against conviction will be allowed. We regard that as a sensible course for the prosecution to adopt having regard to the long history of the case and to matters ... which have arisen since the Crown Court hearing.'

Comment

A sensible decision illustrating that the giving of reasons is an essential requirement of a judicial decision.

R v *Horsman* [1997] 3 All ER 385 Court of Appeal (Waller LJ, Tucker and Bennett JJ)

• *Appeal against conviction – powers of the Court of Appeal in disposing of an appeal – power to substitute a conviction of some other offence under s3 Criminal Appeal Act 1968 – whether power available where defendant has pleaded guilty to offences prior to being put in charge of the jury*

Facts

The appellant had pleaded guilty to two counts on an indictment alleging the obtaining of property by deception contrary to s15(1) Theft Act 1968. He was sentenced to 15 months' imprisonment. Following the decision of the House of Lords in *R* v *Preddy* [1996] 3 All ER 481 the appellant applied for an extension of time for appealing his conviction on the ground that *R* v *Preddy* demonstrated that, despite his admitted dishonesty, no offence under s15(1) could have been committed. An extension of time and leave to appeal were duly granted. The Court of Appeal accepted that, following *R* v *Preddy*, the conviction under s15(1) must be quashed. The issue was whether the Court of Appeal had power under s3 Criminal Appeal Act 1968 to substitute convictions for some other offence.

Held

There was no power available to substitute convictions for some other offence because s3 of the 1968 Act expressly contemplates a verdict from a jury and no such verdict had been available in the present case. The appeal was therefore allowed and the conviction under s15(1) Theft Act 1968 quashed.

Waller LJ:

> '... in relation to this appellant, it should be made clear that under compulsion this court has allowed the appeal, but he should appreciate that he has only the most technical of acquittals, because if the problems, which

were not appreciated when an extension of time for appealing was being granted, had in fact been appreciated, he would never in the circumstances of this case have obtained such leave.'

Comment

The case reveals a significant gap in the power of the Court of Appeal which may require amending legislation. Until such amendment is made applications for extensions of time for appealing and applications for leave to appeal where there has been a plea of guilty (if not simply refused) will be referred to the full Court of Appeal, rather than to a single justice, so that the Court of Appeal's powers to see that justice is done in any particular case are not hampered.

(The implication of this change of practice, advised by the Court of Appeal in the present case, is that the absence of the power to substitute a conviction for some other offence will be a highly material factor in deciding whether to grant an extension of time/leave to appeal.)

R* v *Jones (Steven Martin) (1996) The Times 23 July Court of Appeal (Criminal Division) (Bingham LCJ, Ognall and Smith JJ)

- *Receiving fresh evidence under s23 of the Criminal Appeal Act 1968 as amended by s4 of the Criminal Appeal Act 1995*

Facts

The appellant had been convicted of his wife's murder and had applied to the court to receive fresh expert evidence.

Held

It was expedient in the interests of justice to receive the new evidence. Three forensic pathologists were then orally examined and cross-examined before the Court of Appeal, which also received written evidence. Having received the evidence, the Court of Appeal then dismissed the appeal on the ground that the conviction was not unsafe. The following guidance was given by Lord Bingham CJ on the approach to fresh evidence under the new law.

He stated that s23 as amended made it plain that in the exercise of its discretion whether to receive evidence or not the court had to be guided above all by what it considered necessary or expedient in the interests of justice.

Section 23(2)(d) did, however, acknowledge the crucial obligation on a defendant in a criminal case to advance his whole defence and any evidence on which he relied before the trial jury. He was not entitled to hold evidence in reserve and then seek to introduce it on appeal following conviction.

While failure to adduce the evidence before the jury was not a bar to reception of the evidence on appeal, it was a matter which the court was obliged to consider in deciding whether to receive the evidence or not.

The court had in the past accepted that s23 might apply to expert evidence, and their Lordships would not wish to circumscribe the operation of a statutory rule enacted to protect defendants against the risk of wrongful conviction. But it seemed unlikely that the section was framed with expert evidence prominently in mind.

The requirement in subs(2)(a) that the evidence should appear to be capable of belief applied more aptly to factual evidence than to expert opinion, which might or might not be acceptable or persuasive but was unlikely to be thought to be incapable of belief in any ordinary sense.

The giving of a reasonable explanation for failure to adduce the evidence before the jury, again applied more aptly to factual evidence of which a party was unaware, or could not adduce, than to expert evidence, since if one expert was unavailable to testify at a trial a party would ordinarily be expected to call another, unless circumstances prevented that.

Expert witnesses, although inevitably varying in standing and experience, were

interchangeable in a way in which factual witnesses were not. It would clearly subvert the trial process if a defendant, convicted at trial, were to be generally free to mount on appeal an expert case which, if sound, could and should have been advanced before the jury.

If it was said that the only expert witness in an established field whose opinion supported a certain defence was unavailable to testify at the trial, that might be thought, save in unusual circumstances, to reflect on the acceptability of that opinion.

Comment

The decision provides useful guidance on the circumstances in which fresh expert evidence is likely to be dealt with in future applications of this sort to the Court of Appeal.

R* v *Lee [1984] 1 WLR 578 Court of Appeal (Ackner LJ, Glidewell and Leggatt JJ)

• *Criminal appeals – following trial on indictment*

Facts

Some months after a fire at a house in which three boys died the applicant was arrested and charged with arson. He admitted causing the fire. In due course eleven indictments were preferred against the applicant alleging arson and murder at various places on different occasions. At a pre-trial review by the judge in chambers the applicant's counsel expressed disquiet that the applicant intended to plead guilty but all the reporting psychiatrists agreed that the applicant was fit to plead. On arraignment, the applicant's pleas of guilty to arson and manslaughter by reason of diminished responsibility were unequivocal and were accepted by the court. The defendant applied for leave to appeal against his conviction.

Held

The fact that the applicant had been found fit to plead and had also pleaded guilty without equivocation after receiving expert advice was relevant to the consideration of the question whether the convictions were either unsafe or unsatisfactory, but did not of itself deprive the court of jurisdiction to grant leave and determine the appeal against the convictions. Also, under s23(1) of the Criminal Appeal Act 1968, the court had a general discretionary power to receive evidence if it was thought 'necessary or expedient in the interests of justice'; in the wholly unusual circumstances of the case, those conditions were fulfilled and the court would hear relevant and admissible evidence as to whether the convictions were either unsafe or unsatisfactory.

Ackner LJ:

> 'The fact that the applicant was fit to plead; knew what he was doing; intended to make the pleas he did; pleaded guilty without equivocation after receiving expert advice; although factors highly relevant to whether the convictions on any of them were either unsafe or unsatisfactory, cannot of themselves deprive the court of jurisdiction to hear the applications.
>
> The question we have to answer is, "Is it necessary or expedient in the interests of justice that we should allow – in a case where no evidence at all was called before a jury – evidence which would or could have been called if the applicant had, by pleading not guilty, caused the trial to take place?" Superadded to the applications to call that evidence are, of course, applications to call evidence which has, since the convictions, become available. Obviously the answer to this question must depend upon the particular circumstances of the case.
>
> The decision which we are now making is not intended to provide any general precedent. Indeed, it is our view that the occasions on which this court will allow evidence to be called, after there has been an unequivocal plea of guilty, will be very rare. We regard this case, as indeed do both counsel, as wholly exceptional, if not unique.
>
> We are satisfied that in the wholly

unusual circumstance of these applications, it is both necessary and expedient in the interests of justice that we should, at this stage, hear relevant and admissible evidence called by both the applicant and the Crown as to whether the convictions on the first indictment were either unsafe or unsatisfactory.'

Comment

The case shows that a guilty plea is not an absolute bar to an appeal against conviction if a ground of appeal can be established.

R* v *McIlkenny [1992] 2 All ER 417 Court of Appeal (Lloyd, Mustill and Farquharson LJJ)

• *Court of Appeal, Criminal Division – function*

Facts

The Home Secretary referred to the Court of Appeal under s17 of the Criminal Appeal Act 1968 the convictions of the appellants ('the Birmingham Six') of murder.

Held

The appeals would be allowed and the convictions quashed as, in the light of fresh scientific evidence and fresh investigation of police evidence, the convictions were both unsafe and unsatisfactory.

The Lords Justices of Appeal by turns read the judgment which included the following:

'*The role of the Court of Appeal*

Since the present appeal has given rise to much public discussion as to the powers and duties of the Court of Appeal, Criminal Division, and since the Home Secretary has set up a Royal Commission to investigate and report, it may be helpful if we set out our understanding of the present state of the law.

(1) The Court of Appeal, Criminal Division is the creature of statute. Our powers are derived from, and confined to, those contained in the Supreme Court Act 1981, the Criminal Appeal Act 1968 and the Criminal Justice Act 1988. We have no inherent jurisdiction apart from statute ... Thus we have no power to conduct an open-ended investigation into an alleged miscarriage of justice, even if we were equipped to do so. Our function is to hear criminal appeals, neither more nor less.

(2) Just as we have no powers other than those conferred on us by Parliament, so we are guided by Parliament in the exercise of those powers. Thus by s2(1) of the 1968 Act we are directed to allow an appeal against conviction if, but only if, (a) we think that the conviction is unsafe or unsatisfactory, (b) there has been a wrong decision on a question of law or (c) there has been a material irregularity. In all other cases we are obliged to dismiss the appeal. Where we allow an appeal, we are directed by s2(2) to quash the conviction. Where we quash the conviction, the order operates, by virtue of s2(3), as a direction to the trial court to enter a verdict of acquittal, except where a retrial is ordered under s7 of the 1968 Act. Nothing in s2 of the 1968 Act or anywhere else obliges or entitles us to say whether we think that the appellant is innocent. This is a point of great constitutional importance. The task of deciding whether a man is guilty falls on the jury. We are concerned solely with the question whether the verdict of the jury can stand.

(3) Rightly or wrongly (we think rightly) trial by jury is the foundation of our criminal justice system. Under jury trial juries not only find the facts; they also apply the law. Since they are not experts in the law, they are directed on the relevant law by the judge. But the task of applying the law to the facts, and so reaching a verdict, belongs to the jury, and the jury alone. The primacy of the jury in the English criminal justice system explains why, historically, the Court of Appeal had so limited a function ...

(4) The primacy of the jury in the criminal justice system is well illustrated by the difference between the Criminal and Civil Divisions of the Court of Appeal. Like the Criminal Division, the Civil Division is also a creature of statute. But its powers are

much wider. A civil appeal is by way of rehearing of the whole case. So the court is concerned with fact as well as law. It is true the court does not rehear the witnesses. But it reads their evidence. It follows that in a civil case the Court of Appeal may take a different view of the facts from the court below. In a criminal case this is not possible. Since justice is as much concerned with the conviction of the guilty as the acquittal of the innocent, and the task of convicting the guilty belongs constitutionally to the jury, not to us, the role of the Criminal Division of the Court of Appeal is necessarily limited. Hence it is true to say that whereas the Civil Division of the Court of Appeal has appellate jurisdiction in the full sense, the Criminal Division is perhaps more accurately described as a court of review ... We have no power to upset the verdict of a jury on a question of fact unless we think a conviction unsafe or unsatisfactory under all the circumstances of the case. These words were substituted by s4 of the Criminal Appeal Act 1966 ...

(5) Another feature of our law, which goes hand in hand with trial by jury, is the adversarial nature of criminal proceedings. Clearly a jury cannot embark on a judicial investigation. So the material must be placed before the jury. It is sometimes said that the adversarial system leaves too much power in the hands of the police. But that criticism has been met, at least in part, by the creation of the Crown Prosecution Service. The great advantage of the adversarial system is that it enables the defendant to test the prosecution case in open court. Once there is sufficient evidence to commit a defendant for trial, the prosecution has to prove the case against him by calling witnesses to give oral testimony in the presence of the jury. We doubt whether there is a better way of exposing the weaknesses in the prosecution case, whether the witness be a policeman, a scientist or a bystander, than by cross-examination.

(6) A disadvantage of the adversarial system may be that the parties are not evenly matched in resources ... But the inequality of resources is ameliorated by the obligation on the part of the prosecution to make available all material which may prove helpful to the defence ...

(7) No system is better than its human input. Like any other system of justice the adversarial system may be abused. The evidence adduced may be inadequate. Expert evidence may not have been properly researched or there may have been a deliberate attempt to undermine the system by giving false evidence. If there is a conflict of evidence there is no way of ensuring the jury will always get it right. This is particularly so where there is a conflict of expert evidence, such as there was here. No human system can expect to be perfect.

(8) Just as the adversarial system prevails at the trial, so also it prevails in the Court of Appeal. It is for the appellants to raise the issues which they wish to lay before the court. Those issues are set out in the grounds of appeal ...'

Comment

This is one of the most famous cases in recent English law, involving the notorious miscarriage of justice suffered by the 'Birmingham Six'. The judgments contain a useful historical survey of the functions of the Court of Appeal, the nature of the adversarial system, and the implications of trials by juries: see the Criminal Appeal Act 1995 for reforms introduced as a result of this case.

R v *Maguire and Others* [1992] 2 All ER 433 Court of Appeal (Criminal Division) (Stuart-Smith, Mann and McCowan LJJ)

- *Grounds for appeal in criminal cases: meaning of 'material irregularity' under s2(1)(c) of the Criminal Appeal Act 1968*

Facts

The seven appellants had been convicted and sentenced to imprisonment in 1976 for possessing explosives. One of them had died in prison in 1980. The Home Secretary referred

the convictions to the Court of Appeal under s17 of the Criminal Appeal Act 1968. One of the grounds for the new appeal was the failure of the prosecution to inform the defence of relevant material known to the Crown's witnesses at the time of the trial.

Held

Appeals would be allowed and the convictions quashed.

Stuart-Smith LJ:

> 'The ground of "material irregularity" in the course of the trial was introduced by s4(1) of the Criminal Appeal Act 1966. So far as we are aware the scope of the phrase has not fallen for examination, but in *R* v *Shannon* [1974] 2 All ER 1009 at 1051, [1975] AC 717 at 773 Lord Salmon expressed himself obiter as thinking that it "refers only to procedural irregularities". Mr Butterfield [counsel for the Crown] submitted that so to confine the phrase produced a sensible structure for s2 of the 1968 Act in that para (a) dealt with evidential matters, para (b) with questions of law and para (c) with procedural matters. Non-disclosure, said Mr Butterfield, was not a procedural irregularity. We can at once say that his postulated structure would suppose that the three paragraphs are mutually exclusive. We can see no reason on the construction of s2 why this should be so. ...
>
> We are of the opinion that a forensic scientist who is an adviser to the prosecuting authority is under a duty to disclose material of which he knows and which may have "some bearing on the offence charged and the surrounding circumstances of the case". The disclosure will be to the authority which retains him and which must in turn (subject to sensitivity) disclose the information to the defence. We hold that there is such a duty because we can see no cause to distinguish between members of the prosecuting authority and those advising it in the capacity of a forensic scientist. Such a distinction could involve different and contested inquiries as to where knowledge stopped but, most importantly, would be entirely counter to the desirability of ameliorating the disparity of scientific resources as between the Crown and the subject. Accordingly we hold that there can be a material irregularity in the course of trial when a forensic scientist advising the prosecution has not disclosed material of the type to which we have referred.'

However His Lordship concluded that on the facts no miscarriage of justice actually occurred by reason of the particular non-disclosure and that instead the appeals would be allowed solely on the ground that the convictions were unsafe and unsatisfactory because of the risk of innocent contamination in regard to the forensic evidence used at the original trial.

Mann and McCowan LJJ agreed.

Comment

Another notorious miscarriage of justice case. The particular ground for appeal considered in this case, that of 'material irregularity' during the course of a trial, has been replaced by a single broad ground of appeal based on the safeness of the conviction: see s2(1) of the Criminal Appeal Act 1995.

R* v *Mandair [1994] 2 All ER 715 House of Lords (Lords Mackay LC, Templeman, Goff, Browne-Wilkinson and Mustill)

- *Powers of House of Lords in disposing of criminal appeals*

Facts

The accused had been charged with causing grievous bodily harm with intent, contrary to s18 of the Offences Against the Person Act 1861. The jury acquitted the accused of this charge but, following the judge's directions prior to their retirement, convicted the accused of the alternative lesser verdict of causing grievous bodily harm (but without intent to cause serious bodily harm), contrary to s20 of the 1861 Act. The accused appealed on the

ground, inter alia, that the judge had misdirected the jury. The Court of Appeal, without dealing with the misdirection ground, allowed the appeal and quashed the convictions on the ground that s20 referred to the 'infliction' of grievous bodily harm and that the offence of 'causing' grievous bodily harm was an offence not known to the law. The Crown appealed to the House of Lords.

Held (Lord Mustill dissenting)
(1) The jury had given a verdict of an offence which was known to the law since the reference to 'causing' grievous bodily harm could only mean that what the accused had done consisted of 'inflicting' grievous bodily harm on another person contrary to s20 of the 1861 Act; and (2) in regard to the misdirection issue, left undisposed by the Court of Appeal, the House of Lords had power either to hear and dispose of that issue itself or to remit the case to the Court of Appeal to hear and dispose of that issue. In the particular circumstance the case was remitted to the Court of Appeal.

To that extent the Crown's appeal was allowed. Commenting on the jurisdiction of the House of Lords in criminal appeals Lord Mackay LC said:

> 'It is often the case that a number of grounds of appeal are urged before the Court of Appeal but having reached a clear conclusion upon one which determines the case, the Court of Appeal do not decide the other grounds since such decision is unnecessary to the disposal of the case on the view they have taken of it. It would obviously be highly undesirable and wasteful to require the Court of Appeal in every case to decide all the grounds of appeal before disposing of an appeal before them, on the basis that if a point of law of general public importance is raised in the appeal the House of Lords may take a different view of the point from that taken by the Court of Appeal if leave to appeal to the House of Lords is granted in respect of the decision. …
>
> … In my opinion the statutory provisions under which this appeal is brought make it necessary that a point of law of general public importance is involved in the decision of the Court of Appeal before it can competently be considered by this House but where leave to appeal has been granted which means that the point is to be considered by the House, the House has power not only to exercise all the powers of the Court of Appeal but also to remit the case to that court for the purposes of disposing of the appeal. In his speech in *A-G for Northern Ireland* v *Gallagher* [1961] 3 All ER 299 at 303, [1963] AC 349 at 366 Lord Reid says, after referring to the authorisation in the statute before him of a remit to the Court of Appeal:
>
> > "… but that is only for the purpose of disposing of the appeal to this House. I can find nothing to authorise a remit to the court below directing it to re-open and rehear the case and come to a fresh decision."
>
> He took the view that where a ground of appeal remained undisposed of by the Court of Appeal which was relevant to whether a conviction should stand this House had to go beyond the point certified and decide upon that ground which might have no connection at all with the first. In my opinion it is perfectly reasonable to conclude that where as in this case a decision must ultimately be taken whether the defendant's conviction should stand or be set aside, the appeal to this House cannot be completely disposed of without that question being resolved and I believe that it is natural to read the statutory provisions as enabling this House either to remit the matter to the Court of Appeal or to itself to exercise the powers of the Court of Appeal in relation to grounds of appeal not disposed of by the Court of Appeal.'

Comment
A useful case defining the scope of the powers of the House of Lords when determining an appeal in a criminal case.

R* v *Satpal Ram (1995) The Times 7 December Court Appeal (Criminal Division) (Beldam LJ, Scott-Baker and Stuart-White JJ)

- *Appeals in criminal cases on grounds of negligence or incompetence of defence advocate*

Facts

The accused's counsel at his trial had advised him to base his defence to a charge of murder on provocation when a defence of self-defence was conceivable as an alternative. A case of provocation was then presented. The accused was convicted of murder and appealed to the Court of Appeal.

Held

The appeal would be dismissed.

Beldam LJ said that the appellant had failed to persuade their Lordships that he had been deprived of a viable ground of defence by the advice of his leading counsel.

It was easy, as Lucretius had observed, to stand on the safety of the shore and pass judgment on the work of those battling against the wind and waves in a high sea. It was perhaps even easier six and a half years later.

There seemed to be an increasing tendency to believe that it was only necessary to assert the fault of trial counsel to sustain an argument that the conviction was unsafe or unsatisfactory.

Whether that was due to a mistaken interpretation of the observations on that subject by the 1993 report of the Royal Commission on Criminal Justice chaired by Viscount Runciman of Doxford (Cm 2263), their Lordships did not know but they did see far reaching implications in the commission's suggestion at chapter 9, paragraph 59, that even a reasonable decision of counsel could be the cause of a miscarriage of justice.

The court could not countenance a case in which the defendant was serving a prison sentence for no other reason than a mistake on counsel's part but equally, where counsel's judgment had been reasonable, there was a strong public interest that the legal process should not be indefinitely prolonged on the ground, for example, that a defendant's case advanced within a different framework might have stood a greater chance of success.

The advantages claimed for the adversarial system of justice of necessity depended greatly on the skill and judgment of trial counsel.

Comment

The case shows the reluctance of appeal judges to acknowledge tactical errors by defence counsel as giving rise to legitimate grounds of appeal. It may be that only 'flagrant incompetency' on the part of defence counsel will persuade the appeal judges that the conviction is unsafe: see *R* v *Clinton* [1993] 2 All ER 998.

10 The Legal Profession

Rondel* v *Worsley [1969] 1 AC 191 House of Lords (Lord Reid, Lord Morris, Lord Pearce, Lord Upjohn and Lord Pearson)

- *Immunity of a barrister for conduct of a case in court*

Facts

W was a barrister and had on a dock brief represented R who had been convicted and sent to prison. R then brought an action against W for professional negligence. The case reached the House of Lords on the legal point of whether such an action could lie. The question of negligence never came before the court.

Held

An action did not lie against W as a barrister cannot be sued for negligence for the conduct of his case in court. This is not due to the absence of any contract but is a rule based on public policy. (At one time it was thought that this was because of the absence of a contract. However, since *Hedley Byrne* v *Heller* this alone could not be a sufficient ground). Their Lordships differed slightly on the exact points of public policy but they agreed with the four heads adverted by Lord Denning MR in the Court of Appeal which were:

1. Independence: 'that he may do his duty fearlessly and independently as he ought and to prevent him being harassed by vexatious actions', and
   'If a barrister is to be able to do his duty fearlessly and independently he must not be subject to the threat of an action for negligence.'
2. Professional obligation to act: 'A barrister cannot pick or choose his clients. He is bound to accept a brief for any man who comes before the courts. No matter how great a rascal the man may be. No matter how given to complaining. No matter how undeserving or unpopular his cause. The barrister must defend him to the end.'
3. Duty to the court: 'He has a duty to the court which is paramount. It is a mistake to suppose that he is the mouthpiece of his client to say what he wants: or his tool to do what he directs. He is none of these things. He owes allegiance to a higher cause. It is the cause of truth and justice ... He must disregard the most specific instructions of his client, if they conflict with his duty to the court.'
4. Protraction of litigation: 'If a barrister could be sued for negligence, it would mean a retrial of the original case ... If this action is to go for trial, it will lead to dozens of like cases.'

Their Lordships discussed the problems as to how far immunity should extend and the majority expressed the opinion that it could extend to cover work done whilst litigation was pending (eg pleadings) but that it should not extend to work done outside the context of litigation. (Lord Pearce favoured wider immunity). However, none of their Lordships defined precisely the limit of immunity. The liability of solicitors was discussed by way of obiter and their Lordships opined that they should be immune when doing work for which a barrister would be immune.

Comment

The leading authority on the scope of advocates' immunity. Are the reasons advanced for the immunity cogent bearing in mind that other professionals enjoy no such immunity for their professional work? It has been sugg-

ested that the need to prevent constant re-litigation by disappointed losers is the only real justification for shielding advocates from action: see further *Saif Ali* v *Mitchell* (1980) (below).

Ross* v *Caunters [1979] 3 WLR 605 High Court (Megarry V-C)

- *Liability of solicitor to third parties*

Facts

Solicitors who prepared a will for a testator and sent it to him for execution failed to warn him that the will should not be witnessed by the spouse of a beneficiary. When the testator signed the will, one of the witnesses was the husband of a residuary beneficiary under it. After the testator's death the solicitors wrote to the beneficiary advising her of a possible defect in connection with the witnessing of the will and enclosing a copy of s15 of the Wills Act 1837 which provided that where a beneficiary or a spouse of a beneficiary attested a will, the gift to that beneficiary was void. The beneficiary claimed damages against the solicitors for negligence in respect of the loss of the benefits given to her by the will. The solicitors admitted that they had been negligent but contended that the only duty of care which they owed was to the testator alone and that they had owed no such duty to the beneficiary.

Held

There was no longer any rule that a solicitor, negligent in his professional work, was liable only to his client in contract, for he could also be liable for the tort of negligence not only to his client but to others where a prima facie duty of care towards them could be shown.

Megarry V-C:

> 'Today negligence has long been established as an independent tort and not merely a constituent element in certain other torts. Further, it is difficult today to see the logic in the proposition that if A employs B to do an act for the benefit of C, the existence of B's contractual duty to A to do the act with proper care negates any possible duty of B towards C, since B has no contract with C. Why should the existence of a contractual duty to A preclude the existence of any non-contractual duty to others? If one examines the facts of the case before me to discover whether the three-fold elements of the tort of negligence exist, a simple answer would be on the following lines. First, the solicitors owed a duty of care to the plaintiff since she was someone within their direct contemplation as a person so closely and directly affected by their acts and omissions in carrying out their client's instructions to provide her with a share of his residue that they could reasonably foresee that she would be likely to be injured by those acts or omissions. Second, there has undoubtedly been a breach of that duty of care; and third, the plaintiff has clearly suffered loss as a direct result of that breach of duty.'

Comment

Although this decision on the scope of the duty of care in the tort of negligence has been much criticised it has been followed in recent case law: see *White* v *Jones* [1995] 1 All ER 691 (HL). The decision illustrates that the professional immunity enjoyed by lawyers is restricted to advocacy work (and work intimately connected with it) because of the special public policy factors affecting the conduct of trials: see *Rondel* v *Worsley* (1969), above.

Saif Ali* v *Sydney Mitchell & Co [1980] AC 198 House of Lords (Lords Wilberforce, Diplock, Salmon, Russell and Keith)

- *Immunity of a barrister for pre-trial work – scope of immunity*

Facts

The plaintiff was injured in a motor accident in March 1966 whilst a passenger in a friend's

van. The car was driven by Mrs S but owned by her husband and it was clear that she was to blame, possibly entirely. The plaintiff and his friend consulted solicitors who instructed counsel who advised and settled pleadings against the husband (this was on the grounds of agency). The writ and statement of claim were issued but not served. Negotiations took place with the insurers who indicated that there might be contributory negligence and that agency might be disputed. Counsel was notified of this information but did not advise that the parties should be separately represented or that both drivers should be sued. In 1969 the three year limitation expired. In August 1969 the writ and statement of claim were served on Mr S and shortly after that counsel advised that the plaintiff should be separately represented. Mr S initially entered a defence admitting that his wife had been his agent but subsequently withdrew the admission. The plaintiff's new advisers advised him to discontinue the action. This left the plaintiff without an action as he was statute-barred from bringing proceedings against the other parties. He therefore brought an action against his former solicitors for damages alleging negligence in that they had failed to advise him to take proceedings against Mrs S or his friend or both. The solicitor issued a third party notice and a statement of claim against the barrister claiming that he was entitled to be indemnified for any such damages payable to the plaintiff on the grounds that the barrister had acted negligently in advising who should be joined in the proceedings and in settling the proceedings in accordance with that advice. The barrister applied to have the third party notice struck out as it disclosed no reasonable cause of action. The registrar granted the application, his order was reversed by the judge, and the Court of Appeal reversed the judge's order.

Held (Lord Russell and Lord Keith dissenting)

The further appeal would be allowed. Public policy required that a barrister should be immune from suit in negligence in respect of his conduct of litigation but such immunity was not to be given any wider application than was absolutely necessary in the interests of the administration of justice. Consequently, a barrister's immunity extends only to those matters of pre-trial work which were so intimately connected with the conduct of the matter in court, that they could really be said to be preliminary decisions affecting the way the case was to be conducted when the hearing took place.

The majority said that although public policy required that a barrister should be immune from suit for negligence in respect of his acts or omissions in the conduct and management of litigation which caused damage to his client, such immunity was an exception to the principle that a professional person who held himself out as qualified to practice that profession was under a duty to use reasonable care and skill and was not to be given any wider application than was absolutely necessary in the interests of the administration of justice. Accordingly, a barrister's immunity from suit extended only to those matters of pre-trial work intimately connected with the hearing. In as much as the barrister's advice and settling of the pleadings in fact prevented the plaintiff's cause from coming to court as it should have done, it could not be said to have been intimately connected with the conduct of the plaintiff's cause in court, and was therefore not within the sphere of a barrister's immunity from suit for negligence. Lords Wilberforce, Diplock and Salmon also said, obiter, that a solicitor acting as an advocate in court enjoys the same immunity as a barrister.

Lord Salmon:

> 'I recognise that it is most unpleasant for a barrister to have to fight an allegation that he has been negligent, but such an experience is no more unpleasant for a barrister than it is for a physician or a surgeon, an architect or an accountant. I cannot understand how there can be any justification for the law affording a blanket immunity to a barrister

in respect of all work done out of court when it affords none to the members of any other profession; nor do I believe that the Bar would wish to claim such immunity.

The theory that because the barrister has no contractual relationship with his client he could not be liable for negligent advice causing financial loss vanished with *Hedley Byrne & Co Ltd* v *Heller & Partners Ltd* which overruled *Candler* v *Crane, Christmas & Co.*

The other theories supporting a barrister's supposed blanket immunity from liability for negligence in respect of any paperwork cannot survive in the realistic atmosphere of the late 20th century. These were based on the fact that (i) a barrister cannot sue his client for fees and (ii) he is obliged to accept briefs relating to a field of law in which he normally practices, providing he is offered a proper fee.

Although a barrister cannot sue for his fees he can demand that his fees be paid before he appears in court. If the barrister does not demand his fees in advance and the lay client does not pay them after the barrister's services have been rendered, the solicitor can sue the lay client for the barrister's fees. It is true that if the solicitor recovers the fees from the lay client and does not pay them over to the barrister, the barrister cannot sue the solicitor; but he can report him to the Law Society, and this as every lawyer knows, would be likely to cost the solicitor far more than the fees he retains. There is no reason to suppose that the Bar incurs more bad debts than any other profession.

The rule that a barrister must accept a brief in the circumstances which I have described was made to ensure that every accused person or litigant could be represented in court by counsel. I do not, however, know of any firm rule which obliges counsel to accept instructions to advise or to draft pleadings.

Unless what seems to me to be an untenable proposition is accepted, namely, that public policy always requires that a barrister should be immune from liability for his neglect or incompetence in respect of all paperwork, he is rightly in no better position than any other professional man who is sued for negligence. The normal rule applied by the law is that if anyone holding himself out as possessing reasonable competence in his avocation undertakes to advise or to settle a document, he owes a duty to advise or settle the document with reasonable competence and care. This duty is owed to anyone he should foresee may suffer loss if the duty is breached.

If in breach of that duty he fails to exercise reasonable competence or care and as a result the person to whom the duty was owed suffers damage, he is liable to compensate that person for the damage he has suffered. The law requires the damage to be borne by the person whose breach of duty has caused it, rather than by the innocent person who has suffered it.'

Comment

The case confirms the traditional immunity from suit granted to advocates but appears to refine the principles of *Rondel* v *Worsley* (1969) (above) by giving more precise definition of the sort of related work also protected by the immunity: the test appears to be that such work must be so intimately connected with the conduct of the trial that it can be said to involve preliminary decisions affecting the way the case is to be conducted.

Yonge v *Toynbee* [1910] 1 KB 215 Court of Appeal (Vaughan Williams, Buckley LJJ and Swinfen Eady J)

- *Solicitor and client relationship*

Facts

A firm of solicitors was instructed to act for the defendant in an action brought against him. Soon afterwards the defendant was certified as of unsound mind but the solicitors, ignorant of this fact, entered an appearance for him and prepared the defence. Subsequently, the trial not having yet begun, the plaintiff in the action applied for the

appearance and subsequent proceedings in the action to be struck out and the solicitors ordered to pay all the plaintiff's costs, on the ground that they had acted without authority.

Held

The solicitors had taken on themselves to act for the defendant in the action and had thereby impliedly warranted that they had the authority to do so and were therefore liable to pay the plaintiff's costs of the action.

Swinfen Eady J:

> 'The manner in which business is ordinarily conducted requires that each party should be able to rely upon the solicitor of the other party having obtained a proper authority before assuming to act. It is always open to a solicitor to communicate as best he can with his own client, and obtain from time to time such authority and instructions as may be necessary. But the solicitor on the other side does not communicate with his opponent's client and, speaking generally, it is not proper for him to do so ... It is my opinion essential to the proper conduct of legal business that a solicitor should be held to warrant the authority which he claims of representing the client; if it were not so, no-one would be safe in assuming that his opponent is authorised in what he said or did, and it would be impossible to conduct legal business upon the footing now existing; and, whatever the legal liability may be, the Court, in exercising the authority which it possesses over its own officers, ought to proceed upon the footing that a solicitor assuming to act in an action for one of the parties to the action warrants his authority.'

Comment

A straightforward application of principles of agency law. The solicitor is treated no differently than any other kind of agent.

11 Legal Aid

Hanlon v *Law Society* [1981] AC 124 House of Lords (Lords Edmund-Davies, Simon, Fraser, Scarman and Lowry)

• *Contributions and charges*

Facts

Mrs H obtained legal aid in divorce – ancillary proceedings. The matrimonial home was formerly in her husband's name and it was transferred into hers. She applied unsuccessfully to the High Court for a declaration that the statutory charge in favour of the Law Society for £8,000 did not apply. Further appeals to the Court of Appeal were also unsuccessful. The issues involved were as follows:

1 Whether property could be 'recovered or preserved' in matrimonial proceedings.
2 Whether any set-off was allowed in respect of maintenance forgone or whether the charge affected the whole of the property.
3 Whether the 'proceedings' were to be interpreted as all the divorce proceedings or only those involving the recovery or preservation of property.
4 Whether the Law Society does have any discretion regarding enforcement of the charge.

Held

The appeal would be dismissed. The legal aid costs of £8,025 were a first charge for the benefit of the legal aid fund on the value of the house as property recovered or preserved under s9(b) of the Legal Aid Act 1974. The Law Society had a discretion to postpone enforcement of the charge on the house or accept a substitute charge on a replacement house. The charge was applicable in matrimonial proceedings: that it applied to the whole of the property and the entire proceedings were included in 'proceedings'.

(No extract from a judgment is necessary on this point.)

Comment

A famous case illustrating the hardship that can be caused by the 'clawback' principle – in this case taking the form of a charge on the family home: see now s16 of the Legal Aid Act 1988 and Regulations made under it (which permit the Board to defer enforcement of the charge).

Hanning v *Maitland (No 2)* [1970] 1 QB 580 Court of Appeal (Lord Denning MR, Salmon and Edmund-Davies LJJ)

• *Assisted party losses*

Facts

The defendant, an unassisted person, was successful in an action brought by the plaintiff who was legally aided. The defendant's costs were £325.13s.9d. but the taxing master refused to award costs out of the legal aid fund. The refusal was confirmed, the judge holding that he was bound by *Nowotnik* v *Nowotnik (Hyatt intervening)* [1965] 3 All ER 167 to hold that the defendant would not suffer 'severe financial hardship'. He was also of the opinion that the defendant had not established that it would be 'just and equitable' that provisions for his costs should be made out of public funds. The defendant appealed.

Held

The appeal would be allowed. On the facts, it was 'just and equitable' (within s1(2) of the Legal Aid Act 1964) that the costs should be paid out of public funds and the defendant would suffer 'severe financial hardship' (within s1(3)(b) of the 1964 Act) unless the costs were so paid.

Lord Denning MR:

> 'My views are as follows. First, the decision in *Nowotnik* v *Nowotnik* was right; but it should be based *solely* on the ground that, apart altogether from the Legal Aid Act 1964, no order would have been made in favour of the husband against the wife ordering her to pay his costs. The husband was barred, therefore, from recovering against the legal aid fund by the exception contained in s1(4) of the 1964 Act …
>
> Secondly, the words "severe financial hardship" were construed in *Nowotnik* v *Nowotnik* so as to give emphasis to the word "severe". But, in the light of experience, I do not think that they should be construed so strictly.
>
> In future, the words should be construed so as to exclude … wealthy folks who can meet the costs without feeling it. But they should not be construed as to exclude people of modest income or modest capital who would find it hard to bear their own costs …'
>
> The plain fact is that the unassisted party is unassisted. It matters not why. He may have too much income or capital. Or he may prefer not to apply for legal aid, but to defend himself as best he can on his own resources. By so doing he puts himself at risk. If he lost, he will have to pay all the costs of the "other side"; and the other side be it remembered, is backed by the legal aid fund. If they win the case, they will get an order for costs against him, and they will come down on him for every penny. Conversely, if they lose the case, it is usually "just and equitable" that they – the legal aid fund – should pay him every penny of his taxed costs. …
>
> I realise that this means that, in many of the cases where the unassisted party will suffer "severe financial hardship", it is also "just and equitable" that he should receive his costs out of the legal aid fund. So be it. It is a good result. But there are some cases where it may not be just and equitable. The defendant may have done a good deal to bring the litigation on to himself. For instance, there are some cases between husband and wife, or father and mother, or beneficiary and trustee, where the unassisted party, even though he is successful may be left to bear his own costs, rather than out of the legal aid fund.'

Comment

A sympathetic judgment from Lord Denning MR which recognised the plight of a successful unassisted party faced with the problem of trying to obtain costs from a losing assisted party. Lord Denning's interpretation of the relevant statutory provisions are typical in showing his reluctance to apply a strict literal interpretation which would cause hardship. Instead his robust 'commonsense' approach ensured that a costs order would be made in favour of those who needed it, even if the Legal Aid Fund (and therefore the taxpayers generally) had to foot the bill: see further *R* v *Greenwich London Borough Council, ex parte Lovelace (No 2)* (1992) (below).

Joyce* v *Sengupta [1993] 1 WLR 337 Court of Appeal (Sir Donald Nicholls V-C, Butler-Sloss LJ and Sir Michael Kerr)

- *Legal aid – choice of cause of action*

Facts

An issue of *Today*, the defendants' newspaper, had a banner headline 'Royal maid stole letters'. This statement was false and the maid, instead of suing for libel (for which legal aid was not available), sued for malicious falsehood and she obtained legal aid to pursue her claim. The judge struck out her claim on the ground that it could not properly be based on

malicious falsehood when it was in essence a case of libel.

Held

The plaintiff's action would be reinstated.

Sir Donald Nicholls V-C:

> '[Counsel for the defendants] submitted that [a] reason why this action is an abuse is that only nominal damages, or at best modest damages of a few hundred pounds, will be recoverable by the plaintiff. The amount she stands to obtain is wholly out of line with the costs each side will incur. In practice the defendants will never recover their costs even if they are successful in defending the action and even if they make a payment into court of an amount in excess of any damages awarded at the trial. [Counsel] submitted that, so far as the plaintiff is concerned, the action is "economic lunacy", given that any damages awarded to her will be swallowed up by the Legal Aid Board's charge over them as property recovered in the proceedings. Public funds are being used to support the plaintiff in a wholly uneconomic way.
>
> With all respect to counsel, this is a hopeless submission ... For the moment let me assume that the defendants are correct in submitting that the plaintiff is unlikely to recover more than a few hundred pounds in damages. I shall make that assumption although I am not to be taken as indorsing it. Even so I do not see how it follows that this action should be struck out as an abuse. The plaintiff's main purpose in bringing this action is to clear her name. If she wins, she will succeed in doing so. Compared with a libel action, the amount of damages she may recover in malicious falsehood may be small, but there is no reason why she should not be entitled to pursue such a claim. I see no justification for the court stopping her action. The defendants, it must be borne in mind, are resisting her claim in its entirety. The prospect that they are unlikely to recoup their costs even if their defence is wholly successful is an unfortunate fact of everyday life for many defendants when sued by legally aided plaintiffs.
>
> The reality here is that the defendants are unhappy that the plaintiff has obtained legal aid to pursue the action. They fear that if this action is permitted to proceed, the floodgates will be opened. The Legal Aid Board will be flooded with applications for legal aid to pursue claims for malicious falsehood against newspapers. Newspapers will be faced with the prospect, not intended by Parliament, of legally aided plaintiffs pursuing claims against them founded on defamatory articles.
>
> As to these fears, it is vital to keep in mind that the decision on whether or not to grant legal aid has been entrusted by Parliament to the Legal Aid Board, not the court.'

Comment

An interesting case (which attracted much media attention at the time because of the Royal Family connection) showing a possible way round the problem facing litigants who cannot afford to sue for defamation (for which legal aid is not available). The decision shows that the very similar tort of malicious falsehood is nevertheless a separate tort and therefore not covered by the restriction on legal aid which affects libel and slander actions.

R* v *Greenwich London Borough Council, ex parte Lovelace (No 2) [1992] 1 QB 155 Court of Appeal (Neill, Stocker and Staughton LJJ)

- *Legal aid – unassisted party's costs*

Facts

With the assistance of legal aid, two members of a council's housing committee sought a declaration that a decision of the council reducing membership of the housing committee was ultra vires. The Divisional Court dismissed the application for judicial review with costs and an appeal to the Court of Appeal was similarly dismissed. The council sought payment of its costs from the Legal Aid Board under s18 of the Legal Aid Act 1988.

Held

The council could recover from the board its costs in the Court of Appeal, but not the Divisional Court.

Neill LJ:

> 'The next question to be determined is whether the council would suffer severe financial hardship unless its costs are met by the board.
>
> In the course of the argument we were referred to a number of authorities in this field [which] tend to show that an order on the grounds of severe financial hardship will not be made in favour of a large financial institution.
>
> It was argued on behalf of the council that a local authority occupies a special position because it owes a fiduciary duty to its ratepayers (or payers of the community charge) and that some local authorities, including the council, are currently adversely affected by rate-capping.
>
> In the present case it is common ground that even on the most generous basis the costs incurred by the council will not exceed £70,000 to £80,000. Against this the council has an income of many million pounds. I do not consider that it would be useful to explore in this judgement the circumstances in which a local authority might be held to have suffered severe financial hardship as a result of litigation. In principle I can see no reason why a local authority or any other large body should not be able to establish in a particular case that the amount expended on costs placed a quite exceptional burden on its resources and that it would suffer severe financial hardship unless the board paid the costs. In the present case, however, the evidence in my view is wholly insufficient to establish severe financial hardship. The sums involved fall short of what would have to be proved to establish such hardship. It is not enough that *some* curtailment of socially desirable expenditure will be necessary. The words "severe financial hardship" are strong words and indicate some real impairment of the ability to function normally.
>
> In these circumstances, though I consider that the court has jurisdiction to make an order in favour of the council in respect of the costs incurred in the Divisional Court, I would not make such an order in this case.
>
> In the case of the costs incurred by the council in the Court of Appeal, however, there is no need to establish severe financial hardship. But on behalf of the board a further argument was put forward ... Thus it was submitted that it was necessary in any event for the court to be satisfied that it was just and equitable in all the circumstances that provision for the costs should be made out of public funds, and that the court could not or should not be so satisfied where the applicant was itself a public body.
>
> For my part I would see some force in this argument if the applicant were a public body funded solely by the general body of taxpayers. But that is not this case. Although a substantial portion of the expenditure of local authorities is met out of general taxation, a further substantial proportion is met by local residents and businesses. These proceedings were made possible because the applicants seeking judicial review were in receipt of legal aid. I consider that it would be just and equitable that the council should recover the costs which they were obliged to incur in defending those proceedings. I would therefore make an order in favour of the council in respect of their costs in the Court of Appeal.'

Comment

The case shows how an apparently wealthy party can nevertheless recover costs from the Legal Aid Fund by showing 'severe financial hardship'. Obviously a local authority may be able to show special circumstances which render it burdensome for it to shoulder its own costs of an action. Each application for reimbursement must therefore be treated on its own particular merits.